A Mother's Dance

One Step Back, Two Steps Forward, Full Circle

Pattie Welek Hall

Georgia

Published in the United States by WriteLife Publishing
(an imprint of Boutique of Quality Books Publishing Company)
www.writelife.com

Printed in the United States of America

978-1-60808-134-9 (p)
978-1-60808-137-0 (h)
978-1-60808-135-6 (e)
Library of Congress Control Number: 2015942451

Book design by Robin Krauss, www.bookformatters.com
Cover design by Ellis Dixon, www.ellisdixon.com

OTHER BOOKS BY PATTIE WELEK HALL

Believe
Released: January 15, 2010

Praise for *A Mother's Dance*

I have read Pattie Welek Hall's book, *A Mother's Dance*, through the lens of a practicing neurointensivist (a physician specializing in the critical care of patients with acute neurological illness) and have learned valuable lessons that years of rigorous academic training cannot provide. Ms. Welek Hall eloquently illustrates in her book our limited ability at determining prognosis after traumatic brain injury and our inability to accurately predict functional outcome. The book allows physicians to see a facet of medical care that is often unrevealed (perhaps ignored?) by busy practicing clinicians who tend to pay little attention to the oppressiveness of being a patient or family member in intensive care or the value of spiritual healing that the family is attempting to deliver.

Mainly the book is a story about hope, resilience, fortitude, faith, and about the value of family and friends—the most important elements in the recovery of any patient. It reminds practicing physicians and nurses that "the little things" matter the most to patients and families, that we often overlook them, that patients and families may have creative ways to improve therapy and should be encouraged to do so, and that the fortitude of our patients can be limitless. Our encounters with patients are brief but Pattie takes us beyond that brief period to see the past and the aftermath of the ICU stay, full of obstacles but also graced with wonderful accomplishments and joys.

Spirituality, an often neglected aspect of patient care, comes about frequently in the book and, without a doubt, will make clinicians (believers or agnostics) stop and reflect about its impact on patient healing. The book is a lesson in acceptance and open-mindedness for physicians who may not embrace mustard seeds, holy water, or flying angels as part of their daily medical armamentarium! **It's a must read for those involved in the care of patients with acute brain injuries.**

~ Julio A. Chalela MD
Associate Professor of Neurology and Neurosurgery
Medical University of South Carolina
Medical Director NSICU

From the moment I began reading Pattie's story, I knew that I was about to embark on a heartfelt journey. Her beautifully written words transported me both into her life and allowed me to step into her shoes, as a mother. My heart was full, not only with sadness as I travelled through the depths of her pain, but with overwhelming joy as I celebrated the miracles and wonderment of her life. Pattie Welek Hall is a beautiful gift and is the perfect person to share hope and joy with the world.

~ Bonnie Compton APRN, BC, CPNP,
Child & Adolescent Therapist
Host of *Wholehearted Parenting Radio*

A beautiful story of a mother's unwavering love for her child and her deep-rooted faith which was tested beyond measure on a daily basis that sustained her during the most tumultuous time of her life. It inspired me to forever hold on to HOPE and to believe that miracles really do happen. I cried and I laughed. A real page turner.

~ Mary Welek McBride

Pattie Welek Hall has turned a mother's worst nightmare into a dance so full of love, your heart will ache. Oh, the lengths she's willing to go to to save her son. Read it, and celebrate love at its most scary—and most beautiful.

~ Bren McClain
Author of *One Good Mama Bone*

Pattie Welek Hall's heart-rending and electrifying memoir sweeps readers into every mother's worst nightmare. Pattie is the rare debut author who tackles big subjects—rock-solid beliefs shaken to the core, bouts of hopelessness, the search for fortitude amid adversity, rejection, redemption, and the boundless love of friends and family—and makes every word ring true.

~ Catherine Underhill Fitzpatrick
Author of *Going on Nine*

Pattie has written a courageous book, one that is both heartbreaking and heartwarming. She tells her story with exceptional grace. Pattie emerges as a strong and admirable heroine who will encourage readers through difficult times.

~ Mary Welek Atwell
Author of *Equal Protection of the Law?* and *Wretched Sisters*

Pattie Welek Hall's book touched my heart. There is something in this book for everybody, no matter your religion. People from all religions can benefit from the healing that is found in Pattie's story. She finds comfort in her religion of origin, Catholicism, and comfort in new thought/age philosophies, which she accurately points out are really old age. If you want to learn to use spiritual principles to turn tragedy into growth, this book is for you!

~ Reverend Ed Kosak MSW
Minister, Unity Church of Charleston, SC

If Pattie Welek Hall's wonderful and moving book, *A Mother's Dance*, proves one thing it is this: when tragedy strikes, a mother's love is surpassed only by God's, the combined power of which can bring about miracles of healing.

~ Edward Grinnan
Editor-in-Chief and Vice President of Guideposts Publications
Author of *The Promise of Hope*

A Mother's Dance is a love story between a mother and her children. Written in exquisite detail with sensitivity, grace, and deep spiritual insights, Pattie's memoir is a must read for everyone who wants to walk the path God sent them long before they were born.

~ Trudy Harris
New York Times bestselling Author of *Glimpses of Heaven*

Nurturing is a lifelong process and Pattie gathered every available resource to guide her family through the most challenging times imaginable. *A Mother's Dance: One Step Back, Two Steps Forward, Full Circle* is a wonderful testament to the power of a mother's love and openness to the healing spirit.

~ Mark Dickson
Vice President Mission
Roper St. Francis Healthcare

A moving and poignant book about a mother's struggle through brain injury and loss. This book provides hope, strength, and faith to those who face the true challenges of life. Thank you to a brave and loving mother.

~ Judy Heath
Author of *No Time for Tears: Coping with Grief in a Busy World*

God first . . .

My children:
Robert B. Hall, Jr., Casey B. Hall, and Annie Hall Vincent

My siblings:
Charlie, Mary, Rita, Geri, John, and Margie

My parents:
Charles F. Welek III and Rita Johans Barry,
who I hope received advance copies in heaven . . .

You are my *everything!*

*Faith dares the soul
to go farther than it can see.*

~William Clarke

Foreword

There is this erroneous belief going around that we end up where we are by chance, or that we end up in our particular families because we had really great luck or really horrible luck—it depends on your story. I think where we end up, and who we end up with, goes a lot deeper than that. I believe that things just don't happen by chance in an orderly Universe.

Is it possible that our soul, in its infinite wisdom, knows exactly what family to land in for its higher evolution and the evolution of those around us? I believe so with all my heart.

And so it is from this place that I am moved by the perfection of Pattie's role as a mother to her children and the role they have chosen to play in her life.

In this book Pattie exposes her soul, her vulnerability, and her strengths in a way that any mother, any parent can relate to—the deep and unconditional love for her child. The willingness to go to the gates of hell to pull her child out; to trust when there's no reason to trust; and to keep getting up when she's knocked down by the pain, the fear, the dismantled hopes and the broken dreams where her child is concerned. And yet, she gets up again and again, unwilling to negotiate when it comes to the wellbeing and ultimate triumph for her child.

That is a mother's love.
Allow the words in this book to touch the core of your being, as it has touched mine.
From one mother to another—well done Pattie.

Ester Nicholson, Author of *Soul Recovery*

PART ONE

ONE STEP BACK

CHAPTER ONE

October 6, 2002

> *The only way to make sense out of change is to plunge into it,*
> *move with it, and join the dance.*
> ~ *Alan Watts*

Shafts of sunlight seep through the shutters and angle down, casting striated patterns of shadow and light across the family room as I'm leaving for work. I can't wait to tell my coworkers at Barnes & Noble that I landed the job as community relations manager in Huntersville. But ten minutes after I arrive and share the news, the high I was riding comes crashing to the ground with one phone call.

"Mom!" Annie's voice is choked with tears. "Dad just called. Casey was in a motorcycle accident at four o'clock this morning."

"What? Is he okay?" I cup my mouth, trying to muffle the animal cries rising from deep inside of me.

"He's . . . he's in intensive care at the Medical University of South Carolina. The doctor had to cut away part of his skull. He was afraid Casey's brain was bleeding." Annie's cries muffle her words. "He was admitted as 'John Doe.' My friends are driving me to the hospital to identify him. Mom, I'm so afraid."

"Oh, sweetie. I'm on my way."

"Hurry, Mom. Hurry. They don't know if he's going to—"

The phone goes dead. I feel like a lightning bolt has pierced my heart. Shock waves are shooting through my body, causing my fears to clap like thunder. My knees buckle. I reach out to grasp hold of the counter when my coworker catches my fall. "You okay? What's wrong?" I recap the worst news of my life.

"Grab your purse. I'll fill everyone in. You need to get on the road. NOW."

I sprint through racks of fiction, mystery, and biography at Barnes & Noble and snatch my purse from the locker. Racing to the front door, I storm past my coworker. "You okay to drive?" she shouts. I don't answer. I keep moving.

At home, I pack a bag, call the dog sitter, and jump back in the car.

Charlotte to Charleston takes three hours. Normally. I press my foot on the accelerator and watch the needle glide past 70, 80, then 85. No sirens blare. No flashing lights blink in the rearview mirror. My foot turns to lead and the needle swings forward. Blinded by my tears, I flick the waterworks from the left eye, then from the right eye, and weave between the traffic until I find an opening.

I sent my spirit 150 miles ahead, 125 miles ahead, then 50. I'm holding Casey's hand, hugging him, telling him how much I love him.

My fears burst into a crescendo of noise. What if I never see my son again? Never laugh or cry with him? Share in his joys and sorrows? Never attend his wedding? Play with his children? *No, I can't go there.* With an imaginary eraser in hand, I frantically try to wipe the thoughts from my mind, along with a haunting image of attending my son's funeral. But when that doesn't work, I bang my sweaty palms on the steering wheel and plead, "Please, Jesus, keep my son alive. PLEASE."

Finally, I spot the hospital exit ahead. I weave through the city's back streets, hardly braking at the continuous row of stop signs, barely feeling my chest rise and fall.

At the medical center, I find an elevator and push button four. When the doors open, there is my Annie, eyes swollen. We grab each other and hold on, our gut-wrenching pain interlocked like vines growing up a tree.

The nurse ushers us into ICU and speaks.

"Your son was hit by a car while driving his motorcycle without a helmet. He was thrown from his bike at a forty-five-degree angle and landed on the right side of his head. An anonymous 911 call came in. An ambulance arrived minutes later. Casey was rushed to the ER."

There's cold pressing against my shoulder blades, and I realize I've slumped against the wall.

The nurse continues.

"The intense impact to Casey's skull caused his brain to swell. During surgery, the neurosurgeon removed a portion of the right side of his cranium to release the pressure. He discovered a blood clot and suctioned it out."

I can feel my body growing numb. I try to ask the nurse; *Is he in pain? Does he know we are here? What do the doctors think his chances are for recovery? Is he going to live?* But my words get lodged in my throat.

"Your son was admitted to MUSC. He didn't have any identification on him. All he was carrying was his cell phone. He was tagged 'John Doe.' At two this afternoon, his cell phone rang. I answered. It was his father. I informed him of the accident." As the nurse is catching her breath, I feel her eyes on me. "Miss Hall. You all right?"

I catch my reflection in the mirror above Casey's sink and gasp. Lines, etched in sorrow, stretch across my cheeks, and my eyes, dark as night, sink into the void. My chin spasms. I press my lips together, but the unwanted pulse of dread persists. Willing myself back to the moment, I banish the image from my mind.

"No. But please call me Pattie."

"I will leave you two alone with Casey. Feel free to stay until someone kicks you out," the nurse whispers. "I have a teenage son. This is a mother's worst nightmare. Let me know if you need anything."

Annie's low keening dwarfs the beeping and humming of the machines. The sound of her sorrow brings me back.

"What is it, honey?"

"Just hours ago I was standing right here, Mom. The nurse asked me, 'Is this your brother?' and I nodded. She left me alone, but I heard whispers from the hall. Something about Casey's chances weren't good. That he might not make it twenty-four hours."

She buries her head deep into the pocket of my shoulder. Slowly,

Annie pulls her face away from my dampened shirt. She continues. "I inched closer to Casey and told him I loved him. That everything was going to be okay."

Lying on a sterile hospital bed is my nineteen-year-old boy. A bulge accentuates the swelling on the right side of his head. I can't tell if that's from the accident or the surgery. God, how did this happen? How could I not have been here, while my child was fighting for his life on the operating table? I can barely discern this face as my son's. The curve of his eyelids and brows is straightened. Nose widened. Lips puffed.

Annie's chin quivers. Her eyes are distant.

"My friends were here, Mom. We walked out to the garden. I couldn't even sit down. I hurt so bad."

I understand what she means. I feel as if I've been stabbed in the chest with a double-bladed knife. Maybe I should have taken a flight from Charlotte, rather than driving. Maybe I could have been in Charleston sooner. Holding her. Comforting her. Absorbing her pain. My God, she's only eighteen years old, a college freshman. This isn't fair, God. You hear me? Not fair.

"Oh, honey. I'm so sorry I wasn't here for you."

Her body rocks now, harder and faster, as if she's trying to shake off the pain.

"Me too, Mom."

I wrap my arms around my girl and pull her close, smelling her sweetness.

"You gonna be okay, honey?"

Annie dries her cheeks with the back of her hands. She doesn't answer. I don't push.

Carts shuffle in the hallway, breaking our silence.

"Mom, I should go." Annie says, tapping her watch. "It's six o'clock. Dad's plane from Louisville arrives in Charleston at seven. Bo's plane lands at eight. Dad is renting a car and picking me up. Visiting hours are at nine o'clock this evening, right?"

I nod.

At a time like this, when our world appears to be falling apart, Annie's warrior spirit and responsible nature—a far cry from her brothers who, more often than not, fly by the seat of their pants—is a godsend.

"Do you want me to—?"

"No. Go. I'm good, sweetie," I lie.

As Annie leaves, I think about how stoic she is. How she has to internalize her feelings before she'll express what's really on her mind. I can't help but wonder; *Will this memory scar her life forever?* Then, I turn and look at Casey and wonder, *Will there be life for Casey?*

It's as if the wind catches my thoughts and carries them away to August, two months ago, when Casey was packing his bags for college.

Music blared from his room, and Casey's voice drifted upstairs as he belted out each word perfectly pitched with the musician. At times, I felt like stuffing cotton in my ears but reminded myself the clock was ticking, and the end of our time together was drawing near. For the next few hours, I washed, folded, and ironed his clothes. Ran up and down the stairs more times than I could count on two hands. Handed him stacks of laundry, freshly pressed shirts, and pants; then watched as he stuffed them into the bag. The phone rang and the doorbell chimed, each time for Casey. Friends came and went. Bobby, my ex-husband, drove into the driveway in a rented truck. He honked, and I yelled downstairs, "Your dad is here."

Casey carried boxes and bags outside to the truck. Hours later, Bobby fastened the lock on the rear roll-up door and slid into the driver's seat. Before hoisting himself into the truck, Casey wrapped his arms around me. "Gonna miss you, Mom." Tongue-tied, I clutched his face and stared into his mischievous, playful hazel eyes. "Gonna miss you too, Son." He pulled me close, and I sank into his burly torso, not wanting to let go.

"Gotta run, Mom. Call you when I get to Charleston." As the truck pulled away, Casey hung his head out the window and yelled through his frisky smile, "Love you, Mom."

With every breath, with every sigh, his words fed my sadness as I entered a house gone empty.

Just months ago, Casey was filled with life. Now, looking at his immobile and swollen body, I can't help but wonder how he will possibly pull through this.

"Please hear me, Son. I can't bear the thought of losing you. How will I survive? How will the family survive? You have to fight, Casey. Use your God-given gifts—determination, courage, and strong will—and FIGHT."

Feeling alone and totally helpless, I pull my rosary from my purse and start whispering in Casey's ear those age-old prayers I learned as a child, hoping they'll spark his memory. After rolling my finger over the final pearl bead, I tenderly kiss my boy on the forehead, not knowing what lies ahead, not knowing if this night will be the last time I get to feel the warmth of his skin on mine. My insides scream—*Wake up, Casey! Wake up. It's your mama. Let me know you feel my touch, feel the depth of my love.* But I sense nothing back. It's as if he's in a realm of his own, a place impossible to reach. I saunter back to the waiting room and talk to the receptionist.

"Vanessa," I say, looking at her name tag. "Quick question. I noticed a stack of pillows, blankets, and sleeping bags in the corner. Given Casey's condition, I was wondering if it's okay for me to bunk here tonight?"

"Of course, dear. When you're ready to go to bed, just locate one of the nurses to get you a pillow and blanket."

At 9 p.m., Annie, Bo, Bobby, and I gather in Casey's room. Bo stands on one side of the bed. His tall, muscular frame shrinks as he takes in the horrific sight of his brother. Just two days ago, Bo was a normal college student at North Carolina State University, and now he's watching a machine breathe life into his brother. Bobby stands at the foot of Casey's bed, his head bent in sorrow. His round-rimmed glasses slide down his nose. He nudges them back in place. Annie stands next to me, her arms pressed into her stomach, as if she's crushing her pain. I want to hit the rewind button to yesterday.

I was heading down the stairs in my condo and stopped at each step to look at the pictures that marked my history. Pop in his World War II Navy uniform, his lieutenant's hat covering all but one inch of his raven hair. Mom in her college graduation photo, looking like Rita Hayworth's twin. Bo, my oldest, sitting inside a red wagon, his chubby legs hanging over the side and his restless toes digging into the carpet. Casey, as a toddler, napping, with his arms wrapped around his matted teddy bear. Annie, my baby girl, lying in her crib with her feet in the air, her fingers clutching her toes.

As my eyes scanned the wall of photos, I thought about all the great memories—birthday parties, graduations, vacations, reunions—celebrated over the years. I gave thanks for how far we all had come through the good and hard times: Mom and Pop each happily remarried, the kids in college and moving forward with their lives, and me, ready to start a new job in a few weeks. My last thought was; *Life is good.*

But that was yesterday.

Today, Casey's on the brink of death.

We say goodbye at 10 p.m., and I take advantage of the quiet time to call my sister Mary.

Mary is second in line of seven. I'm third.

For the first eighteen years of our lives, we shared a room. Shared our laughter. Shared our tears. Shared our most intimate secrets. It's not that we were best friends. We were both caught up in our own worlds. She went to one all-girls Catholic high school, and I went to another. It was important for me to find my own way. But the seeds of friendship were planted back then, and, years later, they blossomed.

Today, Mary is my best friend. My rock.

"I'm so glad you called. I've been worried sick. What happened?"

I recount the horrific details, barely able to get the words out, struggling to believe they still apply to my son.

Neither of us speaks, our words substituted by whimpers.

Mary clears her throat. "How's he doing?"

"Not good. He looks like a mannequin frozen in bed. The right side of his head is swollen. Mare, I'm so scared." I try to hold it together but something snaps. My whimpers turn into moans and thunder through me, sounding like an iceberg crashing into the sea.

Mary, feeling my pain, joins in. When we have no more tears left to cry, she says, "You going to be okay?"

"Yeah. Just torn. All the kids need me now, and I'm feeling like an octopus whose arms are being stretched in different directions. I'm praying I can give them all they need, and that Casey's tragedy doesn't strain our relationships. Oh, Mare, that would break me into a million little pieces."

"Annie and Bo are strong young adults, and from what you've told me, it sounds like they understand the severity of the situation. Rather than pulling all of you apart, maybe this tragedy will bring all of you closer together."

"Maybe you're right, Mare."

"So, what did the doctor say?"

"I didn't get a chance to talk to him. The nurse mentioned he made his final round just before I got there. And he won't be back until morning, unless . . . I just can't talk right now. I feel like my world is wobbling on a three-legged chair. I need sleep."

My new home is the ICU waiting room; my bed is the floor, until the doctor assures me Casey is going to make it through the night. A nurse brings me a pillow and a couple of blankets. I crawl under the receptionist's desk, sandwich myself between the covers, and plump up my starched pillow. My mind settles on a memory of Casey, age five.

I had just whipped up a batch of scrambled eggs for our Saturday breakfast. While squeezing catsup over his eggs, Casey said, "Dad, I want you to take my training wheels off my bike."

"You sure, Casey?"

"Uh-huh. I'm a big boy now." He held up his hand and stretched his fingers apart.

Once Casey shoveled the last fork of crimson mush into his mouth, we set off to the neighborhood park. Lawn mowers hummed. The sweet smell of freshly cut grass and hyacinths filled the air.

Bo, six years old, led the way on his bike. His blond locks sailed in the wind as he disappeared around the curve. Casey followed on foot, trying to keep up with his older brother. Their father ran behind, pulling the bike by its handlebars, and shouted into the wind, "Slow down, boys.

There could be cars coming." Annie, three years old, was nestled in my arms. We were the caboose on that out-of-control train.

At the mouth of the park, a crumbling sidewalk weaved through the rolling hills and ended at the playground.

Bo stood at the top of the yellow slide and shouted, "You can do it, Casey."

Annie clapped.

His father mumbled under his breath. He placed his hand on Casey's padded seat and motioned for him to mount the bike.

"Don't let go, Dad. Promise?" Casey shouted into the wind as his dad ran beside him.

Casey peddled hard, moving faster and faster.

"You're doing great, Case," his dad said. Then he let go.

Casey turned. And crashed under a canopy of trees.

As Casey untangled himself from the bike, his father and I rushed to his side. We brushed the dirt off his arm, pulled pebbles from his skinned knees, and encouraged him to try again.

With his feet and hands in position, Casey said, "This time, Dad, tell me when you are going to let go."

He did, and Casey never looked back.

Hungering for what was, I whisper, "Don't put on the brakes now, Casey. We're still here for you. We're going to help you get back up and dust you off again."

I close my eyes. I try to will my mind to silence the monkey-chatter exploding in my head, but the cage has been left open, and the monkeys are running wild.

What if someone hadn't been at the scene of the accident and called 911? What if Casey had stayed in the street for hours, crumpled, bleeding, unconscious, and alone? What would his chances of survival be? What are they now? What if something had gone awry during the operation?

I rock as if I'm holding Casey in my arms, soothing his pain, soothing my pain. Finally, I manage to fall asleep, knowing that at least if my boy calls, I'll be here.

CHAPTER TWO

October 7

Doctors and nurses—dressed in scrubs with surgical masks hanging from their necks—scurry into the cafeteria to grab a cup of coffee and a bagel. As I watch, I can't help but wonder if one of them had been in the operating room with Casey. I want to stop each one of them and ask, "Did you operate on my boy? Was he conscious when he was wheeled in? Did he call out for his mama like he did when he was a child after he cut his arm or slashed his nose?" I want to ask those questions and more, but I can't. I'm afraid their answers will bring me to my knees.

In the far corner of the room the TV is playing. I sit and start picking at my oatmeal. My thoughts are with my boy. The morning news is on.

"I'm standing at the corner of President and Sprint Street where sixteen hours ago there was a collision involving a motorcycle and pickup truck," says the broadcaster. "An anonymous 911 call was made and the victim was rushed to MUSC—"

The cameraman zooms in. Lying on the asphalt, a few feet from the curve, is a single tattered Birkenstock.

"Oh my God! That's Casey's shoe."

Realizing I just shouted out loud, I turn and look around. Like headlights in the night, all eyes are shining on me.

I need to get out of here. I check my watch. It's only 7:15 a.m.—two more long hours until I can see my boy. Aimlessly, I walk up one corridor and down another, turning at each bend as if I'm walking through a maze, trying to find my way *out*.

A brass sign embossed with the word "Chapel" is affixed to the wooden door ahead. I take a few shallow breaths and ease the door open. Tranquility fills the room, yet the heavy weight of sorrow lingers. A red leather Bible sits open in the center of the altar. Two vanilla candles burn on either side, casting shadows of light against the dark walls. I kneel and bury my head in my hands. I try to pray, but I can't. My tears gush, forming puddles around my elbows.

Over my shoulder, I hear the door squeak then squeak again. An elderly couple, holding hands, kneel in front of me, and a young man sits to my side, his baseball cap tucked under his arm. I bottle up my tears and tiptoe out of the room.

Every hallway on this floor looks the same: cream tiled floors and partially tiled walls, honey-stained wooden doors, some with signs—X-rays, labs, restrooms—some without.

I keep walking, thinking about how surreal life feels. On any given day when my heart isn't drowning in sorrow, I'd be at work. I smile, reflecting on how simple life used to be, and how I landed the job at Barnes & Noble.

My neighbor, Wendy, and I were sitting at the bookstore in overstuffed chairs, sipping on our caffé lattes, when Wendy asked, "How's your interior design business going?"

"Great. But I need another part-time job that pays benefits. My medical insurance is expiring soon."

"You should apply here. Shoot, not only have you read almost every self-help, New Age, and spiritual book on the shelves, you've engaged in conversation with complete strangers and recommended books to read."

She was right! So I did, and weeks later, I was hired.

So for the past year, I have worked as a bookseller. But in three weeks, I am scheduled to step into my new position as community relations manager. That is, if my boss holds my job until—

Feeling nauseated, I step aside and let the nurses pass until the sensation subsides.

At the end of the corridor, light shines from behind a glass pane. The words "Gift Shop" are painted on the window. I step inside. Perched on a shelf is a stuffed teddy bear, a miniature replica of Casey's bedtime buddy as a child. It tugs at my heartstrings. I grab the bear and proceed to the checkout counter.

A box filled with two-dozen iridescent amber stones, each encasing a tiny mustard seed, catches my attention. Attached is a card that reads, "If you have faith the size of a mustard seed, you will tell this mountain, 'Move from here to there,' and it will move. Nothing will be impossible for you. Matthew 17:20." I buy the whole box.

Somehow I make my way back to the waiting room and watch the minute hand on the clock slowly tick its way to nine o'clock—thirty more minutes, twenty-nine, twenty-nine and a half. My cell phone rings. It's my oldest friend, Drace, calling from St. Louis, my home for the first twenty-eight years of my life.

"How's it going, girl?"

I fill Drace in on the morning news, details about Casey, about the dog sitter back in Charlotte, about my final moments at work yesterday, and about the employee's phone calls promising to cover my shifts.

"That's good. So, girl, how are you doing today?"

There's a pause, not an uncomfortable one. Just a pause. I believe we're both thinking about yesterday and my nightmare trip to MUSC. Drace kept checking in on me. She didn't talk long, just asked if I was okay. Then she hung up and called me back every twenty minutes and asked the same question.

"Holding on. I'm not sure why this happened, Drace. God, I wish I knew. But there has to be a reason, some lesson I'm supposed to learn. In time, I'm sure I'll see the bigger picture. Right now, I'm just trying to remember to breathe."

"I'm here for you, girl."

Drace isn't one of those friends who says one thing, and when the time comes to take action, looks the other way. If I have a problem, significant or not, she's there for me. Because to her, that's what friends are for.

I slide my phone into my sweatshirt pocket and pray. Pray that Casey lives. Pray for my family. Pray for the courage and strength to meet today's challenges. I pray and pray.

Bo, Annie, and their dad arrive in the waiting room moments later. I hand each a stone along with the card. Watching their brows furrow as they read Matthew's message, I move in closer, invading their sacred space. "If the faith of one mustard seed can move a mountain, just imagine what we can do if we all believe."

No one responds: shoulders slump, heads drop, and faces go blank. They place the stones in their pockets and head down the hall.

I follow, thinking: *How did I expect them to react? To trust and to believe that miracles can happen? That God will restore all that is broken if they want something bad enough, if they pray hard enough? Maybe I'm asking too much.*

Just two years ago, the kids' fairy-tale dream of their parents living happily ever after was replaced by the Humpty Dumpty nursery rhyme. Even though I sensed they felt the underlying tension—not only during our family therapy sessions, but the times in between—I believed it was important to spare them the details that led to my decision. After all, that was between their father and me.

One month after the divorce papers were signed, Bo informed me that his dad had taken a job in Louisville.

"Is he going to sell his condo in Charlotte?" I asked.

"No. He's keeping it. That way, I can hang my hat at Dad's when I'm not in school, and he has a place to stay when he visits."

"Now you have three homes—my place, your dad's condo, and his new residence in Kentucky. How does that make you feel?"

"Confused, I guess. Just not sure where home is anymore."

His words pierce my heart. I shake my head, wondering how much more instability my son would have to accept in his life.

Due to their father's job, we'd moved from state to state—from California, to New York, to North Carolina—all during the kids' most formative years. Even though I generally embraced the change, the moves were quite stressful for the kids. They had to leave their old friends behind and make new ones, only to say goodbye and start over again.

Some kids adapt easily to change. Mine do not.

I need to talk to them.

"Annie. Bo. Wait up."

They stop and look over their shoulders.

Grabbing hold of Bo's hand, I speak.

"Bo, three years ago you dropped out of high school in your senior year, right?"

"Yes. That's because I had a drinking problem. My head was all messed up. But Mom, you know I turned my life around. I got my GED, and I'm at NC State. Why are you bringing this up now?"

"Just hear me out."

I wrap my fingers around Annie's.

"And you, sweetie, had such a hard time adjusting to our move from California to New York. Your first day in kindergarten, I had to peel you off my leg to get you in the classroom. That was a hard day for both of us."

"I didn't want you to leave. Didn't want to go to a new school. Didn't want to make new friends."

"I know. But before long, you joined Brownies, swam for the swim team, and blossomed."

Still holding Bo's hand, I pull Annie close.

"I know you two have been through a lot. With the moves and the divorce, and now here's one more change that's being pushed on you. But both of you have learned how to take a negative in your life and make it into a positive. Well, that's what we are going to do again, together, as family. Got it?"

Heads dip. Hearts open wide. Tears come. Tears go.

We walk into Casey's room.

Anticipating an unconscious Casey, we're all shocked to see him responsive, at least to our voices.

Annie says, "Case, move your finger if you know I'm here."

His finger moves.

Bo gently brushes his sister to the side and asks, "Case, move two fingers if I'm your favorite brother."

Two fingers go up.

Bobby steps in. "Case, do you know you were in an accident? If so, give me a thumbs-up."

He does.

I touch the arms of my loved ones and whisper, "Hey, sweetie, do you know how much we love you?"

His forefinger points up.

Bo turns and faces Annie. Their palms meet midair, clanking like cymbals. "He's coming back," they burst in unison.

I clutch the mustard seed inside my pocket and nod a silent thank you.

On visits throughout the day, we continue asking silly questions. Casey responds with a pointed finger or an occasional thumbs-up.

By ten o'clock, after a day of tiny victories, it's time for Annie, Bo, and their dad to leave. When the elevator arrives, I wave goodbye over my shoulder and hear an unfamiliar sound: laughter. Wanting to witness my kids' momentary bliss, I turn, but the elevator doors shut.

After a long day, I join my waiting-room cohorts clustered together in the side alcove. Tom and Betty sit with their four adult children. Sue is to the right of Tom. Jack and Sarah occupy the next two seats. I slide into the empty chair, completing the circle.

Tom leads the group discussion, sharing his heartbreaking story about his son, Chris, another brain injury victim. Betty and the children relay their concerns for the family's challenges ahead. Sue follows, imparting her trepidation regarding her mother's quality of health after suffering a near-fatal heart attack. Jack speaks, but his words "spinal injury victim" get suffocated by his pain. Sarah sobs. Rather than sharing, I reach into my bag, grab hold of nine mustard seed stones, and place one into each of their palms. As they read Matthew's verse, I utter, "Nothing is impossible."

Slowly, the group rises, scatters to opposite corners of the room, and bunks down for the evening. Before climbing under Vanessa's desk, a single loose-leaf paper attached above her desk catches my eye.

Waiting room hours drag by like a snail.
You listen to everyone tell their sad tale.
You suddenly realize it's not a bad place to be
'Cause suddenly strangers become family.

Turning, I glance back at the group and realize we are a family now.

With barely an ounce of energy left in me, I curl up in my covers. Sink into the darkness. Sink into my thoughts, and thank God for today's sweet miracle.

CHAPTER THREE

October 8 and 9

The family packs into Casey's small room at 9 a.m. and settles into their spots. Bo stands on the right of Casey, next to the respirator machine, and stares out the window. Bobby's at the foot of the bed in front of the picture window that faces the nurse's station, and Annie and I are on the left with our backs to the sink beside the nurse. She speaks.

"The family's stimulation yesterday triggered Casey's intracranial pressure, or as we call it ICP, causing his levels to rise above 20. That's a red flag for us. High ICPs will cause internal or external herniation of the brain. It's critical that his numbers remain in the teens."

Bo closes his eyes. Annie looks down. Their father stares out through the opened blinds. My face lifts to the heavens.

"The past few hours have been rough on Casey. His fever is rising. We fear the onset of pneumonia."

A fever has never stopped Casey before.

At six years old, Casey was asked to be the ring bearer in our neighbors' wedding. When the day arrived, he was spiking a fever. I suggested that he let Bo take his place. But Casey had no intention of relinquishing his role, much less turning his black tux and shiny black shoes over to his brother.

Three hours later, "Here Comes the Bride" blasted from the organ and the bridesmaids proceeded down the aisle, followed by the ring bearer and flower girl.

I couldn't take my eyes off Casey, wondering if he would make it down the white runner. But my boy never flinched. He just smiled and moved forward.

After performing his little-man role, he climbed into the pew and laid his burning head on my knee. "I did it, Mom. I did it," he whispered.

"You sure did, Son," I said proudly, while wiping the sweat from his brow. "Now we need to get you home and into bed."

I want to shout to the nurse, "Nothing stops Casey. He doesn't let obstacles get in his way. He's a born fighter." Instead, I say, "I need to talk to the doctor."

"The neurosurgeon, Dr. Bailey, sends his apologies for missing you. He checked Casey's vitals this morning and instructed us to put Casey in a medically induced coma."

"What?" Running my fingers through my hair, I look at the family then back at the nurse.

"It's a normal process with brain injury victims, used when there is swelling that puts pressure on the nervous system."

"Is he in danger?"

"Keeping Casey in a coma means he won't have to fight so hard to survive. He'll be able to get proper rest, which will allow his body to heal."

"So, how long will he be—?"

"It all depends on Casey's healing process. It's different for every patient."

Did we do this to him by bombarding him with questions yesterday? Feeling like I'm being sucked into the ocean's rip current, my hands clutch the chair's top rail.

"Can we at least stay with Casey until ten o'clock?" his father asks.

"Of course."

For the next thirty minutes, no one says a word. I'm not sure if everyone is caught up in the sounds of the heart rate monitor beeping regularly with an alert going off halfway through the recording; the respirator pump hissing as oxygen goes through Casey's mask; or if they are caught up in their own thoughts, a place sacred only to them.

The nurse pops her head into the room. "Sorry, but it's time to go."

Bobby, Bo, Annie, and I notice a middle-aged policeman pacing down the hallway. He stops when he hears the sound of footsteps.

"Casey's parents?"

He removes his hat from his balding head and tucks it under his left arm. "I'm Officer O'Brien," he says as he stretches out his hand to Bobby, then me. "I'm so sorry about your son. I heard he's in pretty bad shape."

"Worse than we imagined," Bobby says. "But he made it past the first twenty-four hours, which I hear is a miracle in itself."

"This can't be easy for either of you." He clears his throat. "I would appreciate it if you could give me a few minutes of your time."

Bobby nods.

Officer O'Brien pulls his notebook from his pants pocket, flips through worn pages, and stops toward the bottom of the pad, "Let's see." He skims over his notes. "The gentleman driving the pickup truck, who is doing fine by the way, says your son ran a red light. Since it's his word against your son's, who is unable to give his side of the story—"

I can't be a part of this. Not now. I need to be alone. I excuse myself and collapse into a chair in the waiting room, knowing Bobby can handle the logistics. My God, I'm still trying to digest that Casey's in a coma.

Sometimes I just have to take a step back, get away from the madness for a few moments; the first time I remember doing this, I was ten years old.

The family was already seated at the dinner table. I was late. As I walked in, the sibling chant started, "Pattie fatty, two-by-four, can't get through the kitchen door."

I froze. I wanted to run back upstairs, but I didn't. I sat down.

"Please pass the food around the table," Mom said, her brown eyes fixed on mine.

Then someone whispered the chorus again while passing the mashed potatoes.

"Stop," Mom said in her gentle yet stern voice. But it was too late.

I pushed my chair back. Excused myself. And ran upstairs. Mom didn't stop me. I grabbed my pink diary from its hiding place. Planted my trembling body against the side of the bed and scribbled in large print: "Dear Jesus, make them stop. I can't stand it when they are mean. I can't stand it when I hurt. I feel so alone. Please take this pain away, Jesus." My tears exploded onto the page, smudging every word.

That's how I coped then and still do now. When life gets complicated, when I hurt like my guts have been yanked out of me, I write. I pray.

I clasp my Mother Mary medal.

"Please, Mother, I turn my precious child over to you. He is yours. He has always been yours. His wings are clipped right now, and he needs you. I need you."

Determined to turn my upside-down world right-side up, I dial my loved ones, alerting them to Casey's present condition. After Masses are promised and prayer groups notified, I make my final call to my Healing Touch instructor.

Healing Touch is a nurturing energy therapy. Gentle touch of the hands assists in restoring and balancing one's physical, mental, emotional, and spiritual well-being that has been depleted due to illness, injury, surgery, and stress.

For most of my life, I've felt heat radiating from my palms, but I never knew what to do with it. Sensing the energy could speak, taste, touch, hear, and feel in a language all its own, I felt driven to explore the mysterious phenomenon. When I found an ad for Healing Touch, with a picture of hands opened and white light radiating from them, I knew I had to take the course. Last month, I completed Healing Touch Level 1 and discovered my instincts were accurate.

God must have known what loomed on the horizon, that the medical field would do all they could to save Casey's life. Must have known Casey could benefit from alternative healing methods. Must have known I would do everything in my power to save my son's life.

My instructor, Joan, picks up and the sound of her voice immediately soothes me. "Joan. Can you send distance healing Casey's way? He can use all the help—"

"I'll start a phone chain immediately. When the moment is right, use the techniques you learned in class. Casey's energy fields hold the memory of what has happened. Clearing the disturbances will help promote healing. Don't worry, honey. We'll do all we can from this end."

"Thank you, Joan. I have to run, the family just arrived. Be in touch soon."

Nothing during our morning visit prepared us for tonight. Casey's head is the size of an over-inflated basketball. His facial features are stretched to the max: The underneath lining of his lips is raised and visible, his nostrils are flared to the width of a quarter, and his ears are inverted, resembling patches of cauliflower.

Casey's ICP levels are up. His hands are ice-cold.

My breathing grows shallow.

Annie weeps.

Bo paces nervously around the room.

Bobby stands solemnly at the end of Casey's bed, his hands folded over his leather belt. He appears to be blinking back his tears, but a single droplet glides past his glasses.

How did this happen? How did yesterday's highs turn into today's lowest lows?

Just as I start to hope for progress, things are even worse than before. Will I ever again hear my boy's infectious laugh and quick-witted statements? Will I watch him dance, listen to him sing, feel his larger-than-life presence when he enters a room, or have those tender heart-to-heart moments I've come to treasure?

The doors to the ICU open. Bo, Annie, Bobby, and I walk to the elevator—only tonight, our footsteps are slow and thoughtful. Bobby breaks the silence with the police report.

"Due to Casey's situation, the policeman felt there was no need to pursue this case."

"Great," I murmur, half listening, wrestling with my thoughts.

"I can't help but wonder if Casey was drinking when he crashed—"

"Maybe he was. We can't beat ourselves up over this, Bobby. Casey's a sophomore in college now. We can't hover over him every second, forcing him to make right choices. Right now, we have more important things to worry about."

He sighs. I continue.

"Sometimes we have to learn through experience. Let's just hope Casey's been given that opportunity."

The door opens. Annie steps to the back, her hand fluttering above the brass railing. Bo fixes his gaze on the ceiling. Bobby stands dead center.

"Bobby, thanks for taking over earlier today."

He nods.

I crawl under Vanessa's desk, my makeshift sleeping quarters, and think about what it means to be a mother. We love. We support. We listen. We guide. But, no matter how hard we try, our children's choices are their own. But yet, I question. Have my priorities been askew with me returning to work, juggling two part-time jobs? Have I allowed the struggles of raising a teenager deter me from spending quality time with him? Maybe it's true: Life needs to hit us over the head with a two-by-four in order to get our attention. I just hope through it all, I loved Casey *enough*.

> I cry for yesterday . . .
> I cry for today . . .
> and for a new tomorrow.
> I cry for my son . . .
> his lessons, choices, and pain.
> I cry, knowing I have no control . . .
> that there are no guarantees in life . . .
> that I must let go.
> I cry for my family's suffering . . .
> and all the other families.
> I cry and I cry.

After finishing my morning bathroom routine—brushing my teeth, washing my face and body, changing my clothes—I walk into Casey's room at nine. My stride breaks when I lay eyes on the nurse. Her head is down. Her cheeks are pasty white. Strands of strawberry-blond hair cling to her forehead. She's mumbling while folding and tucking clean sheets around him. "Casey's ICP levels are elevated and rising. His fever lingers," she says, wiping her brow.

Does she realize I'm in the room? Does she know I can hear every word she is saying? Is she aware her words are piercing my already punctured heart?

She stops. Looks up. And continues. "Getting Casey's ICP levels under control is paramount to warding off any threats of further brain damage."

Further brain damage?

Feeling faint, I reach for the chair. No one said he's suffered brain damage.

"You know, Casey is lucky he survived twenty-four hours," she says, patting my shoulder before walking out of the room.

I agree. But can't someone just say, "Casey's going to beat the odds. His life will return to normal?" *For God's sake, somebody give me something to work with here.*

I drag the wooden chair over to Casey's bedside and rest my head on his arm. I inhale, wanting to smell my boy again. But the familiar scent of his Armani is gone, replaced by the foul scent of medicine.

"I'm not going to give up on you. I am going to grasp every straw, pull the low-hanging fruit from every spiritual tree, and call on God and His angels, seeking healing for you. I promise not to leave a stone unturned. You hear me, Son?"

Casey sleeps.

I dig into my bag, pull out my journal, and manage to write two words: "Dear Jesus." For moments on end, the words stare back at me. Finally, I underline the salutation several times, each line heavier than the one before. Then my hand freezes.

My emotions whirl inside me like leaves on a windy day. Unable to pluck them from the air, I close the diary. It slips off my lap and fans open to an older entry. My mood shifts as I flip the pages, reading about how life used to be: daily runs and meditations, spiritual books I had read, papers I had written for an online course to get my masters, characters I had met when my interior design business was in full swing, notes I had taken from psychic readings, lunches and parties I had attended with friends, and lastly, the watercolor class I had signed up for and was in the middle of . . . when life stopped.

I stuff the journal into my bag and look at Casey—gauze wrapped around his swollen head, needles in his bruised arms, a tube between his puffed lips—wondering if life will ever return to normal for him, for me.

Right now I'm adjusting to a new normal, where every breath I take centers on Casey. I've promised myself that I will give until there appears to be nothing left, and then I'll dig into my reserve and give some more. If it sucks the life out of me, so be it, because I'd die taking my last breath for my child, giving him all I've got.

My stomach growls. I eat. Folks chat in the waiting room. I join in. Someone cries. I hand her a tissue. The hospital phone rings. I answer. People walk down the hallway for the 5 p.m. visitation. I follow.

Bo and Annie catch the last leg of the visit.

"Sorry we're so late, Mom. I had to drop Dad off at the airport, so he could catch a flight back to Louisville," says Annie with Bo standing by her side.

"Oh." I can feel my forehead stretch like a rubber band then relax.

Some things never change.

Due to Bobby's line of business—selling heavy equipment internationally—his travels can stretch from three days to three weeks.

But even now?

Hearing footsteps in the hall, Annie, Bo, and I join the others. Starved, we catch a quick bite to eat at Basil Thai Restaurant, in downtown Charleston. In the middle of dinner, the phone rings. I check the area code. It's my cousin Tim, a neurologist from Boise, Idaho.

I excuse myself, step outside, and flip open the phone.

"Tim! Thanks for getting back to me so quickly. Were you able to get in touch with Dr. Bailey?"

"Yes. I also reviewed Casey's CAT scans that he forwarded."

"And?" I hear my heart beating against my ribcage.

"I'm so sorry," Tim says, as if the mountains echoed.

"Thanks."

The word drags on. I want to say more . . . to thank Tim for his time . . . for being there for me, but my fears strangle my words. I snap the phone closed and feel the cold metal against the back of my legs. I slump into a bench outside the café. My world goes black.

"Mom. You okay?" I hear Bo ask. "You never came back into the restaurant, so I had the waitress box your dinner."

We paid our bill and went back to the hospital. While we were sitting in the waiting room, Bo's voice cut through the eerie silence, and he said, "Mom, what are the doctors saying about Casey's chance of recovery?"

Not willing to share what I believe Tim implied when he said, "I'm so sorry," I blurt out, "The doctors don't know what God knows. I promise you, I am bringing Casey home with me. Nothing is stopping me, Bo. Nothing."

Bo fingers his lower lip, as if he's thinking. Is he having a private conversation with Jesus? Is he asking him to save his brother, the brother he has watched over since he walked into his life, sometimes to a fault?

Talking to Jesus wasn't uncommon for Bo, especially when he was young. Often, when a situation presented itself that was out of control, he would grab his statue of the Sacred Heart and talk to him. The first time I witnessed Bo in action was when he was five years old. Casey was four, and Annie was two.

San Francisco was experiencing unusually hot temperatures that summer. The boys, who bunked together in one room, had just awakened. While I was tying their shoes, a gust of wind roared through the opened window and slammed the door shut. It stuck. Knowing Annie was sleeping across the hall, I panicked and crawled out on the roof and yelled for help.

"Mom. I have to go to the bathroom," Casey screamed from inside as he squatted, his legs seamlessly connected.

"Hang in there, Case," I shouted as I paced across the shingles, praying that a neighbor would drive by.

Bo stuck his head out the window, the Sacred Heart statue in his hands. "Don't worry, Mom. I just asked Jesus to help us. Everything is going to be okay."

In the background, the sound of an engine grew louder as it approached the cul-de-sac. Frantically, I screamed, "Help!" My arms flapped furiously, like a fledging learning to fly. "Up here."

The neighbor caught sight of the madwoman on the roof. He parked his car, ran up the stairs, and opened the door.

Bo tugged on my shirt. "See, Mom? I told you Jesus would help."

As Bo grew older, he held onto his faith. It wasn't something he proclaimed publicly. But on many occasions, our conversations would lapse into spirituality, and I would get a glimmer of his soul's light. It's been a gift I've treasured over the years. Now, like then, a situation exists that's out of his control—life and death, blessing or curse—and I'm confident Bo has returned to the place where he finds solace.

I place my arm on Bo's shoulder. He speaks. "You know, Mom, I've been thinking. Not sure if I've been a good example for Casey. I've made a lot of stupid choices in my life."

I nod and wait for Bo to continue. Instead, he stares ahead.

Bo had mastered early the art of not getting caught drinking or smoking during those awkward teenage years. But the moment I remember most, the moment that will be forever etched into the core of my being, was the night Bo woke me from my sleep and spilled his guts.

"Mom. MOM. Wake up." Each word was laced with panic.

"What is it, Bo? You okay?" In the blink of an eye, my body moved into fight or flight. I tossed back the covers and sat up, ready to protect my boy from harm.

The moonlight streamed through the window and shined on Bo, the darkness and light coexisting as one. His body was shaking. Tears blanketed his face.

"Take this. I can't do this anymore, Mom. I'm so scared. Help me. Please."

Bo shoved a bag of pot and a pipe into my hand, and I sat there staring at the drugs in disbelief, haunted by the demons from the past. *No, God. Not my boy.* I'd been down this addiction road with my dad and alcohol, and I couldn't bear the thought of doing it again. I wanted to scream, but I knew my boy was hurting. Instead, I wrapped my arms around him. He shook. I shook. He cried. I cried—each tear riddled with guilt that this awful gene had been passed down to my son at the ripe age of seventeen.

"Sweetie, don't worry. I'll make some calls in the morning. Okay? I'll help you get through this. I promise." Even though I didn't know where to begin, I knew I wouldn't stop until I got the answers I needed and found a treatment center.

"Okay, Mom. I love you. I'm so sorry."

"I know, sweetie."

I can't recall if I ever shared this story with Annie and Casey. If not, I should have the next day, every damn painful life-sucking moment of it. If I had, maybe it would have made an impact on Casey.

Yet Casey, longing for his brother's approval, mimicked his ways. The only problem was: Casey was a rookie.

One night Casey grabbed my car keys and sneaked out of the house. After a night of binging, he got behind the wheel and headed down the highway, hoping to return the car before sunrise. But he fell asleep at the wheel, went down a ravine, and crashed my Toyota into a tree.

No longer could we ignore the pediatrician's voice. "With alcoholism on both sides of your family, your boys have a higher chance of carrying the gene."

It seems Bo has inherited the disease. He's only twenty-one, but he's been in and out of treatment for four years. It's been a roller coaster ride for all of us, the kind you never want to buy a ticket for.

Bo nudges me. "Mom."

"It's time to go," Annie whispers tenderly.

I see two nurses as we enter Casey's room. One is standing at the head of his bed, studying the ICP monitor. "His levels are escalating," she reports.

I clear my throat. The nurse to Casey's right glances up. Her name tag reads "Cathy." She nods.

"The ice mat isn't helping. His temperature is rising. It's past 103 degrees. Call the doctor. Now!" Cathy commands.

Like a tsunami brewing in the ocean, everything in ICU changes in a matter of hours, sometimes minutes.

The other nurse dashes out of the room. Annie, Bo, and I are caught in her downdraft.

I turn my head back to my boy. He's dressed in plaid boxer shorts. The blankets and sheets hang from the bed rails.

My breathing grows heavy, as if my insides are being squeezed through a mechanical vice.

I hear the sound of gut-wrenching pain. Annie and Bo are behind me, weeping.

Enough already, God. ENOUGH.

I feel like I'm riding on a runaway train. Desperately, I want the wild mechanical beast to come to a halt, but I fear the lever is broken.

The head nurse offers tissues to Bo and Annie. "I know it's hard seeing your brother in this condition. Would you rather come back tomorrow?"

Bo and Annie nod through their sniffles. They leave, and their feet drag, heavy, like their hearts.

After we hug and say goodnight, I crawl into my campsite under Vanessa's desk and start writing in my journal.

Casey, my sweet boy, I just want to hold and rock you in my arms. Not being able to comfort you, to hear where you hurt, to make things better is tearing me to pieces, bit by bit. My job as your mother has always been to be there for you—to pamper you with love, offer guidance, and shield you from harm. I feel so lost not being able to give you all you need. From the sidelines, I soak up all your pain; but even that, my son, is not enough.

Aching inside in places I didn't even know I had, I continue writing faster, my handwriting illegible.

Case, as I try to make sense of the past few days, Caroline Myss's book, Sacred Contracts, *keeps popping into my head. She writes about the ancient notion that our souls make a contract before birth in which we agree to have various human experiences and encounters with certain people in order to learn our life lessons.*

I believe that before you took your first breath, you agreed to write this chapter in your life-book. This pact is between you and God.

My pencil goes limp between my fingers and rolls onto my lap. I pick it up and continue.

Maybe my role in your contract is not to deviate one degree from my deep-rooted faith. If so, I accept the challenge.

Drained, I try to sleep, but my mind starts searching through the archives of home movies. And stops. The reel begins to play.

A seven-year-old Casey digs into his back pants pocket and retrieves a brown paper bag. He hands it to me.

I slowly pull apart the wrinkled paper and slide my hand inside. Fingering the bottom of the bag, I pull out two items: a cross and small card embossed with my favorite poem, "Footprints in the Sand."

"Do you like them, Mom?" he chirps.

"Casey, I don't just like them, I love them," I say, while pulling down on his baseball cap. "Would you like me to read the poem to you?"

"Okay." He snuggles close to me on the bottom step.

The tape ends and I clutch my journal.

I hold onto my promise. I hold onto my faith.

CHAPTER FOUR

October 10

At noon, Maggie pulls up in front of the hospital in her old Toyota, waving and honking.

Maggie is a sophomore at the College of Charleston, and a good friend to Casey and Annie. She's also the daughter of my dearest friend, Drace.

Drace and I grew up in St. Louis and have known each other since we were six years old. Over the years, our lives have become so intertwined that the line between family and friends has completely disappeared.

"Thanks, sweetie, for picking me up."

"You okay?"

"Better. It's just that—"

"What?"

"I sit in Casey's room listening to the monitors. Every beep makes my heart stop. STOP. I have to remind myself to breathe."

"Aw. You sure you want to leave?"

"It's not that I want to. It's that I have to for my own sanity. I need to connect to the outside world. I need to laugh. I need to feel alive again. Even if it's for one short hour."

"Well, say no more." Maggie slides the gear into drive.

We cruise down Broad Street, swerving between cars and running yellow lights while taking in the city's historic sites and three-hundred-year-old mansions. Maggie takes a sharp left and almost skims the bumper of the car next to us. "Are you having fun yet?"

"Yeah, but could you slow down? I'm not going to be much good to Casey if I end up in the bed next to him. Who taught you how to drive, anyway?"

She laughs. We careen along Market Street. I grip the dashboard.

A few more turns, and we say goodbye to the city. Maggie presses on the accelerator. We fly over the Ashley River Bridge. I close my eyes and pray the drawbridge doesn't rise. Seconds later, Maggie comes to a screeching halt in West Ashley. She parks and tosses her hands in the air.

"We're here."

I stretch my head out the open window and look back.

"What's wrong?"

"I'm looking for my lost soul parts. But I think they jumped into the Ashley River."

"Oh, stop." She points toward a sign that says "New Age." She says, "I thought you would like to go here since you're into all that spiritual stuff—crystals and tarot cards. Plus, I'd like to learn more."

New Age? Baloney. It's more like Old Age.

After the family moved to Charlotte in 1994, I visited a store in the Dilworth area filled with crystals, tarot cards, statues of Buddha and other deities, and bookshelves filled with ancient wisdom—some merchandise familiar, some not. Driven to learn more, my visits became more frequent. I bought, wore, and educated myself about crystals and their healing properties. I purchased boxes of cards: *Angel Blessings* and *Rider Waite Tarot*. I read books: *The Law of Life, Books I & II*; *Life and Teaching of Jesus and Mary*; *Saint Germain*; *New Moon Astrology*; The *I Ching Workbook*; *Love Is in the Earth*; and many more.

It was inside those printed pages that I learned that crystals were first used for their healing properties in Egypt in 1500 B.C. For centuries, certain cultures—the Incas, Native Americans, and Chinese—integrated crystals into their daily lives. The sacred Hindu scripture, the Vedas, along with St. Hildegard, discuss their healing powers. And they are referred to over two hundred times in the Bible. The ancient divination text, *I Ching*, goes back to the eighth century B.C., and tarot cards were created in the mid-fifteenth century.

We open the door. Chimes jingle. The intoxicating aroma of jasmine incense fills the air. The sound of monks chanting plays in the background.

Chanting is a weird choice of music for a New Age store, I think. But my senses come alive as if the chants triggered long-lost memories stored in my DNA from a past incarnation. Time stops. In my mind's eye, I time-travel.

The organ plays. The procession of nuns advances to the altar. I'm positioned in the middle of the flock, dressed from head to toe in black. My head is lowered. My hands, pointed to the heavens, press into my breastbone. Rubber-soled shoes pad to the hand-carved pews. Petticoats rustle as they brush against the wooden kneelers. Long wooden crosses, affixed to each nun's waist, jangle. We kneel. Incense clouds the air. Gregorian chants sound from the choir loft. Heads bow, looking like hundreds of penguins clustered together in the Arctic. We pray.

I blink and can't help but wonder if my past lifetime has provided the faith I need to meet today's challenges.

The voice of the petite clerk behind the glass counter grounds me in the present.

"Welcome, ladies. Let me know if you need any help."

"Look at all these crystal pendulums." Maggie pulls one with a rose quartz off the rack. "How do these things work?"

"You ask it a question and wait for it to answer."

"Huh?"

"If it swings clockwise the answer is yes, and counterclockwise is no. Well, that's the way it works for me."

Maggie's eyelids flutter. "Am I ever going to meet the man of my dreams?"

The pendulum says yes.

"I'll take this one." She hands it to the clerk.

"Look, Mags. Angel cards. I have to get these."

"Open the box. Pick the card on top. Who is it?" Her breath warms my neck.

"Adriana."

"Read what it says."

"We've heard your prayers. Pay attention to your intuition, thoughts, dreams, and feelings. Follow divine guidance."

"Perfect message for you."

"Your turn."

I hand Maggie the deck. She shuffles the cards and picks angel Astara. "I think this card is for you. Listen. 'God and his angels want you to have more fun.' Well, that's not exactly what it says, but close."

The chimes jingle again, but this time without the door opening.

"See?" Maggie beams. "The angels agree. Ready to go? We still have time to swing by Walmart. Their clothes are inexpensive and will fit your budget."

When I packed to come to Charleston, my mind was 250 miles away with Casey. Haphazardly, I filled my suitcase with T-shirts, jeans, overalls, turtlenecks, and sweatshirts. Four days into my stay, my clothes are dirty. With no time to sit at a laundromat, picking up a few items to stretch my humble wardrobe makes sense.

While we're browsing through the clothes racks at Walmart, Maggie asks, "Do you want to hear about my most embarrassing Walmart moment?"

"Sure," I say, clanking the plastic hangers together, looking for my shirt size.

"A couple months ago, my friends and I popped in here to pick up suntan lotion. I really had to use the bathroom. The girls told me to be quick because they wanted to get to the beach. When I came out of the bathroom they all started laughing."

"Laughing. Why?"

"Because toilet paper was hanging, you know." Maggie points to her backside.

I cup my hands over my mouth and shriek. "Really?"

Her words pick up speed.

"So I ducked inside a clothes rack. Grabbed the toilet paper. Wadded it into a ball. Tossed it in the trash can. Rushed out the door. And never looked back."

Maggie bursts into laughter. I join in. It's a welcome sound. A sound I've forgotten.

"Hopefully your humiliation wasn't caught on camera, Mags."

"God, no. But my friends will never let me live it down. My new nickname is 'Toilet Trail.'"

Maggie shaves five minutes off our travel time back to the hospital. She parks in front of the revolving entrance doors that are covered by an extended roof, open on three sides. Red brick pillars, matching the exterior of the rectangular building, are scattered from end to end, supporting the structure. Visitors are clustered around the ashtray next to the front door, chatting and smoking. I lean over and kiss Maggie on the cheek.

"Thanks, sweetie, for allowing me to feel whole again. For one precious hour, the weight was lifted."

"I really had fun. If you need anything or just need a break, please call me," she says, while tying her wind-beaten black curly hair into a ponytail.

Every time I reach my lowest lows . . . when I think I don't have the strength to put one foot in front of the other . . . friends come along and let me climb out of my world and into theirs, filling me with enough energy to carry on.

When I walk into Casey's room, it's like entering an air traffic control tower, crackling with intense, efficient activity. A squadron of nurses checks his vitals, reads the machines, and scratches notes in his chart. The cleaning lady gathers trash and swishes the mop across the floor.

The last time I saw this many people gathered around Casey was in Long Island, New York, in 1990.

It was Huntington Bay Club's first swim meet of the year. The eight-and-unders were positioned behind the block and ready to compete in a freestyle race. Casey mounted the end block. The gun went off. All his competitors dove into the water and furiously flapped their arms, except Casey. One of the mothers in the stands burst out laughing.

Pointing at him, she cried, "Look!"

All heads turned at once. We watched his body playfully roll to the left then sway to the right, catching the wake of his rivals, looking like a dolphin at sea. Getting to the other side was the furthest thing from his mind.

The race ended. He pulled himself from the pool's edge. Water cascaded down his stocky frame. His coach handed him his ribbon and cheered. "Great job, Casey."

Prize in hand, Casey clopped his small flat feet on the wet pavement and headed toward me. Beaming, he waved his ribbon in the air and shouted, "Mom, I got sixth place."

What I wouldn't give to see my boy smile, to hear the sound of his voice, the sound of his laughter again. Instead, each hour rolls into the next, like waves breaking on the shoreline. Nothing changes.

Tennis shoes squeak across the tile. I see the night shift nurse standing behind Casey, replacing his insulin bag.

"Alone again?"

"For now. But several hours ago, Casey's room was filled with his buddies from Charlotte," I say proudly. "Do you think Casey heard their voices? Felt their handshakes?"

"I do. We talk to the patients all the time, telling them we're ready to prick their finger, take their pulse, or give them an injection. We don't want to scare them."

"So, it's possible he hears me whisper prayers in his ear?"

"I believe so. I've been doing some research, and studies show that even when patients are in comas, they are aware of their surroundings. Keep talking to your boy," she says as she walks out the door.

I clear my throat and begin recapping the day's events, hoping Casey will hear my words.

"The nurses brought your ICPs down to fourteen this afternoon. Later, your high school buds—Karl, Candace, John, Hillary, Allie, and Jeremy—arrived. I gave each of them a mustard seed stone and made them promise to keep their thoughts positive. As we walked into your room, their bodies froze and their faces went white."

I believe the absence of Casey's magnetic smile, mischievous nature, and colossal personality was more than they could bear. But they became warriors as they approached his bedside.

"Hillary and Allie gave you a photograph collage with high school memories. It's up on your bulletin board. John wanted you to have something. He put his football sweatband in your hand. I hope it's clean! Even tough-guy Karl said, 'I love you, bro.'

"While I was walking your buds down the corridor, Karl mentioned Charlotte Catholic's first junior varsity football game. It made your mama's spirit fly high as we reminisced over that game." I pause and can feel myself back in the stands rooting for the team, caught up in the excitement of the game. "Remember how huge the opposing team was? Country boys and corn fed, I believe. The coach put you in for one of the final plays. Your goal was to block a guy twice your size. The whistle blew. Your opponent rushed toward you. You broke to the right and ran through the opening. The coach immediately pulled you out of the game.

"While we were walking to the car, I asked you, 'Case, why didn't you nail number 63?'

"You said, 'Mom, did you see the size of that guy? He would have killed me.'"

I gaze at Casey and gently brush back a few stray hairs. A single tear courses down his cheek, and I know my boy has heard every word I said.

CHAPTER FIVE

October 12

Surprises come in all sorts of sizes and shapes. And this morning, mine is dressed in a lab coat.

"Dr. Bailey? You're doing your rounds a bit late today," I say, tapping my watch, the hands fixed at 9 a.m. sharp.

Under his moustache, he reveals a smile. "Allow me to introduce the residents." Dr. Bailey's arm slowly fans the group of doctors, pausing briefly as he rattles off names, titles, and areas of expertise.

"Nice to meet all of you. So, how's my boy?"

"Better. The nurses haven't had to drain Casey's brain fluids since yesterday afternoon. His ICP levels have stabilized under twenty and are still holding. He still has an infection in his blood. We're treating it with antibiotics. We inserted a feeding tube this morning, but his stomach refused it. We're feeding him intravenously."

"Is it normal for the stomach—"

"When a patient experiences the amount of trauma Casey did, the heart and brain are the first organs to come alive, and then the lungs kick in, followed by the liver and kidneys. The stomach is the last organ to awaken."

"I see."

"We're bringing him out of the coma to check his vitals. By one o'clock, he should be completely weaned." Dr. Bailey tucks Casey's chart under his arm.

A moment after the doctors leave, I wish I'd asked a hundred more questions. What if Casey wakes up and he can't speak? Can't move? Can't remember? What if he's a—

Knowing my thoughts paint life as I see it, and my beliefs are the stepping stones of experience, I erase the negativity from my mind and go for a walk.

The city's sidewalks, slanted and cracked from the root structures of hundred-year-old trees, swarm with people. Hospital employees carrying Styrofoam containers weave between the pedestrians. Local businessmen and women duck inside cafés. Visitors stop and take pictures.

At a fast pace, I snake through the crowds to the Charleston City Marina. It's one of those cloudless autumn days when the air smells of dried leaves and the trees are pumpkin-colored.

A vacant bench, weathered from the sun's heat and ravages of nature, faces the river. I rest there and watch the sailboats dance upon the crests as seagulls dive for their lunch. A sudden calmness washes over me, and my first sailing adventure—with Casey, age twelve, on Huntington Bay— comes to mind.

It was parents' day at Huntington Bay Club, late August. The intoxicating sea aroma filled the air. The soft breeze and warm temperature were perfect conditions for sailing. The long pier clattered and shook as family members crossed the warped planks, anxious to witness their child's mastery of sailing skills.

A few feet from our designated Opti, I spotted a sea jelly floating in the water and yelled ahead. "Case, I thought you said there weren't any jellyfish this time of the year?"

"Oh, Mom, he's dead."

"Then why was he going *blub, blub, blub*?"

He grinned and offered his arm for support. I placed my right foot in the hull, and the boat rocked. I froze. Casey gently edged me forward. "I promise, Mom, I will take you on the ride of your lifetime, if you just get in and sit down."

Once in position, I gripped the rim of the fiberglass boat. I panicked and felt my lifelong fear of drowning paralyze me. I had never quite recovered from my five-year-old self, who'd fallen into the fishpond cleaning her tea party plates, who flapped and screamed so furiously she had to be rescued by the passing milkman.

I watched as Casey gracefully maneuvered the dingy over the waves. Convinced that the only thing I feared was fear itself, I tilted my head upward and welcomed the sun's warm touch and the salty sea breeze upon my face.

Casey helped me sail through one of my greatest fears on that warm August day. Now I'm here to help my boy walk through his.

Seagulls squawk. The wind brushes against my face. Footsteps crackle on the dried leaves behind me. I'm back in Charleston. I glance at my watch. It's 12:45 p.m.

My heart quickens as I rush into Casey's room. His eyes are closed. His body is motionless.

"Isn't Casey supposed to be out of his coma?" I blurt, startling the nurse who is taking his temperature. "The doctor said he would be weaned off the drug by 1 p.m."

"It takes time, honey, to wash the drugs out of his system."

"Time! How much time are we talking about—minutes, hours, days?" I can feel the color drain from my face.

The nurse pats me on the shoulder. "Honey. I know this isn't easy. Why don't you have a chat with your son? I'm sure you have a thousand stories to tell. And hearing his mom's voice is good medicine."

I turn inward, like I've done before and think about whose clock we're on: the doctor's, mine, or God's? It triggers a memory from childhood, a memory so embedded in my mind that I've sketched it on paper to keep it alive.

"Case, I'm going to tell you a story about how I remember Heaven.

"It was such a magical and whimsical place. There were fields of wildflowers that stretched for miles, sprinkled with oak and red-leaf maple trees. The sounds of nature rang through the air, from babbling brooks to the *purdy, purdy, purdy* whistle of cardinals. The air permeated with the fragrant scent of roses, lilacs, and honeysuckle.

"Grown-ups and children of every color played and laughed together. The animals and fairies were our friends. Harmony was our brother. Love was our breath. And peace, our vibration.

"Angels, sages, and prophets were our companions. My favorite was Jesus. I loved sitting on his knee and listening to him speak.

"One day he told me that my earth mother and father were waiting for me. He picked me up, held me tight in his arms, and we journeyed down a long, winding road. Soon we came to what looked like an oversized cornucopia with an enormous opening. Jesus, still holding me, stepped inside."

I stop and reposition myself in the chair. Sunlight seeps through the window, casting shadows of Casey lying in bed against the wall. I swallow hard and continue.

"At first there was a gentle breeze, and the angels' voices rang in our ears. But as the tunnel narrowed, the music stopped, the light dimmed, and the wind roared. Even though Jesus' long hair pelted against his face, he kept moving.

"A strange feeling stirred inside me. I thrust my arms around Jesus. Why did I need a new family? I already had a huge one in heaven. Maybe I should tell Jesus to turn around. But it was too late.

"He stopped at the mouth of the tunnel. I tightened my grip, not wanting to say goodbye. How would I survive without my best friend?

"'I will never forsake you,' Jesus said, as if he could read my mind. 'Just call my name and I'll be there.'

"Well, Casey, that memory stayed fresh in my mind as a youngster. Oh, how I longed to go home. Almost daily, I'd sit in my bedroom windowsill and stare high above the sycamore tree and call Jesus. 'Hi, Jesus. It's me again. I really don't belong here. Please come and take me home.'"

I pause and check Casey's ICP levels. "Would you believe, Case, that my insistent cry to go home lasted till I was forty-six?" I say lightheartedly, realizing how crazy that sounds.

I bend over the rails and examine Casey's face. His eyelids don't flutter. His muscles don't twitch.

"Well, if this wasn't a one-way conversation, you'd probably pipe in and ask, 'What made you stop, Mom?'"

My mood shifts. I slump back in the chair, remembering that I was at a place in my life when I was uncomfortable with me, uncomfortable with my marriage, and uncomfortable with certain circumstances surrounding the children. My daily calls to heaven increased, and again I begged to come home.

I close my eyes and think about my conversation with Casey. It appears that giving time, time, is a thread that runs through my life. Whether it's walking through fears, desiring to return "home," finding the courage to move on, or waiting for Casey to emerge from his coma . . . they all revolve around time.

And God doesn't wear a watch.

CHAPTER SIX

October 14

The clock stops. Ticks backward. Stops again. And holds.

Just when I think I can't breathe and can't feel, something happens that turns my "cannots" into "cans": Family.

At 1 p.m., I walk into the waiting room with my head down.

My cell phone rings.

"Pop, is that you?"

I envision Pop—olive complexion, hazel eyes, silver hair—sitting on the lanai, dressed in his Florida attire: white T-shirt, gray cotton shorts, and sockless leather loafers. In one hand, he's holding the phone, in the other, a cigarette. His athletic legs, lined with varicose veins, are crossed.

Ever since I was a little girl, I've thought Pop was rather handsome. But I think he already knew that.

One story he loved to boast about happened years ago, in 1978.

He and one of his buddies were walking into a casino in Las Vegas. A tour bus filled with older women pulled up alongside them. The first lady off the bus made eye contact with Dad. "You sure look like George Peppard." Her words rang through the crowd: "George Peppard! George Peppard!" Soon Dad was surrounded by a busload of women asking for his autograph.

Even though Pop loved being the center of attention and making women's heads turn, young and old, what he loved most was family.

"Sure is, honey. How ya doing? How's our boy?"

"Oh, Pop. Not so good."

"What's wrong?"

"Remember yesterday when I told you how good Casey was doing? Well, everything backfired today. Dr. Bailey informed me this morning that Casey's prognosis is worse than yesterday. The nursing staff had to drain his brain fluids through the night. His fever won't drop."

"So, what does that—?"

"It means the doctor is putting Casey back in a coma. And running more tests."

"For what?"

"I'm not one hundred percent sure. Something about testing his blood and brain fluids."

"Wish I could be there with you, honey. If it makes you feel any better, I went to church yesterday."

Church was never Pop's thing. He fulfilled his weekly obligation on Sunday with the family. But he usually lingered closer to the door and occasionally sneaked outside to shoot the breeze with the men. Then twenty years ago, he joined AA and replaced dogma with spirituality. He attends weekly meetings, reads his daily reflections, and trusts in a Higher Power.

"I bet the Big Guy was surprised to see you."

"Yeah. Been a while. I slid into a vacant pew and buried my head in my hands. Your old man cried like a baby. I wiped my tears with my handkerchief, and asked Him if he would be kind enough to grant Casey a miracle."

"Aw, Pop. What would I do without you?"

"I'm here for you, kiddo. Okay? You call me if you need anything. Promise? I love you. Hey, your brothers are here visiting. They want to say hello."

As Pop rounds up his boys, my mind plummets into the past.

Growing up, Pop was harder on his sons than he was on his daughters. He pushed them to be better at school, better at sports, almost to the point of perfection.

I'd almost get sick watching the interaction between Pop and my brothers, especially at the dinner table when Pop pointed out the goal they missed, the block they didn't make, the punt that lost the game. And I often wondered if their stomachs were in knots, too.

But Charlie and Johnny never said a word, at least that I remember. They just kept giving life their best. Today Charlie is a real estate agent, and Johnny owns and operates a construction business.

Over the years, Pop softened, and I came to realize that it wasn't that he didn't love his boys, because he did. He was just doing the best he could with the tools he had, the tools that had been passed down from his father. Knowing they are all together, picking up the lost pieces and starting anew, makes me happy.

Pop comes back on the line.

"Sorry about the wait, sweetie. Here's your brother."

Charlie, the oldest, promises prayers and tells me to call him if I need anything. As he clears his throat several times, sounding like he swallowed a frog, I can't help but wonder if his emotions have gotten the best of him.

"Life was much easier when we were growing up, wasn't it, sis?"

"Yeah. But sometimes you were such a jerk. Remember when you scared the wits out of us girls?"

One night when my parents were out of town, the five sisters—ages twelve and under—were gathered in a bedroom. We heard noises coming from the main floor and ran to the banister.

"Who's there?" we shouted into the darkness.

No one answered.

The sound of a door closing trailed upstairs. We ran into the bathroom, turned the lock and hid. One sister climbed into the hamper, another in the tub. The rest of us crammed in the shower and closed the curtain. The stairs in the hallway creaked louder. "He's coming up the steps," said the voice inside the hamper, teeth chattering between each word. We held our breath. There was a rap at the door. It stopped. A heavy fist pounded into the wood. Inside the shower, the whites of our eyes shined like strobe lights in the night sky. Someone squeaked like a mouse, "Whooo's there?" The silence lingered. Then laughter seeped beneath the door. We knew in an instant it was Charlie; his

contagious laugh gave him away. "Not funny," we said, as we filed out of
the bathroom, still shaking from fright.

Like then, Charlie's laughter bellows through the air. "You girls were
so gullible and so easy to tease. Sorry about that. Listen, here's Johnny.
We'll talk soon."

"I'd like to come to Charleston to be with you."

My fingers press into my sternum.

"I can catch the next plane out of Florida." His voice breaks. "I don't
think you should be alone."

Johnny, the second youngest of seven, wears his heart on his sleeve.
He can't stomach seeing those he loves in pain. After Mom had open-
heart surgery, Johnny took one look at her and walked out of the room.
He leaned against the cold, tiled wall, and his unbridled tears broke free.

"Stay, Johnny. Have fun with Dad and Charlie."

"Are you sure?"

I lie. "I'm sure."

Even though Johnny is willing to give up his first vacation in years, I
don't have the strength to hold up one more person. Not now.

"Bro, one more thing . . . I'll never forget your offer. Never."

I hang up the phone and memories of my childhood overwhelm my
defenses.

Growing up with six siblings in a nine-year span presented its own
set of challenges, as well as advantages. Early on, we each inherited a
nickname. I'm not sure who christened each of us with our new names,
but they stuck. Charlie was Blockhead. Mary was Chicken. I was Fatty
Pattie. Rita was Chiquita Banana. Geri was Rubber Teeth. Johnny was
Pumpkin Head. Margie was Crow's Feet. On more occasions than I wish
to remember, the family loved rubbing salt in the wound. For some of
us, the sarcasm only added fuel to the fire of our own insecurities. I was
one of them.

It took years of work, digging deep inside and learning to love myself,
before I came to realize that the voices I carried in my head and claimed
as my own were just that: voices. Voices that had no power over me
unless I gave them power.

It was then that I realized we all come into this world whole, get broken, and spend the rest of our lives putting the pieces back together; that siblings can be cruel at times, which comes from immaturity; that dads can be tough on their boys, which stems from wanting the best for them. But in my heart of hearts, I don't believe any of us intentionally causes harm to hurt others. We just act from inexperience. Over the years, that inexperience ebbs away. Healing begins. Hearts open. Forgiveness comes. Love prevails. And we become whole again.

Today, my family are my stars in the night, my sun in the day, and my rainbows after the rains.

CHAPTER SEVEN

October 17–19

"Come on, Mom," Bo shouts, bracing his body against the open door. "We're going to be late. Dad and Annie are already in Casey's room." Smiling, he pats his cargo pants and says, "Got something for Casey."

"Give me a minute, Bo."

I write my prayer and slide it into the box on Vanessa's desk.

Bo twists and stretches his neck, looking like an anhinga, a water bird. "What's that?"

"A God box."

"Where did it come from?"

"Vanessa made it. I wanted the family members to have a place to put their prayers."

Bo squints. "What's it say on top?"

"When your cross is too heavy to bear, give it to God. He will take care of the rest."

"Mom, are you crying?"

"A little. Casey didn't have a good morning. His blood and lungs are riddled with infection. He's still running a high fever. His ICPs are skyrocketing."

Bo grabs my arm, we start running down the hall, I barely feel my feet touch the ground.

Inside Casey's room, Bo releases his grip and pulls out a crumpled piece of loose-leaf paper from his pants pocket, clears his throat, and reads.

"To my brother:

'Because You're My Best Friend . . .
When you are sad,
I will dry your tears.
When you are scared,
I will comfort your fears.
When you are worried,
I will give you hope.
When you are confused,
I will help you cope.
And when you are lost
and can't see the light,
I shall be your beacon,
shining ever so bright.
This is my oath
I pledge till the end.
Why, you may ask?
Because you're [my brother], my friend.'
—Monica Maichua Lo, 'Because You're My Best Friend . . .'"

Bo tucks the paper under Casey's pillow and squeezes his brother's hand.

"Love ya, bro."

Watching this sweet moment with Bo reminds me of a tender scene from long ago—older brother meets baby brother for the first time—which happened almost twenty years ago.

Bo had been number one for twenty months before Casey came along, and like an only child, he got all of his mom and dad's attention.

A little nervous about sibling rivalry, Bobby and I stopped by a toy store on our way home from the maternity ward. Once home and inside the door, I handed my eight-pound, eight-ounce bundle of love over to my mom. I bent down until I was eye level with Bo and hugged him. After we finished playing our verbal ping-pong game of, "I love you. I love you more," I handed him the present from the toy store. He pushed down on the giraffe's head and watched him glide across the tile floor. "I want to see my brother," he said.

We walked into the den where Casey lay on my mom's lap. Bo crawled up on the ottoman, snuggled next to his grammy, and anxiously waited for permission to touch this living doll. She nodded. Bo laid his head on his brother, and Casey grabbed his hair. In his squeaky toddler voice, Bo said, "I love my brother."

That was then.

Today, some things have changed—Bo's hands are bigger, his voice has matured—and some have not: his love for his brother.

As the family walks down the hallway, Bo motions for Bobby and Annie to go ahead.

"Mom, I have to tell you something. This weekend is Lisa's wedding. Dad is leaving tonight for St. Louis."

His niece, Lisa? What is that man thinking? For God's sake, Casey's in a coma.

"I was thinking that I might go with him. But, I'll stay, if you want me to."

Taken aback, I carefully examine my words before I speak.

"Bo, I can't tell you what to do. You're twenty-one and able to make your own decisions. But before you do, ask yourself one question: 'If something happens to my brother, will I be able to live with the choice I made?' Only you can answer that question honestly. Listen to your heart, Son. It never lies."

We stop at the elevator. Bo steps in, joining his dad and Annie. "See you at five," I say. But before anyone can answer, the doors close.

Outside Casey's window, the sun slips below the horizon, sending rays of amber, peach, and burnt orange outward and upward like spokes of a wheel. I turn as Bobby walks in, alone. After spending thirty minutes with Casey, I duck out of the room to give Bobby time with his son; I stop in at the nurse's station.

"Is it possible to extend visiting hours until six-thirty? My sister is due in from Atlanta any minute now. I know she'd love to see Casey."

"Of course."

As I'm walking into the waiting room, Tom, one of my waiting room cohorts, is broadcasting his good news to his camping partners. "Chris had a tracheotomy this morning. He also had a feeding tube administered. There's a possibility he's moving to the step-down floor later this evening."

Sue chimes in. "Mom turned the corner last night, and she's moving out of the ICU tomorrow."

We all cheer.

While huddled in our group hug, Sue, Tom, and his family pull their mustard seed stones from their pockets and whisper, "Thank you."

Humbly, I nod.

My waiting room buddies and I haven't talked about the mustard seed stones. We never have to. Volumes of unedited compassion are communicated each time we pass one another in the hallway, showcasing our stones. Can it be that those iridescent stones, anchored in prayer, wrapped in faith, and cradled in hope are responsible for these pivotal healings? I wonder.

Five minutes later, the elevator *dings*.

Mary, impeccably dressed in her perfectly pressed white sleeveless cotton shirt and coral shorts with matching leather sandals, steps into the hallway, dragging her suitcase behind. I rush to her side, wrap my arms around her, and squeeze her so tight that I ruffle her short, frosted hair.

"Aw, Mare. So happy you're here."

"Me too."

We loosen our grip. Mary fingers her hair as she scans me from head to toe. "You look like a bag lady."

"What? You don't like my overalls? I thought they were in style."

"For farmers. I need to get us a hotel room."

"Not now. ICU is giving us thirty extra minutes tonight. We need to move fast."

Mary parks her red suitcase, and we run down the hall. She stops a few feet outside Room One and grabs my hand. "Just give me a minute." She breathes.

Bobby walks out of the room. "How was your trip, Mary?"

"Not bad. How's Casey?"

"Still in a coma." He turns and points to Casey lying in the bed.

Mary stretches her neck, peeks in, and winces.

"Let's go." I pull Mary by her shirt. Over her shoulder, she waves goodbye to Bobby.

Mary sandwiches Casey's hand in hers.

"Hi, Casey. It's Aunt Mary. I love you."

Mary has always had a soft spot for Casey, and Casey has much love for his Aunt Mary. Maybe it's because their personalities are similar: quick-witted. When the two of them banter, it's like listening to a tennis ball whoosh across the court at full speed. Yet when it comes to looks, Casey has a few of his mama's characteristics—olive skin, thick brown hair, heavy brows, broad smile, and a long torso with short legs.

But none of that matters today.

Like paper dolls, Mary's hand and my hand connect. For the next thirty minutes, neither of us speaks.

Back in the waiting room, Mary chats with Vanessa, her chin resting on her hand.

"Any nice hotels close by? I'd like to get my sister a room."

"The Marriott Courtyard is just a few blocks away. Would you like me to call them?"

Mary slides her elbow across the desk. "Please. And thank you."

While Mary and Vanessa make arrangements, I drop into my thoughts. For eleven days, I've been minutes away from my boy. What if he takes a turn for the worse? What if he miraculously says, "Mom," and I am not here? Realizing I'm heading down a dead-end street playing the "what if" game, I beeline it to the ICU, explain my dilemma to the nurses, jot down my cell phone, and ask them to call me if there is any change in Casey's condition. Next, I stop at Vanessa's desk to request the same.

With detailed directions from Vanessa in hand, Mary and I drive to the Marriott. Every time we are together, it turns into the Lucy and Ethel Show. She's Lucy, I'm Ethel—so says Mary.

"Go right. No, I meant left. Oh no, we're heading down a one-way street. Watch out for that car." Scream. Shriek. Honk!

Inside the hotel lobby, my arms collapse on the check-in counter, and my head follows, a culmination of sheer emotional weight from the past eleven days. Given how I'm dressed, I let Mary do the talking.

"Is it possible to get a room with a bay view?"

With pursed lips, the clerk looks up.

"The hotel provides rooms at a discounted rate for patients' family members. Honoring your request isn't feasible."

Mary doesn't give up. She fills the clerk in on the details of Casey's accident, his current status—blood and lungs riddled with infection, high fever, and skyrocketing ICPs—and my latest sleeping arrangements.

The clerk hands us the keys. "I did the best I could," she says.

Inside our room, we toss our purses on the bed, open the sliding door, and step out on the large deck. Waves gently brush against the shore. Sailboats and yachts, tied to the weathered docks, rock. The gentle breeze gathers the scent of fish and blows it our way.

Mary and I don't talk. Instead, I think both of us are saying a silent prayer of gratitude.

We step back inside, and my eyes lock on the queen beds.

The body is an astonishing mechanism. It holds itself together as stress mounts, keeps fighting, pushing forward until a miraculous window of opportunity presents itself. I'm thinking my time has come. I fall on the mattress and close my eyes.

Mary pulls out the TV control.

"Why won't this thing work?"

"Are you sure you're pushing the right button?"

"Yes. See? I pushed this button, then this one, and this one. The TV is broken. I'm calling the front desk."

I roll my eyes, thinking this won't be the first time she's called for help.

Over the years, I've witnessed Mary's technology skills, or lack thereof. Whenever some device—computer or controller—doesn't work fast enough, she calls for her husband. "Kevin, I can't get this to work. You need to come fix it." And he does.

She hangs up the phone and clamps her hand around her suitcase. "Let's go."

"Where?" I mumble.

"Down to the front desk. The clerk said the hotel's handyman, Michael, has gone home for the evening. She's getting us a new room with a working TV."

"You've got to be kidding me, Mary? Leave this room with a view?"

"Sorry, but I can't fall asleep without the TV playing in the background."

Reluctantly, I gather my belongings and follow Mary. Just as we are ready to step into the elevator, Michael steps off. Within minutes, there's a picture and sound coming from the TV.

Mary unzips the top pocket on her suitcase and hands me two cards: one from her tennis team, the other from her and Kevin, both with cash tucked inside.

"Now you can extend your stay in the hotel a few extra days."

"Aw, Mare. It feels like angels are falling out of the sky—the hotel clerk, the handyman, your tennis team, then you and Kevin."

"And I bet there are more on their way, sis." Mary checks her watch. "It's eight o'clock. Let's grab something to eat before we go back to the hospital. Will I get to see Bo?"

"No. He went to St. Louis with Bobby."

"St. Louis? What for?"

"Lisa, Bobby's niece, is getting married this weekend."

"Really?" Her mouth gapes open. "How do you feel about that?"

"Truthfully, Mary, I was hoping Bo would stay."

"Did you tell him that?"

"Told him he needed to ask himself, 'If something happened to my brother, would I be able to live with the choice I made?'"

Mary shakes her head.

"What?"

"You're too nice. I would have been in his face. I would have said there are no options. You're here to stay. Your brother is fighting for his life. And we have no idea how this is going to work out. So, when did you first hear about this?"

"This morning. Bobby mentioned he was thinking about going to the wedding."

"And what did you say?"

"He didn't ask for my opinion. So, I didn't offer."

We eat something quick at a burger place, head to the hospital, and sit with Casey. Visiting hour flies by, and soon we're back at the hotel.

Before crawling into our beds, I hand Mary a mustard seed. Tears race down her face as she reads Matthew's verse. We hug, say goodnight, and slip our exhausted bodies between the sheets.

"Hey, Mare," I say, through the darkness. "Do you remember when Mom used to pick all five of us up from school and drive us to Carmen Thomas Dance Studio?"

"Smoking one cigarette after another with the windows closed!" Mary coughs and chokes, as if her lungs remember.

I can feel an updraft as Mary rises in her bed.

"Miss Carmen would pace those scuffed floors commanding, 'Plié, one, two, plié, one, two,'" Mary mimics. "Then she'd follow with, 'Now, up on your toes girls. Up. Up. Higher.'"

How can I forget that? As a child I rolled up on my toes, listened to my bones crack, winced in pain, and rolled back. I still feel the burn.

"My fave was performing at Kiel Auditorium—tapping across the stage, wearing makeup and—"

"Giving orders for us to follow your lead. Mary . . . you—" I'm choking on my laughter.

"Oh, be quiet," Mary grimaces. "So I turned in the wrong direction. Big deal."

Called The Lemon Drops and dressed in yellow-sequined leotards, we five sisters marched in single file across the floor and stopped center stage, waiting for our cue. As the music began, we clanked our metal tips against the scuffed hardwoods—in front, behind, and to the side of us—in perfect harmony. But when it came time to tap in a circle, Mary tapped clockwise as the rest of us tapped counterclockwise.

I think we're done talking as the silence lingers, but then Mary starts singing softly. I pipe in and our voices join as we sing the lyrics from Gypsy, "Together Wherever We Go," the song The Lemon Drops danced to over forty years ago.

Our voices grow faint. "Goodnight, Mare. Glad you're here."

Every chair in the waiting room is taken this morning. Grown-ups cluster in groups. Children sit on the floor, reading books and playing board games. The room hums with the sound of cell phones, laughter, and tears.

Mary and I lean against the corner of the receptionist's desk.

"I sure could go for a good cup of coffee," Mary says through her yawn.

Before I get a chance to speak, Vanessa whispers from behind.

"You might want to take the elevator up to the ninth floor. They have specialty coffees there. It's kind of a secret."

In the elevator, Mary and I are so engrossed in conversation that we don't notice we're going down rather than up. Suddenly the doors open, and a guy who is the spitting image of George Clooney steps in. Our jaws drop. Mary studies his hospital badge. "So, you're a cardiologist?"

Mary is every stranger's best friend.

"I am," he says, rather abruptly.

"Well, Doctor, I have high blood pressure. I think it's hereditary. Our family is riddled with heart problems. I was just wondering . . ."

Mary's prattling on and on. Finally, the doors open. I have never seen a doctor exit so fast.

But Mary's not finished, not by a long shot. Before I know it, she's right on his heels.

". . . what do you think my chances are of having a heart attack?"

The doctor stops cold and turns to face us.

"Didn't you ladies mention you were going up? I think you got off on the wrong floor."

As the elevator climbs to the ninth floor, Mary and I are laughing so hard that we double cross our legs.

My jaw drops as we walk into the spacious room. Round tables, surrounded by leather chairs, sit on navy-blue carpeting. A large picture window, overlooking Charleston, fills the left wall, while watercolor scenes of the city line the right. Ahead, a mahogany cabinet stretches from floor to ceiling and serves as a coffee bar.

"Check this place out, Mare. I don't even feel like I'm in the hospital."

We each grab a cup of coffee and sit in front of the window.

"Breathtaking, isn't it, Mary?"

"Sure is. So, what do you like most about Charleston?"

"The people. The slower lifestyle. The beaches are definitely a plus. Oh, and I love that Charleston is a historic town—the wars, the hurricanes, the earthquake. It all makes Charleston special. Hey, wanted to thank you."

"For what?"

"For that last episode. The last time I remember laughing that hard was when Casey had to interview me back when he was in grade school."

"Pray tell."

"Casey and I sat on the edge of my bed. He asked nine questions. I answered. But then he asked the tenth one: 'Mom, are you spontaneous?' And my mind went blank. Not blank because I couldn't remember. Blank because I couldn't think of a time when I acted on a whim. I could hear Casey's pencil drumming against his notepad. Finally, his voice cut through the silence. 'Mom, if you have to think about it that long, you're obviously not spontaneous.' We both fell back on the bed and couldn't stop laughing."

My smile weakens.

"Mare, what if Casey and I never have the opportunity to laugh like that again?"

Mary puts my hand in hers. "You will."

"Are you sure?"

Mary puts her coffee cup on the table and places her hand on my knee, her eyes glued to mine. "Now is not the time to let go of your faith, Pattie. It's a gift you came into this world with, a gift many of us wish we had."

"I know, Mare. But sometimes it's so hard."

"Well, life wasn't meant to be easy. We all came here to learn. You know that. You've told me that a million times. Sure we're going to fall. But when we do, we'll get back up, dust ourselves off, and start all over again." Mary slides back in the chair. "And, sis, don't forget, I'm always here for you."

I smile through my tears, remembering a conversation Mary and I had years ago about promises we both made before we journeyed to earth.

We were sitting on the back porch, sipping a glass of wine, talking and laughing like sisters do, straight from the heart.

"I don't know why God gave you so many challenges in this life," Mary uttered.

"I do."

"Why?"

"Well, I believe Jesus gathered all the souls who were ready to journey to earth. There were thousands of us. I was sitting in the front row, and you were behind me. Jesus asked for volunteers to undertake some rather difficult tasks while on earth."

"Like what?"

Whenever Mary is engaged in conversation, she asks a million questions, not to be annoying, but because she's genuinely interested. I've always admired her gift of staying in the present, something I'm still working on. Usually, my restless mind can fly from topic to topic in the blink of an eye, as if it were a kite dancing in the wind.

"I can't remember, Mare. All I know is that I loved Jesus so much, that every time he presented a new opportunity to further one's spiritual growth, I raised my hand."

"Yeah, and I was probably pushing your hand higher, saying, 'Give it to her. Give it to her.'" Mary pressed her feet into the cushion and hugged her legs. "I guess that wasn't very nice of me."

"Oh, Mare, it was perfect."

"Perfect. Why?"

"Because I believe that you, too, made a promise to Jesus."

"I did. What was it?"

"That you'd stand by my side through the good times, bad times, and in-between times."

And today, as in the past, Mary has kept her promise.

Hours later, the walls outside the ICU are lined with families. Heads are low. Bodies still. In silence, we wait for the signal to enter.

"Mary." I whisper. "Want to help me do a Healing Touch treatment on Casey?"

"Who? Me? You're kidding, right?"

"No. I could really use your help."

"But I don't know the first thing about energy work. What if I screw up?"

"You can't. I'll guide you through the steps."

"Let me think about it."

The doors open, and within minutes we are standing at Casey's bedside.

"Hi, Case. It's Aunt Mary. You're going to make it through this. People from all over are praying for you. Keep fighting." She kisses him on the forehead.

"Hi, sweetie. It's Mom. I love . . ." My words get stuck.

Mary places her arm on my shoulder and draws me close.

"The sight of Casey is more frightening than I ever imagined. I wanted to tell you yesterday, but I couldn't." She pauses briefly. "Okay. I'll do that energy thing with you. But, we're closing the curtain."

Mary takes her place on Casey's right side, and I am on his left.

"You ready?"

"Not really, but go ahead. I'll watch."

"The goal of Healing Touch is to restore balance to Casey's energy system—spiritually, mentally, physically, and emotionally. The first thing we want to do is set our intention for Casey's highest good."

"Got it. Then?"

"You're going to place your hands like mine, six inches above his head, with your fingers spread apart."

"Uh-huh."

"Slowly we are going to move our hands down over Casey's body. You may come to a spot where your hands feel like they've hit a wall. That's his blocked energy. But just keep moving your hands over his body until you get to his toes."

"So, then we're done?"

"No. We start all over again."

"For how long?"

"Fifteen minutes. At that point, we should have cleared his stagnated energy."

Mary's eyes widen. Her poker face melts.

We've raked our fingers through a quarter of Casey's energy field when Mary stops.

"I don't know if Casey feels any better, but I think I cured Piglet of his stomach ache." Mary bursts out in laughter.

Stuffed Piglet arrived on the scene after a group of Casey's friends came to visit and now shares his bed with Teddy.

"Mar-y-y-y."

"Okay. Okay. Let me move Piglet out of the way. He's breaking my concentration. Ready."

Finally, we finish. I spritz Lourdes holy water over Casey.

Mary throws back the curtain and walks to the nurse's station. Half-bent, she crisscrosses her hands over her legs and cries, "My sister is making me do the hokey pokey."

I watch, smiling, knowing how Mary loves an audience.

Mary can take an ordinary moment and turn it into an extraordinary one. At least that's what she's done for me, my whole life. Whenever I'm sad, she makes me laugh, giving me a reason to smile when I thought there was none.

"Want to do another Healing Touch treatment on Casey again tomorrow?" I say, as we return to the room, give Case a kiss, and pick up our belongings.

"That was a one-time show. All tickets are marked sold. There will be NO repeat performances."

"Got it. What do you think the nurses thought about our voodoo and me spritzing Casey with holy water?"

"Judging by the expressions on their faces, I'd venture to say it's not something they've seen before."

"Oh, they'll come around."

"Mmm. Not sure about that," Mary says while searching for the car in the parking lot.

Minutes later, Mary swipes the hotel key, and we step inside the room. "Look. You have messages." She pushes the button on the hotel phone.

"Honey, this is your dad and Ginny calling. Buzz us when you can."

"Sweetie, this is your mom. Call me."

Mary and I slip into our pajamas. I dial Dad and press speaker. Briefly, I describe the past few days: that Casey's still in a coma and that we checked into the Marriott, thanks to Mary, Kevin, and her tennis team's generous donations.

"Listen, kiddo. Ginny and I have been talking. We're going to pick up your hotel bill. We want you to stay as long as you need to. Casey's your number one priority right now. We don't want you worrying about money."

"Pop. I'll make it up to you."

"Don't you even think about it. Just take care of our boy, okay? Keep up the good work. We love you."

We hang up the phone, dial Mom, and press speaker again.

"Hi, Mom."

"Oh, honey. Good to hear your voice. How's Casey?"

"No change since yesterday."

"Well, at least he's not any worse, honey. Wish I could be there with you, but I still can't walk very well. Still shuffling around in my slippers."

I cringe, thinking about the day Mom burned her foot with hot grease.

"Don't worry, Mom. I've stepped into your shoes," Mary shouts from her bed.

"That's good, sweetie. Can't tell you what it means to me knowing the two of you are together. All I ever wanted, all I ever prayed for, was that you kids would grow up and be good friends. Proud of both of you. How's the hotel?"

"Oh, Mom, it has been a godsend. The staff is kind and loving. This morning, Mary and I were having breakfast in the dining hall and our waitress, Connie, promised to start a prayer group for Casey."

"That's wonderful, sweetie."

"Mom, you sound tired. I'll give you a buzz tomorrow."

"Okay. Wait. You need anything?"

"I'm good."

"Oh, you wouldn't tell me if you did. I'm going to send you some money. Use it toward food, clothes, or the hotel." She goes on to say Bud, her husband, is going to add to the kitty. "Give Casey a big hug and kiss from his grammy. Tell him I love him, and I'm praying for him. Love you girls. Sleep tight."

The morning breeze blows through the open door, and the sheers dance like a ballerina's arms moving to the beat of music. The graceful movement reminds me of Mary's stay. For the first time since my outings with Maggie, I feel a sense of ease flow through my chaotic life, my spirits lifted.

Yet this morning Mary packs, and my heavy heart returns. I want to beg her to stay, but she needs to get home to her family. This is my obligation, not hers.

It's never been easy for me to ask for help. I've always felt what comes my way, belongs to me.

After Mary zips up her bag, we begin her final leg down the Marriott's hallway. Two hotel maids approach us.

"Good morning, ladies. I'm Clemi. This is Clare. We heard about your boy from Connie and joined the prayer group. You need anything? Coffee? Towels? Laundry?"

"I'm good with the first two, but I'll take your last offer."

After I hand Clemi my laundry, she promises to have my clothes back in the room tonight.

Mary tosses her bag in her car and follows me to MUSC.

Inside Casey's room, we observe that his eyes open and close.

"Mare, did you see that? I think Casey knows we're here."

"Wouldn't that be wonderful?"

"It would." My eyes well up. "Mare, it's so grueling—watching and watching. Not knowing if Casey does wake up, what his quality of life will look like."

"I know, sis." Our chins quiver in turn.

I spritz Casey with holy water and give my boy a kiss. Mary follows and wipes her tears off his face. As we're walking into the hallway, the nurse motions us to the desk.

"Hey, girls. I noticed at the end of every visit, you spray something over Casey's body. What is it?"

Mary steps forward and answers.

"Holy water."

"Holy water? Does it have some kind of healing powers?"

Mary continues. "This particular one does. It comes from a shrine in Lourdes and has been known to heal people physically, emotionally, and spiritually."

"Lourdes, France?" The nurse asks, her eyes still on Mary.

"Yes. I have a friend in Atlanta who goes there every year. When she heard about Casey's accident, she gave me a big jug."

"You wouldn't happen to have a spare bottle on you? I think our patients could use a spritz or two?"

I dig into my purse and hand her two bottles.

While walking to the car, I lean over and whisper to Mary, "See? I told you the nurses would come around."

"Yes, sis, everyone is searching for a miracle."

Mary unlocks the car. "I really hate leaving you."

"Me too." Tears flow from my heart as I touch the edge of her compassion. "Thanks for being here for me. I don't know what I'm going to do without you. Who's going to make me laugh? Who's going to wipe my tears? Whose shoulder am I going to lean on?"

"Wish Mom or Dad could come be with you. But Mom has a burned foot, and Dad, well, we all know how much he hates hospitals."

"I'm good, Mare. Annie and Bo stop by when they can, and right now that's all I need."

Mary pulls me close. We hug. We cry.

"Just call me if you need me, okay?"

Mary slides into the driver's seat. We kiss and hug one last time through the open window. "Love you, sis."

"Love you, too, Mare."

I wave until Mary's car disappears into the distance, all the while humming the lyrics from Gypsy, "Together Wherever We Go."

The day drags on without Mary, and I feel like a piece of me is missing. When I'm not with my boy, I'm sitting in the waiting room watching people step up to the God box. One lady presses her fingers to her lips, then to her note, and then she feeds it through the slot. A middle-aged man dressed in a business suit writes his message, pulls bills from his pocket, and stuffs both into the box. I wonder if they are writing something similar to what I've written. "Please God, take this excruciating pain away. I'm trying so hard to be strong for my loved ones, but I could use a little help. Oh, and Casey could use healing from the angels. If they're not too busy helping someone else, could you send them his way? Thank you."

Drained after an emotional day, I head back to the hotel. Once inside the dark and empty room, I'm engulfed by Mary's lingering perfume. "I miss you, sis," I say aloud.

I sit on Mary's bed to ease my heartache. My laundry and two notes fall to the floor. I pick up the first note and read it. "No Charge. Love, Clemi and Clare." Then, I read the second one. "We're praying for your son. Hope the two of you had a good day. We'll see you at breakfast. Yours, Connie, Rosie, and the gang."

Filled with mixed emotions, both of sadness and gratitude, I tilt my head upward and whisper, "Thank you."

CHAPTER EIGHT

October 21–22

For the past fifteen days, I've endured the valleys, celebrated the peaks, experienced patience, and persisted on this journey. Yet what I've come to realize is that there are no guarantees. The final outcome from this tragedy is still under construction.

"I have news. And I think it's going to put smiles on your faces." The nurse looks at me then Annie. "The doctor decided to stop the Diprivan drip."

"Is that the drug the doctor used to put Casey back in his coma?"

"Yes. It's used in intensive care units with patients who are on a ventilator, as Casey is. It works on the brain and acts as a depressant on one's central nervous system. It basically puts the entire brain to sleep."

"So, his fever is gone?" My hands fan open.

"Not gone. But under control."

"Do you . . ." I take a deep breath, "think he's going to make it this time?"

"All the nurses have their fingers crossed. We'll see how he reacts."

"Does that mean Casey will be waking up soon?"

She winks. "He's already wiggling around."

"That fast?"

"Once the drip is turned off, a patient can awaken in ten minutes. See for yourself." The nurse points toward Casey's room. "Holler if you need anything."

Annie, dressed in frayed jeans and a blue T-shirt, moves from one side of Casey's bed to the other, not taking her eyes off her brother. "Casey, do you know who I am?"

He blinks.

Annie holds his hand. "Mom, Casey just squeezed my fingers."

I copy Annie. Both of us start giggling. Casey smiles. Yes, smiles!

"Mom. We need to ask him questions. Casey, can you give us a thumbs-up?"

"Oh, Annie, can't you think of something else? I'm terrified that grilling him again will cause a relapse. I can't go backward one more time. I just can't."

"Okay." Annie grabs the stuffed animals off Casey's pillow. "Casey, we're going to play baseball with Piglet and Teddy. I want you to think of them as baseballs. If they hit the wall, it counts as a strike. Got it?"

Casey blinks.

Annie tosses her long, blond hair over her shoulder and wraps Casey's fingers around Piglet's belly. "Okay, Casey, throw."

Casey lifts his arm at ninety degrees and tosses Piglet across the room.

"Strike one." Annie thrusts her arm in the air.

Her adrenaline kicks in. She grabs Teddy. "Throw, Casey, throw."

Caught up in Annie's exuberance, I skyrocket back in time to the North/South swim meet on Long Island, 1993, the first time I witnessed my daughter's competitive drive.

In position on the middle block, she shook her arms, along with her five competitors in the ten-and-unders age group. The official pulled the gun's trigger, and she dove into the water. When her head emerged, she swam the length of the pool, looking like a frog on steroids, her opponent to her side. Knowing she wasn't favored to win the meet, the family yelled and clapped until our hands turned blood-red. "Come on, Annie. You can do it. Push." A fire lit inside her, and she blew through the water. Her hands smacked the pool's edge seconds before her rival. "You did it, Annie. You won!" we shouted as she placed her goggles on her cap and pulled herself out of the pool. The coach high-fived Annie and slipped the gold medal over her head. She beamed, proud of her victory.

But no matter how hard one tries, sometimes the end result doesn't go as planned. Teddy lands at the footboard.

"Annie, you need to stop. I think Casey's getting tired."

"Oh, Mom. He's fine. Stop worrying."

I'm not sure if Annie realizes the ramifications of her brother's brain injury. Does she think if she dares Casey, like she has done in the past, that she'll get the same results today as she did back then?

My anxiety grows like cancer, invading every cell. But before I can say another word, I hear Annie say, "That's okay, Casey. I'll give you that one. Strike two. Now all you need is one more strike, and you win the game. Do you think you can do that, Casey?"

He blinks. Again.

I hold my breath.

Piglet is in place. Casey drops his arm to forty-five degrees, glides it forward, and throws. Piglet smacks against the wall with a thud and crashes on the floor.

I exhale.

"He did it, Mom. He did it. Casey, you did it! Good job. You struck those guys out."

As I watch Casey celebrate his win, arms in the air and a smile stretched across his face, it takes me back to his early school years.

No matter how hard he studied, his grades rarely reflected his efforts. When he failed, he felt the anguish of defeat. When he succeeded, he savored his success.

But my boy never gave up. Not then. Not now.

Our laughter seeps into the hallway, drawing the nurses in.

"What's all the ruckus?" one of the nurses shouts.

"Watch this," Annie shrieks, placing Piglet back in Casey's hand.

"Slow and steady, Casey," the nurses say gingerly, trying not to overstimulate him.

His arm springs forward. He releases and scores again. The nurses applaud. "Emergency in Room 6," streams through the door. The nurses respond to the call.

I look over at Casey to congratulate him but stop myself.

"Annie, look. He's closed his eyes. I think we need to stop. He's exhausted." I pull out the Lourdes water, give him a spritz, and call on Mother Mary. Casey sleeps.

As Annie and I are walking to our cars, I pull her close. "We've been through a lot together, haven't we, sweetie?"

"Uh-huh. Especially these past few years. Just one thing after another."

"I know, Annie. If I were a sponge, I would soak up all your pain."

"I can handle it, Mom."

When Bo was in outpatient treatment, Annie went to every family meeting. When Bobby and I divorced, she never picked sides. When three of her high school friends died suddenly, she wept. When Casey was admitted as "John Doe," she was the first one by his side.

"I'm proud of you, Annie."

"I know, Mom."

"Thanks for coming tonight. It meant the world to me, to have you by my side."

"So glad I was here and got to see Casey smile for the first time. It was the best day ever, wasn't it Mom?"

"It sure was, sweetie."

Later that night, while lying in bed, I wonder what made Casey turn the corner. Was it the constant care from the ICU nurses and doctors? The power of prayer that circled the globe like a holy boomerang? The family's undying faith? The daily repetition of Matthew 17:20? The miraculous water from Lourdes? The healing angels? Or my sister's Healing Touch treatment?

Maybe it was all of the above.

The world turns and dawn breaks.

I'm standing at the bottom of Casey's bed, watching the nurse remove the respirator tube; he's gagging. Finally it's free. Casey chokes. His lips move. I don't know if he's trying to talk or if he wants to barf. I grab the nurse's arm like a bird's talons clutch a branch. "Listen. I think Casey is trying to talk."

"Honey, what you hear is him clearing his throat. Patients do that after the breathing tube is removed."

Tuning into my motherly instincts, I blurt. "I'm telling you, Casey is trying to say something."

She leans down and puts her ear to his mouth. "You're welcome, Casey."

"What did he say?" I ask, my fingers nervously tapping the footboard.

"He said, 'Thank you.'"

"My son said, 'Thank you!'"

He smiles. He tries to speak again, but nothing comes.

"It's okay, Casey." I press my fingers to his lips. "The words will come. Rest, sweetie."

One minute Casey is relying on a machine to breathe for him. The next, he is breathing on his own. And then . . . he speaks.

Who can sit at a time like this?

I rush down to the waiting room to call Annie and Maggie. I tell them the good news. They both promise to stop by in a few hours.

Maggie is the first to arrive.

"Honey, Maggie's here. She's come to the hospital more times that I can count. She'd love to hear you say something."

Casey opens his eyes. "Thank you-u-u."

"You're welcome, Casey. You're worth it. I have to go to work now. See ya tomorrow, okay?"

Casey waves.

Minutes later, Annie steps in and kisses her brother on the forehead.

"So, Case, Mom said you're talking. Can you say, 'Annie?'"

Blankly, he stares ahead.

"See this, Casey?" She waves her hand like a windshield wiper on high speed in front of his eyes.

He doesn't blink.

"Hear this?" She smacks her hands together.

He doesn't flinch.

"You're not getting off that easy, Casey. I came to hear you speak. Say something. Anything. I know you can do it."

The dynamics between Casey and Annie have evolved over the years. No longer does Casey see Annie as his younger sister, but as his equal. He's learned that she'll tell him when he's out of line, fight for him when he's right, and push him to be his best. Like now.

Casey looks at his sister.

Annie bends down and listens. "I think he asked, 'Where am I?'"

"You're in the hospital, Casey."

As clear as day he says, "HO-O-LY SH-I-I-T."

Every mother remembers the first time her child does something—crawls, walks, or speaks. Even though Casey's four words, "thank you" and "holy shit," are a far cry from his first word, "Mama," my emotion is the same: sheer exhilaration.

"Mom, what's wrong with Casey? I keep fanning my hand in front of his face, like this." She waves. "See his eyes? They're frozen. It's like my hand is invisible." She turns and looks at the wall behind her. "What the heck is he staring at?"

"I'm no expert, Annie. Maybe he's communicating with an angel."

"You mean telepathically?"

"Maybe. I've read hospitals are filled with angels. So, why wouldn't they be here with Casey?"

"Guess that makes sense. Freaky, though."

Over the years, I have never tried to force my beliefs about angels (a carryover from my religious upbringing), meditation, and spirituality on my children. But on many occasions, I have shared my passion freely. Sometimes they roll their eyes and laugh, and other times they listen, curious. But mostly, I believe they think their Mama is Shirley MacLaine in shades of *Out on a Limb*. Truthfully, I don't mind the comparison. In her book, Shirley portrays a spiritual seeker. Her own inner voice challenges her to explore the realm of infinite possibilities.

Even though the foundation of my faith is rooted in Catholicism, I've always wanted more—answers to questions never answered; insight into other religions, philosophies, and age-old wisdom. It's been this internal thirst that has paved the way for my soul's journey.

I want to tell Annie that I felt the presence of an angel in Casey's room this morning while I was doing a Healing Touch treatment with him. A powerful, yet soothing energy had come from behind and gently pushed me aside. Within a matter of seconds, other angels joined him and clustered around Casey's bedside. I couldn't feel myself breathe. I felt honored God had sent his finest to heal my boy. But I don't tell Annie what happened. I know she would just roll her eyes, like she's done before.

CHAPTER NINE

October 23

Eighteen days ago, Casey was admitted to the hospital. He measured four on the Glasgow Coma Scale, in the severe range, signifying no voluntary activities, no meaningful response. He was essentially blind, deaf, and mute. He couldn't lift a finger or wiggle a toe. He lay in a hospital bed, still as death, existing somewhere out of time, somewhere impossibly distant and unreachable.

I didn't think he would live.

No one did.

This morning, I walk into Casey's room. He's sitting in a chair. His head rests on his right shoulder. Drool drips onto his hospital gown.

I squat and rub his knee.

"I love you, Casey."

He doesn't move. Doesn't talk.

Out of the corner of my eye, I see an arm outstretched. It's the doctor. "Need some help?"

Our palms connect, and he pulls me up.

"Doctor, I'm so glad you're here. Casey looks so tired."

"Trauma fatigue. It's caused by the extra effort and attention it takes to do simple tasks like sitting in a chair. Physically, his muscles are weak. Mentally, his brain function isn't as efficient as it was before the injury." The doctor taps Casey on the shoulder. "Would you like to get back in bed?"

He nods.

The doctor beckons a nurse in the hallway to assist him.

Casey's gone from taking his first steps to running, jumping out of trees, playing sports, and driving a car. Now he needs help getting out of a chair.

"Don't worry," the doctor says as he watches me roll one hand over the other. "Fatigue is normal. He'll probably rest for the remainder of the day. Why don't you go get some fresh air?"

A part of me wants to go outside and feel the warmth of the sun on my face and the gentle autumn breeze against my skin. But another part of me wants my mom. Wants to feel her arms around me. Wants to hear her say, "Everything is going to be okay."

My cell phone buzzes as I walk into the waiting room.

"Happy birthday, Mom. I was just thinking about you."

"How's it going, sweetie? How's Casey?"

"He has his peaks and valleys, and so do I. But this I know, Mom, God will see us through."

"Yes, He will. Just keep holding onto your faith, honey."

My faith. Where did it come from? Was I born with it? Or did I learn it from my mom?

On Sunday mornings, Mom made sure her seven children were dressed in their best for church: boys in their suits and girls in navy-and-white-plaid skirts, starched white shirts, navy blazers, and black patent shoes. At five minutes to nine, we scrambled out the door, clumped down the steps, and piled into the station wagon, where we sat squashed like sardines.

"Now, when we get to church, remember 'no talking.' We go to church to pray," Mom said over her shoulder.

Pop parked the car. Mom ushered us into church like a mother duck escorts her ducklings across the road. She knelt down and pulled out her prayer book. For the next hour, she was in a world of her own, a world that didn't include her children, the loves of her life. She bent her head in reverence. Beat her hands against her breast. Stared at the statue of Jesus, the other love of her life, and wept.

As a young child, I didn't understand what drove Mom's deep devotion. All I knew was that I wanted what she had.

Was that seed planted in my subconscious prior to my incarnation? Was Mom's example meant to stir up that lost memory? Or was she here to teach me something I needed to learn? It's hard to say.

What matters is that my faith feeds my soul as it did my mom's back then, as it does today.

"You're right, Mom. Have anything special planned for your big day?"

"Your brothers are coming into town in a few hours. Bud's going to take us all out to dinner. And your sister Rita stopped by this afternoon. There's nothing I love more than spending time with my kids."

"I know. Sorry I didn't get a card in the mail this year."

"Don't you worry about that. You have enough on your plate. Just hearing your voice is my present."

"Mom, I hope someday I can be half the mom you've been to me. You've stood by my side every step of the way, loving me unconditionally as you have the rest of the bunch. We're all still trying to figure out who's your favorite."

Mom has always been fair. What one got, the others got.

"Thanks for the compliment. And I'll let you in on a secret. You're all my favorites. Talk tomorrow. Make the most of every moment with Casey, okay sweetie?"

I hang up the phone and think, when was the last time Casey and I spent quality time together? Two months ago?

We were running around, picking up some last-minute items for school. Dave Matthews was playing on the radio. Casey turned up the volume, strummed his finger on an imaginary guitar, and sang like he was Dave Matthews's backup. The song ended.

"Did you like the lyrics, Mom?"

I shared my thoughts. He shared his. Music was our means of communication, our way into each other's hearts.

Those months turned into weeks, weeks into days. Right now, all I want is one more car ride . . . one more song on the radio . . . one more heart-warming moment between a mother and her child.

As I'm sliding my phone into my purse, Vanessa's eyes connect with mine. She motions me to her desk.

"I have someone I want you to meet." She waves a woman over to her desk. The woman is in her early twenties, with chestnut hair down to her waist, dressed in an ankle-length, flowered pleated skirt and white gauze shirt. "Teresa. This is the lady I was telling you about. Why don't the two of you have a chat in the lobby?"

"How can I help you?" I ask as we find a seat.

Teresa sits and nervously bunches up her skirt, bringing it to her knees. "I gave birth to a baby girl a few days ago. The doctors want to do surgery on her heart, but—"

"It's okay. Take your time."

She pats her face dry. "I don't want her to have the surgery. I'm afraid she won't make it. Vanessa told me you do some kind of energy stuff, and you have miracle water. Can you help my baby?"

"I'll try. Where is she?"

Teresa guides me to the baby's room.

"What's her name?"

"I haven't named her yet. I'm afraid . . ."

I set my purse down on the chair. "Would you like for me to explain what I'm going to do?"

"No. Just do it."

After gently working on the baby's energy field, I spray Lourdes water over the child and pray.

"Our Lady, may your water provide healing for Teresa's baby girl. I trust that you will either grant this baby a miracle or help her to endure surgery. Thank you."

Teresa bends down and kisses her tiny little miracle. "How long before she's better?"

"It usually takes a day or two for the energy to shift. I hope by then your baby will be strong enough for surgery or strong enough to stay for her mama. This is in God's hands, not mine. Keep praying, and use this bottle of holy water on your baby," I say, while placing it in her hand.

Then, mother to mother, we hug.

With my fingers clasped around my mustard seed, I walk back to the lobby, thinking about Teresa and her baby. My tears become my prayers. Footsteps sound from behind and stop.

"Do you mind if I sit down?" A woman extends her hand. "My name's Maureen."

"I'm Pattie. Glad to meet you. You okay?"

"My grandson was just admitted into ICU with a brain injury. The doctors aren't sure if he's going to make it. I don't know what to do." She buries her head in her hankie.

I reach into my purse and pull out a bottle of Lourdes holy water. "Take this and spray it over your grandson."

"What is it?"

"Holy water. It's believed to have miraculous healing powers. I've been using it on my son in ICU. He's not out of the woods yet, but he is getting better."

"Bless you. I'm going to use it on him now. You coming?" She glances at the clock on the wall. "Visiting hours started five minutes ago."

"Go ahead. I'm right behind you."

I take a few minutes and thank God for sending complete strangers my way. A grandmother who aches for her grandson. A mother who is searching for a miracle. Strangers who have taught me that we never walk alone.

When I enter Casey's room, the nurse flashes me a rare smile.

"What?"

"Casey is improving so quickly that the doctors want to move him to the step-down floor in the next couple of days."

"Really?"

"Yes." Her ponytail bounces.

From behind, I hear clapping. I turn, and the nurses are gathered around the desk. Smiles stretch across their faces.

"So, you know?"

Thumbs go up.

"Well, it's been a long road, ladies and gents. One I hope I never have to travel down again."

A nurse chimes in. "He sure did surprise us. We never thought your boy would make it past his first twenty-four hours."

"And he did. But Casey wouldn't be where he is today without your around-the-clock care."

With my hands pointed to heaven, I bow to the nurses while thinking about Maya Angelou's quote: "Let gratitude be the pillow upon which you kneel to say your nightly prayer."

PART TWO

TWO STEPS FORWARD

Chapter Ten

October 25

> *Life isn't about waiting for the storm to pass;*
> *It's about learning to dance in the rain.*
> ~ Vivian Greene

"Just got word. Casey's moving to the step-down floor this morning," the nurse blurts when she sees me.

Thoughts roll across my mind like a scrolling marquee at the bottom of a TV screen. Yes, he's talking, barely. He's thrown stuffed Piglet and Teddy across the room; encouraging. He's had visions of angels; enlightening. But—

A sudden dread fills my gut, running the show. What if he can't speak in coherent sentences? Think with the best of them? Walk and run again? What if his charismatic personality, compassionate heart, and determined spirit are gone, and all I have to hold on to are memories of the boy I once knew?

Years ago, Charlotte Catholic Middle School offered a one-hundred-dollar bill for the student who sold the most candy bars. Casey wanted to win; he wanted to hold that Benjamin in his hands. I'm pretty sure he knocked on every door in our neighborhood, trying to sell boxes of chocolate bars. The kid could turn on his charm. He even convinced a diabetic woman to buy two bars.

One victory led to another, and soon the day came for the principal to announce the winner.

Back at the home front, I was hoping he would come in first place. I knew how hard he had worked to achieve his goal, and I wanted him to win. When he walked in the door, his head hung low. I slid my arm around his waist. "I'm so proud of you. You gave it your best. That's all you can do, Son."

"I know, Mom."

Casey stuck his hand inside his cargo pants pocket, rummaging through God knows what, and pulled out the next best thing to a Benjamin, a check for $100.00. He laughed. "Got ya."

I grab Casey's hand and recite the story aloud. Then, I whisper in his ear. "I'll give you a hundred for every damned milestone you cross."

Casey's legs and arms move under the sheets as if he's a marionette. Did he hear me? Does he understand?

I rush back into the waiting room, feeling a skip in my step, to share the good news with my extended "family." Almost all the original people have moved on—to another floor, rehab, home, or to the Other Side. But Vanessa, our rock, remains. She listens as the words cascade off my tongue.

"That sure is a miracle, honey."

"It is, isn't it? Do you think he's ready? I mean, it's a big move going to the step-down floor. He won't have nurses hovering over him, watching his every move."

"Honey, you have to trust. The doctor wouldn't be taking the leap unless he believed Casey was ready."

"Oh, Vanessa. I'm going to miss you. You've been my anchor when my ship wanted to set sail more times than I can count."

Vanessa reaches out her arm. I tuck myself under her wing.

"Now, what do you want me to do with that God box and all those prayers?"

"Can you keep it here? I feel it's important to the families."

"It certainly is. Promise you'll stop by now and again."

"You got it." I swing my foot under Vanessa's desk. "Thanks for my little campsite, my refuge."

She smiles.

Up on the seventh floor, hospital staff hurries in and out of Room 721 this afternoon. I notice a doctor frowning when checking Casey's vitals. Technicians are staring stone-faced at the monitors. Nurses are feverishly adjusting tubes. Panic is in the air. Casey's face is ashen.

"Excuse me." Hands keep moving and the soft jabber continues, yet no one looks up. I clear my throat. "Excuse me. What's going on?"

The doctor raises his chin slightly, and our eyes briefly connect. He fastens the stethoscope to his ears and listens. "Casey's heart rate is accelerating—"

"His respiratory numbers are plummeting," the technician says, his voice on the razor edge of urgency.

"He's extremely agitated," the nurse utters. She presses the call button, requesting additional help.

Casey's body flails in a zigzag motion across the bed. Loud, painful moans explode out of his mouth.

I grip the nurse's arm and beg, "Please, do something for my boy. Now."

A new nurse wedges herself between the two of us, needle in hand, "Ma'am, please step aside." Grasping Casey's upper arm, she inserts the needle. He squeals.

"It's not working," I shout. "He's still in pain. Listen."

I knew he wasn't ready for the step-down floor.

The nurse turns and places her hands on my shoulder. "Honey, it takes a few minutes before the sedative takes effect. Why don't you let us do our work? Take a walk and come back in ten minutes."

I step back and mutter, "I'm not leaving Casey." My boy lay almost dead by the side of the road, and I wasn't there. My boy had his skull cut open to save his life, and I wasn't there. I'm not going down the hall. I'm staying right here. Period.

For the remainder of the day, I sit next to Casey. Sometimes I read aloud to him. Other times I write in my journal.

The night nurse walks in and spots me sitting under the dim light.

"I heard your son had a rough time when he arrived on the floor today."

"Really tough. He was delirious. Is that normal?" I ask, wishing I had a book about the stages of traumatic brain injury so I'd know what to expect. Instead, I feel like I'm traveling down a raging river in a canoe without any oars.

"Change can do that to patients. We are monitoring him closely. But he should be fine after he has some rest. You need anything?"

"I'm good."

"Honey, go back to the hotel. Get some sleep. We'll call if we need you."

On the drive back to the Marriott, knowing my positive thoughts are prayers answered, I repeat mantras I memorized from Louise Hay's books. "Today is the best day of my life. Everything is in divine right order. Everything I need to know will be revealed to me in the proper time and space sequence."

I pull into the underground garage and park. Before opening the door, I scan the faintly lit area, checking for moving shadows, still not comfortable with my late-night hours. Confident I'm alone, I gather my belongings and press the lock button.

I weave between the parked cars into the open space. The elevator is ten feet ahead. Almost there.

Soft footsteps sound from behind, elevating my heart's rhythm. Rather than breaking into a run, I turn and squint into the night. A figure keeps approaching.

Are you crazy? Go, before it's too late. Go.

Instead, I freeze.

Within seconds, a middle-aged man dressed in khakis, a collared shirt, and a lightweight jacket is standing face to face with me. His turquoise eyes, like round magnets, pull me into his soul. His aura is sage-like, gentle, and peaceful.

I feel as if I'm in a hypnotic trance, being held captive by something bigger and more powerful than I am. Time stops.

Normally I'd be scared, but for some unknown reason, I'm not.

"I'm your guardian angel," he says proudly and with great tenderness. What?

But before I can give his words much thought, fear and doubt look the other way. My hands reach outward, as if they're on autopilot, and cup his face. I hear myself ask, "Where the heck have you been? I could have used you weeks ago!"

Am I nuts? I'm standing in a dimly lit garage, hands on a stranger who says he's my guardian angel, asking him questions.

"I'm here for you," he says, not really answering the question. "Just call me if you need me." He turns and walks back into the darkness, the same odd way he arrived.

I blink my eyes several times, as if I'm trying to wake up from a dream.

Aren't guardian angels supposed to be luminous beings? Tall and white-winged? Don't they appear out of puffy white clouds? Or come to you on your deathbed?

Maybe my guardian angel is different. No wings. No white feathers. No halo. An Earth angel. And maybe it's true—angels appear to confirm that divine love and intelligence work through all creation, becoming revealed at the perfect time.

CHAPTER ELEVEN

October 27

Casey sleeps this morning. I move from one chair, to the next, then back again, waiting for him to wake up. Waiting to learn if his memory is intact. At my wit's end, I clasp his hand and speak.

"Casey. You awake?"

He blinks.

"Good. I need to know what you remember and what you don't. Several months ago, you walked into my room late at night wanting to talk.

"You asked, 'Why aren't my friends always there for me, like I am for them?'

"You mentioned you called your friends, needing to talk, but each of them said they were busy. They promised to get back to you 'tomorrow,' but tomorrow wasn't good enough.

"I asked, 'Is it about a girl? Your job? A friend?' But you assured me it was just normal teenage stuff.

"You talked about the hurt, the disappointment. Remember, Case?"

For over an hour that night, Casey had chopped at his words, as if he were turning a Cuisinart on and off. I believe he was hoping to shred his pain into pulp, easier to swallow. He diced and cut. I hung on to his every word.

He blinks. Again.

"Good. Well, the issue was never resolved. You walked out of the room carrying the same baggage you came in with. There was so much

I wanted to say that night—that life isn't always the way it appears, and that sometimes we get so caught up in our own anguish that we can't see the forest through the trees."

Casey rolls his head toward the window. I guide his face back and start talking really fast, not sure how much time I have before he checks out.

"You still with me, Son?"

His head dips.

"Do you remember your friends coming to visit you at the hospital?"

His eyes rotate left, then right, and stop dead center, as if his mind is searching through three stacks of dusty files. He nods, barely.

"Once your friends got word about your accident, they drove from Charlotte to see you. They knew you needed their support, and they didn't want you to go through this horrific tragedy alone. You can't get more loyal than that, Case.

"When push comes to shove, you can always tell who your friends are. They are the ones who move into action when life throws you a curveball. They run right beside you, just in case you fall and need help getting back on your feet again. They aren't sitting on the sidelines thinking, 'I shoulda' helped him—I coulda' been there for him—I woulda' offered a hand.' Heck, those are a bunch of da's that don't mean a damn."

I grab my water bottle and take a few swigs, my throat dry from probing his memory.

"So, see, Casey, it wasn't the way you thought it was that night. Your friends care about you. Just wanted you to know that."

He smiles.

"That was a great conversation. Don't you think?" I pat his hand like Thumper taps his hind foot. "Well, I did most of the talking. But Casey, you're remembering."

"Mhmm. I'm tired, Mom." He whispers in his husky voice.

"Me too, sweetie."

An hour later, Annie arrives.

"Case. Feeling better today?"

"I guess."

"Got a story for you. Think you'll like it. See this bruise?" Annie lifts up her pale, freckled leg and shows him her purple foot. "Well, I was at the bar last night with my friends, and some gal dug her stiletto heel into my foot and it hit a nerve. I screamed and pushed her off."

Even though Annie is a very conscientious student, she likes to let loose on the weekend. She can party with the best of them, usually pays the price the next day, and swears off booze until the next weekend rolls around.

Casey laughs.

Yes, Casey laughs!

Annie's face lights up, and I realize the many blessings I have taken for granted—the sweet sound of my boy's laughter and the pure delight of Annie's jovial spirit.

Bo walks in.

Bo has been blessed with many gifts: intelligence, compassion, sensitivity, creativity, good looks, and an overabundant exuberance. When he walks into a room, his energy ricochets off the walls like a racquetball in play.

"Bo! Casey laughed!"

"He did, Annie?"

"Yep. I told him about this dumb girl who stepped on my foot. For some reason, he thought it was funny."

Anxiously, Bo moves around the room, looking for props. He spots a stack of extra-large diapers sitting on top of the metal tray. "What the heck?"

Annie cackles. "They put those under Casey's butt as a protective liner. You know, in case he wets himself."

Bo fastens the diaper over his jeans and starts parading around the room like a jester. He struts over to Casey's bed. With one hand on his waist, he holds his pose and then pivots half-circle, holding his pose again, and returns full circle. "Like my outfit, Case?"

Casey explodes into laughter, spitting between his bellowing sounds, feeding Bo's exhibitionism. Bo gallops over to the door, ready to step into the hallway. I scream.

"Bo, you can't go out in the hallway dressed like that! Some of the patients are on their deathbeds. One look at you and they may think they crossed over to the wrong side. Close the door."

I press my fingers into my forehead, wondering how Bo can be so bright yet so immature at the same time.

Seconds later, there's a knock on the door. I wave to the kids to quiet down.

In walks Tom, my waiting room cohort, pushing his son, Chris, in a wheelchair.

Tom and his family slept in the ICU waiting room alcove while I slept under Vanessa's desk. When visiting hours ended each evening, we sat in a circle. Together, we shared our pain and our struggles. We gave each other hope when there was only despair.

"I told you we would visit when Casey moved upstairs." Tom fastens the lock on the wheelchair.

I introduce Annie and Bo.

"Casey, this is Chris. He was in ICU with you and also suffered a brain injury."

"Hey, man."

Chris doesn't speak. Doesn't wave. His head hangs to the left. Drool slides from the corner of his open mouth onto a towel. His hands, resting on the arms of the chair, are curled like claws. His eyes are lifeless.

"He's tired." Tom lifts Chris's head and straightens his pose. "We'd best be going."

"Thanks for stopping by." I wrap my arms around Tom. In our hug, I can feel his brokenness, sadness, and courage.

Plagued by the grief of Tom's journey, I step into his shoes. Casey could have been Chris. I could have been Tom. Silently, I pray.

Please, God, help me to be grateful that my cup, Casey's cup, is half full. Give me the courage and strength to walk tall each day, no matter what obstacles lie ahead. And may I never forget to end my day saying a prayer for Tom, Chris, veterans suffering from post-traumatic stress disorder, and all the thousands of other brain injury victims who have not been as fortunate as Casey. God bless them. God bless their families.

Bo and Annie are snickering in the corner.

"I hope you aren't making fun of Chris. That could have been your—"

"Mom, we—"

Not willing to listen to what Bo and Annie have to say, I feel my hand shoot up.

The sound of silence hums through the air, momentarily. Annie moves over to Casey's closet door and stands in front of Hillary and Allie's collage.

"Hey, Case. Want to play a game?"

"Okay."

"When I point to a picture, name who you see. Who's this?"

Watching Annie, my mood shifts. The doctor mentioned the importance of using pictures to trigger Casey's memory. Annie was present then and obviously paying attention.

"Allie and me." He laughs, "I'm pulling her hair."

"Good. This person?"

"That's John and me wearing braces."

"And you should know who this is," Annie says, pointing to our lab-chow-husky mix, sitting on his hind legs, sporting a red baseball cap.

"Duke—my buddy. Where's Duke? I miss him."

The mood in the room has shifted about six times. Casey's worn out. Now he's reminded of past friendships, and it's all too much for him. Just too much. I've been watching. He's been frowning, pursing his lips, trying not to cry, not to give in to the overwhelming sadness and uncertainty of his condition. Now, tears spill down his cheeks.

Annie drops the props and goes to her brother. "Don't cry, Casey."

Like all brothers and sisters, Annie and Casey have had their disagreements. But if he pushes too hard, she doesn't go down without a fight. With strong conviction, she speaks her mind and points out his irrational thinking. Deep inside, Casey knows she's right and backs off. But when he hurts or he's sad, she's there to comfort him.

Bo walks across the room and pulls me up on my tiptoes. "Annie's going to leave in thirty minutes and meet me for lunch. I'll probably come back later. You mad? We weren't making fun of Chris, Mom. Annie made a joke about me wearing diapers. I laughed. Sorry—"

Holding a grudge only weighs me down, preventing me from embracing the new. I let it go.

"I know, sweetie. It's just been an emotional day. Love you." Standing on the balls of my feet, I kiss my boy.

The door clicks closed behind Bo. The room feels just a little empty in his wake.

"Bathroom!"

It's Casey, suddenly frantic.

"BATHROOM!"

I press the nurse's button. No one comes. Annie panics as Casey rolls onto his side, attempting to raise himself off the bed.

"Where do you think you're going, Casey?"

"Annie, I have to go to the bathroom. Now." He scoots toward the edge of the bed.

"But you can't walk. You could fall and hurt your head!"

Fearing for her brother's safety, Annie places her hands on his shoulders and presses her body against him, holding him down.

My heart beats faster, and I can't catch my breath. I run out into the hall. "We need help in Room 721."

"Hurry, Mom. Casey has one foot on the ground."

Vinnie, a male nurse, rushes out of a room a few doors down. He reaches Casey just in time and takes him to the bathroom.

Relieved, I feel my body collapse like a balloon pricked with a needle.

Vinnie tucks Casey in bed and leaves. Annie follows. Casey sleeps. I settle in the chair, exhausted and ever watchful, until just before midnight.

Casey awakens mad.

"I hate this bed. I'm tired of being stuck in it. I want out." He sits up, throws his covers back, and swings his leg out of the bed.

Looking like a wishbone, I press my legs flush against Casey's and hit the call button. A nurse arrives and sticks his arm with the needle.

"You'll feel better in a few minutes, Casey," the nurse says tenderly while rubbing his hand. "That's it."

With my eyes fixed on the nurses, I whisper. "What if he tries to break loose tonight?"

"We'll need to restrain him. We can't have him falling on his head. The right portion of his skull is stitched together. There's no protection between his brain and skin."

My stomach does a backward flip. "Could you do that after I leave?"

"Of course."

The church bells ring twelve times in the distance. I spritz Casey with holy water. I pray.

Sweet Mother, come and hold your son. Keep him safe during the night. Wash away his discomfort . . . I turn and spritz myself . . . *and mine, too.*

When my guardian angel arrived on the scene yesterday, I thought he was late. But maybe his timing was spot on!

CHAPTER TWELVE

Still October

There's a knock on the door. Dr. Bailey walks in and drops a bombshell.

"Casey, due to your latest oxygen levels, we need to reinstate your breathing tube."

"No way. That hurts."

"Casey, your respiration rate is low. Your numbers need to be stabilized." Dr. Bailey stuffs his stethoscope into his pocket as if he's taking time to collect his thoughts. "If I put the tube back in, will you leave it in?"

"Yeah right." Casey smirks.

"This is what I'm going to do. I'll have the technician monitor your levels closely. If your numbers stabilize, I'll cancel the order."

"My numbers will be good, Doc. I promise. 'Cause no one is sticking that tube down my throat again."

After Dr. Bailey leaves, Casey nods off, and I reflect on how parts of the old Casey are still intact. Even though his brain has undergone significant trauma, the neurons that control his drive are still firing.

There's a soft rap on the door. My attention shifts.

"Hi, Mom. Casey has company." Annie looks to her side. Standing inside the doorframe are two of Casey's college roommates, one wearing a black toboggan and the other a blue jean baseball cap that reads Gap. "You remember Ryan and John from ICU?"

"Sure. Come on in. Casey just nodded off, but I know he'd love company. I'll wake—" Before I finish my sentence, Ryan drops to his knees at Casey's bedside, bows, and recites an old family prayer aloud. I'm moved to tears.

Casey's eyes flutter. He looks around the room, and his arm goes up. Hands smack in midair.

John pulls a folded paper from his pocket and clears his throat. "Want to hear the poem I wrote you?"

Casey nods, so John reads:

> *"Yesterday was like today,*
> *filled with disjointed thoughts.*
> *From pen to paper,*
> *it renders confounded memories.*
> *While I look at a shell*
> *and talk to a soul,*
> *the clandestine speech flows . . .*
> *Like ink during the metaphysical metamorphosis*
> *occurring before my eyes and behind yours.*
> *You are battered physically,*
> *yet spiritually intact.*
> *Reminiscent of our first year's*
> *formalities, or lack thereof,*
> *evokes a strong desire*
> *for just one more hour*
> *of balcony or bunk bed banter*
> *in our thoughts and prayers."*
>
> ~ John Joseph Kruzel

Casey knuckles a falling tear. "Thanks, man. Those were pretty crazy times."

"And lots of laughs," John adds. He makes eye contact with his buds. Laughter bounces off the walls.

Annie and I join in. Not because we understand, but because we know their unspoken words contain stories we will never hear about or read about. Yet for me, my enthusiasm goes deeper: Casey remembers.

As soon as the boys walk out the door, Casey blurts. "Annie, Mom's a potato chip."

"A potato chip? Why?"

"Because she's on crack."

Annie looks at me to see if I'm hurt by his comment.

I shrug.

"On crack? What are you talking about, Casey?"

"I don't know." Casey starts laughing, and Annie follows.

Is this what lies ahead? A bunch of broken childlike outbursts and twisted humor? Sure it's funny now. But what about later? Who will be laughing then?

Casey falls into a deep sleep. Annie pulls up a chair next to me. Her thumb glides over the protruding veins on my hand. "You doing okay, Mom?"

Annie is the quiet, sensitive type. She feels every moment of happiness, sorrow, pain, and hurt, and every moment in between. Nothing slips by her. Even though she doesn't always articulate her feelings, her delicate actions—a gentle touch, a big lingering hug, the look that says "I understand"—convey her compassion and understanding. Right now, I know she's worried about me.

I want to tell Annie that I'm tired. Tired from trying to hold it together. Tired from not knowing what lies ahead. Just damn tired. Instead, I smile and mask my feelings.

"Hangin' in there, sweetie."

"Did you sleep here last night? I mean, you're wearing the same white turtleneck, grey sweatshirt, and jeans you had on yesterday."

"I did, sweetie. I was just worried about Casey."

"He's in good hands. Go rest, Mom."

An hour later, the nurse walks in the room.

"I need to put the straps on Casey. You sure you want to watch?"

"Uh-uh."

What if my boy wakes and sees himself bound to the bed, his dignity lost like an animal caught in the wild? Love hurts.

This morning, dark clouds hang low in the sky. Rain pelts against my windshield. Chilling winds seep through the car window. My gut somersaults. *Something isn't right.* I park the car and rush to Casey's room.

His covers are hanging from the bed. His head is buried in his pillow. He's sobbing.

I wrap a blanket over his shoulders.

"Honey. You all right?"

"I had lots of dreams last night, Mom. Really scary dreams."

I grab a towel and wipe fragmented beads of sweat off his forehead. "Everything is going to be okay, sweetie."

Casey's shaking stops. He lies perfectly still, gaping at a point on the wall, just above the closet door. The room grows still.

It's happened before, this weird drifting off, but I tell myself the angels are visiting my son, as they have in the past.

I drag the chair to his bedside, sit, and wait. Three minutes pass, then five. Not big on patience, I squeeze Casey's hand. "Honey, is someone here?"

"Mother Mary."

"Will you tell her I said, 'Hi?'" I ask, not sure what to say. This isn't exactly an everyday occurrence. Not even a once-in-a-lifetime happening!

Casey doesn't respond. I'm almost ashamed that I barged in on their time.

Moments later, with his eyes still centered on his focal point, Casey says, "Hey." He pauses, as if he's waiting for a response, then speaks.

"Mom, Mary wants you to know that she's always here."

I don't know if I should get on my knees, bow in reverence, or weep with gratitude. I do all three.

Years ago, I read a book about Medjugorje and the apparitions that have been taking place there since the '80s. It said the visionaries didn't react to light, to any earthly sound, or to any touch. While they were in the presence of Our Lady, they felt like they were outside time and space, as Casey appears to be now. If Mary's just appeared to my gravely ill child, and I believe she has, I'm humbled.

"Please tell her I said 'Thank you.'" I want to say more—to thank her for holding, healing, and loving my son, for being here for him in his time of need—but my emotions, like weeds, choke life out of my words.

Casey's legs bend and straighten, as if they're yawning.

"How ya feeling, Son?"

"Fine. Why?"

"Do you remember anything about the last half hour? You told me Mother Mary was here."

"I did? Don't remember."

All I want to do is sit and savor the miraculous event that just occurred. But I can't. The hospital's speech pathologist walks through the door.

"Casey, we are going to work on your swallowing, so you can start eating some real food."

"All right!"

She dips a teaspoon into a cup of water. "Try to swallow this."

He does.

"Let's try a bite of pudding."

"Mmm. Pudding is good."

"Great job, Casey. Now I need you to identify a couple of objects. What's this?"

"Spoon."

"And this?"

"Glass."

"Next, I want you to swallow the contents of this spoon. What is it?"

"Hardee's Ice."

The speech pathologist snickers. "That's the first time anyone ever got that descriptive. Now let's see if you can drink water from a straw."

"Mmm."

"Here's a piece of a graham cracker. You haven't had solid food for twenty-three days. Don't chew. Just let it melt in your mouth."

Casey bites. Gags. Swallows.

"Last thing for today, Casey. I'm going to tell you a story. I want you to listen very carefully. When I'm finished, I'm going to ask you a question."

"Anna's husband gave her a ruby ring for her birthday. She took it off and put it in her pocket. Later she was looking for it and couldn't find it anywhere. She reaches in her pocket for a tissue and finds the ring."

"So, Casey, can you tell me anything about the story?"

"Yeah. That girl is really dumb."

Does he understand the story? Or is this a sign of his limited abilities to process information?

As the speech pathologist is packing up her things, the occupational therapist strolls through the door. She walks over to Casey and starts asking questions.

"How many fingers do I have up?"

"Three."

"Can you raise your right arm?"

Effortlessly, Casey swings his arm above his head.

"Good job. Lift your left arm."

He raises it only inches then says, "I can't."

"Don't worry, Casey. I'm going to help you build those muscles over the course of the next couple of weeks. What's this?"

"Lip balm."

"Very good, Casey. What I want you to do is take the top off and put some on your lips. Do you think you can do that?"

He nods. With the tube in his right hand, he tries to remove the cap with his left. Frustrated, he puts the tube to his mouth, cap still intact, and swipes his lips. "Done."

"Take this washcloth, and clean your face. When you finish, you can rest."

Casey sweeps the cloth over his face, barely catching skin, and drops it. "You can go now."

Casey sleeps. But not for long. Grace Somebody-or-other arrives.

The first time I met Grace—ninety pounds soaking wet, with long brown curly hair and eyes to match—Casey was in ICU. She strolled in. Spent a few minutes with Casey then left without engaging in conversation. I never quite understood her aloofness, but I came to believe she was just shy. When I asked Annie about her, she mentioned Grace was just a friend. Because I was simply grateful that Casey's college friends took the time to visit, I never pushed. But today I realize that there's a fine line between "friend" and "girlfriend."

She sits on the bed and runs her hands across Casey's partially shaved head. He opens his eyes. Within seconds, their bodies are tangled like honeysuckle vines. Casey frees an arm and swats the air, signaling for me to leave the room. Grabs a blanket. Tosses it over their heads.

I want to say, "Really? I'm right here." Instead, I walk down the hall to the nurses' station.

"Excuse me. Is it normal for Casey to be thinking about sex? You know, brain injury and all. Because he and his friend or girlfriend, I'm not quite sure at this point, are . . ."

"Sexual desires get heightened after brain injuries."

"How long does it last?"

"It's different for each patient."

Minutes later, I step inside Casey's room and am caught in Grace's updraft as she races out of the room, looking a bit disheveled. Casey's lying on his back, arms tucked under his head, smiling.

"You know, Mom. This accident isn't all bad. When I came into the hospital, I wasn't even dating. Doc put me into a coma, and when I came out I had a girlfriend. How cool is that?"

"Pretty amazing."

"I think I'm in love with her."

"In love with her?" My eyes open wide and freeze. "Do you even know her last name?"

"Can't remember. Ask Annie. She'll know. Met her at a party we went to."

Because this conversation is the longest one Casey and I have had since he moved to the step-down floor, I want to keep probing, but Casey closes his eyes. Not for long, though.

The physical therapist rouses him. Her assistant stands by her side.

"You want to walk? You start with the walker."

Reluctantly, Casey swings his legs over the side of the bed, and the physical therapist helps him to his feet, her hands around his waist.

"Place your hands on the bar. Good. Lift the walker, and step forward. Good, Casey. Let's keep going."

I follow at a snail's pace down the hallway.

Casey stops in front of the nurses' station. Smiling with childlike innocence, he fans his hand as if he's giving the Queen's wave. The nurses applaud. He turns his head and spots a tall, half-naked man dressed in a green costume at the end of the hallway.

"Who's that?"

The physical therapist chuckles. "It's Halloween. Staff members like to dress up and visit the patients."

"Cool. Mom, can you take my picture with him?"

He parks his walker. The assistant grabs hold of Casey's waist and guides him toward the green man.

"Hey, dude. Nice outfit. Who are you supposed to be?"

"You don't recognize me? 'Ho, ho, ho.' I'm the Jolly Green Giant."

Just as I snap the picture, Casey's thumb points toward the giant. Judging by the expression on Casey's face, it appears he's thinking, *Check this guy out. He thinks he's the Jolly Green Giant. Right!*

The physical therapist and her assistant tuck Casey into bed, and he mutters, "I'm so tired."

I want to say, "And so am I."

Over the past three weeks, I've watched Casey go from languishing in the twilight of an induced coma, to gazing at a vision on a wall, to making out with a girl, to attempting strenuous exercise—physically and mentally. What's next?

A technician strolls into the room. He checks Casey's respiration rate and makes notes in his chart. On his way out the door, he stops, and introduces himself as Christopher.

"You know, your boy is the hospital's miracle story."

"What?" The word stretches as if I'm sounding out each letter.

"It's true. He's had all of us scratching our heads. He shouldn't have lived twenty-four hours."

Even though the severity of Casey's injury indicated he wasn't supposed to live, in my heart of hearts, letting my boy go was never an option.

"Yes. I've heard."

"Who knows why he made it this far?" Christopher wonders. "Maybe it has something to do with the angels. When I'd go into his ICU room to check his numbers, Casey would say, 'The angels are here.' I never caught a glimpse of them, but I believe for Casey they were real and present."

Christopher tilts his head upward, as if he's trying to snatch his thoughts from thin air.

"It's all about karma, you know? Cause and effect. Casey's reaping what he sowed in this lifetime or another. What goes around comes around. He's being given another chance, and his angels are here to help him through it. Well, that's my take on things. You may think differently. Gotta run."

If all of this is karma, Casey's wake-up call, and I'm an integral part of it, does that mean that I, too, am being guided to reassess my life?

CHAPTER THIRTEEN

First days of November

Over the years, Drace and I have supported each other through critical changes in our lives. We strategized our career opportunities. We booked psychic readings and laughed until we peed in our pants. One time we elaborated the bitter truth that birthing a baby hurts like hell. We've been there for each other every step of the way.

This afternoon, I'm standing on Marriott's veranda, overlooking a fountain surrounded by mums, waiting for my friend to arrive.

Maggie, Drace's daughter, circles the driveway in her old Toyota. Drace waves out of the passenger window, her ebony hair tousled in the wind. "Girl, I'm here for you." Maggie brakes. Drace throws the door open and runs up the steps. We lock arms and jump like we're bouncing on a pogo stick.

"Girl, why aren't you at the hospital?"

"I just came from there. Wait until I tell you how the morning went down. Mags, can I help you with the bags?"

"I'm good, Aunt Pattie."

Because Drace and I are more like sisters than friends, our kids put "Aunt" in front of our names. Drace's first name is Anne, so my kids call her Auntie Anne. But in high school, I got in the habit of calling her by her last name, Drace, which stuck.

"Who's with Casey now?"

"Bobby's in town. He's filling in this weekend so I can spend time with you."

"But I want to see Casey."

"Is tomorrow okay? Thought we'd get you settled in, eat, and do a little shopping. I need a break."

"Sounds like a plan."

Drace unpacks. I talk.

"So, what do you want to hear about first? Casey's first attempt to bathe himself and brush his teeth? My talk with Bobby? Or the phone call I had with Danny? You know, my future boss at Barnes & Noble."

"I don't know. They all sound intriguing. Just start at the beginning."

"Okay. So, the occupational therapist walks in the room and tells Casey he's going to learn how to bathe himself. Casey says, 'I can't even stand up. How am I supposed to take a bath?' Then he starts shaking his head."

"Why?"

"Can't say for certain. But, knowing Casey, he was probably thinking that she had the brain injury, not him."

Maggie and Drace's voice become one. "So Casey."

"Anyway, he puts the washcloth in his right hand, swipes the left side of his body, and says, 'Done.'"

"Wait. That reminds me of a story you told me about Casey. I think he was about five. He was playing goalkeeper on a soccer team, and he shouted from outside the net, 'I'm done.'"

"Good memory, Drace! The coach motioned for him to stay put. The ball gained speed and was headed for the goal. Seconds later, the opponent shot high. The ball caught the rim, and the other team scored while Casey sauntered toward the sideline."

Drace chortles. "Then the coach said, 'Casey, why didn't you stay in position?' And he shot back—"

Our voices merge. "I told you I was done."

Bouts of laughter fill the room.

Drace opens the closet and hangs up her clothes. "So, was he done washing his face?"

"Not by a long shot. The therapist made him wash the right side. That's when it got more difficult. He really messed up his upper left arm in the accident, so gripping items presents challenges. He went to grab the washcloth, and his hand curled inward as if it were riddled with arthritis. Finally, he managed to hold the end of the cloth and blotted his face."

"Aw." Drace taps her heart.

"I know. But it got worse with her next request. 'Unscrew the toothpaste cap, put paste on the brush, and clean your teeth.' He couldn't unscrew the top, so he used his teeth. He tried to squirt paste on the brush, but his left hand kept shaking. Then paste fell on his pants, and he scooped it up. Drace, I'm not even sure if I breathed as I watched."

"Girl." Drace sits next to me on the bed and rubs my back.

"It's like I mimic each of his gestures, only internally. Sometimes I want to shout, "Not fair."

Maggie breaks the silence. "Anyone hungry?"

"You okay, girl? You up for getting something to eat?"

I nod and stuff my feelings inside, like I've done before.

"Great. You can tell me Part Two over lunch."

Connie greets us in the dining room. I introduce her to Drace and Maggie, and tell them she's the one responsible for Casey's prayer group. "Would you ladies like to sit outside? The view is spectacular."

She shows us to our table, and we order Caesar salads with grilled chicken and sweet tea.

Drace grabs my arm. "I needed to see the water. I know this isn't the beach, but it's the next best thing. Just look at those cabin cruisers and sailboats. Smell the air. Feel the sun. Shoot, it was freezing when I left St. Louis." She takes in a deep breath and then releases a long-winded "ah-h-h."

"So, what did you and Bobby talk about?"

"I'm not so sure if it was really a conversation. More like an exchange. I asked him for money, and he wrote me a check."

"A check for what?"

"I haven't worked for a month and have bills to pay. Mortgage and utilities. Just needed help defraying my expenses."

"I'm glad you asked. Heck, you haven't left Casey's side since you got here. So, that's it? That's all you talked about?"

I dig my fork into my salad. "He asked me for the latest update on Casey. I told him that his son's potty mouth was a full-blown sewer. That he salivates at anything that walks by in a skirt. And that it was a good thing he wasn't showing any leg today."

Maggie spits out her tea.

"Right, Maggie? You've seen Casey in action."

I grab Drace's arm and switch the subject.

"Do you know how wonderful your daughter is? She's taken me on outings. Opened her apartment so I could shower. Made me laugh when I wanted to cry. Showed up almost every day at the hospital with a smile on her face. And never left without giving me a hug."

Simultaneously, we grab our napkins and wipe our eyes.

Connie approaches our table. "More tea? Girls, you okay?"

Drace clears her throat. "Just having a girlfriend moment. When you have a minute, can you bring me the bill?"

After Maggie goes back to school, Drace and I go shopping.

The chatter never stops. We duck in and out of the shops along King Street, trying on dresses, skirts, tops, and shoes. When our feet grow tired, we stop at the coffee shop. I order a café mocha, and Drace orders a sweet tea. Just when I think life can't get any better, Drace suggests picking up ribs at Sticky Fingers and taking the to-go boxes back to the hotel so Mags can join us.

Much later, after our feast, the three of us climb into our beds.

"I forgot to ask you about your conversation with your new boss. Danny, right?"

"We didn't talk long. I thanked him for holding my job and told him I'd be back in town in a couple of weeks."

My job? I haven't given it much thought. Under normal circumstance, I'd be excited. I was about to move forward with my career. It was going to be great to use my creative talents. Plus, I'd be of service to the community. But the unforeseeable and unforeknowable future squelches my excitement.

"A couple of weeks? You didn't tell me that."

"I talked to Dr. Bailey. Because Casey continues to improve, he guesstimates his departure in two weeks, maybe three. But I don't want to go there now. I want to savor this day."

"Did you talk about anything else?"

"I asked him if he knew of any good rehabs in Charlotte. He mentioned he had a friend who worked in the neurology department at one of the hospitals. He promised to investigate the matter and get back to me."

"Girl. I love how everything is coming together."

"Me too. Piece by piece."

Light filters through the room's sliding glass door at sun's first blush. I roll over and gaze at Drace and Maggie sleeping in the bed next to me, cuddled up like mama and her baby cub.

Drace opens her eyes. "Sleep okay? We probably need to get moving."

"It's almost seven. I'd like to get to the hospital and spend time with Casey before Bobby arrives. Missing my boy."

A little time later, Maggie drives back to her apartment. Drace and I head over to the hospital.

Drace knocks on Casey's door and peeks in.

"Auntie Anne! Mom said you were coming. How long you staying?"

"Going home tomorrow. But I had to come and see my guy." She hugs and kisses Casey.

"Oh no." Casey stares over Drace's shoulder. "They're back."

"Who?"

"The therapist and her friend."

"Thought we'd try to walk today, Casey."

The PT's assistant helps Casey to his feet. "Put your hand on the walker. Good. Hold it steady so I can tie the belt around your waist."

"What if I fall?"

"You won't. I'll have a firm grip on you." He kicks the walker to the side.

Casey slides one foot then the other. He wobbles. The assistant tightens his grip.

"Slow and steady, Casey. That's good."

My heart sinks into my chest. One minute Casey's actions are that of a child; the next, of an old man.

My phone beeps in my pocket. There are two messages.

"Drace. I need to give Mom and Dad a quick call. I'm sure they're looking for today's report."

"Go ahead. I'm going to step outside and get some fresh air."

Ten minutes later, I slide the phone back into my pocket. Casey's groans grow louder. The therapists guide him to the bed, remove the belt, and tuck him in. "Big workout. He's going to sleep good."

Bobby and Drace pass the therapists on their way into the room, giggling between their words.

"Look who I ran into outside."

Does he miss not being with his son daily? Does he think of him, pray for him during his busy day? I'm sure he does. Any father would.

Bobby glances at Drace, then at me. "I got it from here, girls. Go and have some fun."

The November sun hangs low in the sky. Gentle winds blow in from the north. Seasoned docks, thirty feet in front of us, rattle and squeak.

Annie and Maggie swim in the Marriott's pool. Drace and I lounge poolside.

"You know what today is?"

"Yes. Another day from heaven. Wait. That wasn't the answer you were looking for?"

"Good answer, though. Just thinking. Ten years ago today, my dad passed."

"Oh, Drace. I'm sorry for being so selfish. With all that's been going on, I have lost track of everything outside my bubble."

"It's okay. Do you remember my phone call?"

I'd never forgotten. I was cleaning the kitchen in Huntington, New

York. The phone rang; Drace was on the other end, choking out her words: "My dad passed away today."

We didn't say much. Mostly we cried like little girls do when they say goodbye to their daddies as they go off to work. But this time was different; we cried big tears and felt deep sorrow. Her daddy wasn't coming home. There would be no more hugs, kisses, and late-night chats discussing the latest novels. No more shared memories, only ones to hold on to.

I ached for my friend then, as she aches for me now. Together we will ride out yet another storm.

"Yes, friend. I do."

"Anyway." Drace clears her throat. "How's it going with Bobby? You two getting along?"

Drace doesn't like the spotlight on her for long, especially when it comes to her emotions. I don't know if it's because she was born under the sign of Cancer—when things get too emotional, the crab likes to retreat back into its shell—or because she feels too deeply. Probably it's both.

"We're cordial. But seriously, we don't spend much time together. He comes and goes, spends a couple days with Casey, then he's off again."

"How do you feel about that?"

"I don't dwell on it. Every minute of my day, every breath I take, and every thought I think revolves around Casey." I shrug. "Guess we're both doing the best we can."

Sensing I need space, Drace gets up and joins the girls. I lean back in my chair. My thoughts return to my boy.

Later, the sound of laughter brings me back to the present. I turn and follow the noise. Drace is sandwiched between Annie and Maggie. She's flipping through *Style Magazine*, commenting on the latest fashion. The girls give their input. They laugh, turn the page, and start all over.

I marvel how the seed of our friendship, planted in 1956, has grown and withstood time. Now our children are reaping the benefits of our harvest, one sowed and tilled with love.

CHAPTER FOURTEEN

November 5 and 6

"Mom. Last night was so scary!"

I drop my purse and rush to Casey's side.

"What happened?"

"I watched someone being raped."

"What? Oh honey, you probably had a bad dream."

Since Casey was a toddler, he's had nightmares. When he screamed out in the middle of the night, I scooped him into my arms and tried to comfort him: I bounced him on my hip; distracted him with a toy; even sang verses of "Brahms's Lullaby," albeit a bit off-key. He pressed his fingers into my lips, said "shhh-hh," and calmed down.

My singing had a way of bringing Casey back to the present . . . my voice probably worse than his nightmare . . . but now probably isn't a good time to sing a verse or two.

I rub his back.

"It wasn't a dream. It was real. I called the police and told them to get to the hospital quickly."

What kind of drugs is he on?

"People were coming through the window. They were screaming and fighting." His hands flap. His voice grows louder. "Blood was splattered everywhere. The window, the floor, and the bed."

Casey's hysteria fills the room and sucks me in. I can't calm him down. I can't calm me down.

"I screamed like mad. The angels came and rescued me."

Casey's voice wafts into the hallway. A nurse walks in. "What's wrong, Casey? Something I can help you with?"

Without looking up, he shakes his head, as if he has a nervous tick in his neck.

The nurse takes out her false teeth and clanks them together.

Casey laughs momentarily, but his eyes are wide with fright.

The nurse puts her teeth back in her mouth. "Looks like Casey needs to get out of his room. How about a ride in the wheelchair? Would you like that, Casey?"

I get a vision of myself raising my hand, saying "I would. Take me."

He nods, so Beverly loads him into the wheelchair.

I look around, hoping there are two.

"Ever been to the children's ward, Casey? Good medicine for the soul."

The nurse pushes the chair slowly through the halls, talking.

"Look at all these children. Aren't they sweet? See that little girl?" The nurse points to the child's room, her bed filled with stuffed animals. "She had her tonsils out yesterday. I'm sure her throat hurts. But she's smiling." She wheels forward a few feet. "See that little boy?" She points to another room filled with balloons. "He had a lump removed from his arm. The doctors are checking to make sure it isn't cancerous. But listen to him laughing. Mm-mm. Just something about children that makes you feel all good inside."

Casey smiles.

"You see, life isn't always easy, not for kids, teenagers, or old folks like me. It has its ups and downs. Yessiree. But the good thing is that God lets us pick the way we want to live our lives, happy or sad. Don't you think?"

Casey nods.

Hours after Casey's return from the children's ward, the daily parade of therapists begins. First the speech pathologist introduces Casey to more foods. She's followed by the physical therapist, who takes him on a walk. By the time the occupational therapist shows up, Casey is anxious, irritated, and cursing a blue streak. Rather than tossing the beanbag with his left hand, he switches the bag to his right and throws, defeating the purpose of the game—to strengthen his left arm.

Frustrated, the occupational therapist packs her bag and brushes arms with Dr. Bailey as he walks into the room.

"How you feeling, Casey?"

Casey shrugs.

"According to our records, you are progressing nicely. So, next week I will be operating on your skull again. It's time to close up the opening. Because we can't use the original skull piece, I'll be using a durable plastic. There are two ways we can handle this. One, I can send it to a dental lab and have them construct the piece. The advantage is that it's smoother to the hand's touch. The disadvantage is that it takes ten days to create."

"Ten days? Too long, Doc."

Dr. Bailey laughs. "Another option is to make the mold while you're in the operating room. Do you care one way or the other?"

"Well, Doc, since dentists work on teeth and you do skull work, I think I'll go with you. When?"

"I can perform the operation on Friday or next Monday. That would put you in a rehab center by Wednesday or Thursday of next week."

"Let's do it. As far as I'm concerned, you can put all the nuts and bolts you want in my head, as long as I can get out of here."

After Dr. Bailey leaves, there's a knock on the door. It's the nurse who took Casey to the children's ward.

"I'm going off duty soon. Just wanted to check on you. Did you enjoy your outing?"

"I did. I love kids."

He does like kids. Whenever we are around families with little ones, the children gravitate to Casey. They sit on his lap, climb on his shoulders, and wrap their arms around him so tight he coughs. He tickles and wrestles with them. He doesn't mind getting on the floor to play board games, action figures, and Legos. From the sound of laughter in the room, it's hard to decipher who's having the most fun, Casey or the kids.

Mom has said over the years, "You can get a glimpse into a person's soul when you watch him interact with children." I believe Casey's nurse instinctively knew that about him.

She winks. "Remember, you get to choose if you want to be happy or angry. I'll see you bright and early in the morning. You sleep good, you hear?"

Good nurses are a rare breed. They're compassionate, patient, and confident. They know how to think on their feet, be calm under pressure, and tune in to their patients' needs. It's as if they've been blessed with a sixth sense.

Casey's nurse brought order when there was chaos, harmony when there was conflict, and stability where there was none. For that I am eternally grateful.

Morning comes and goes. While Casey rests after his workout with the therapists, my thoughts jump the fence into the past.

Twenty years ago, just before midnight, the second miracle in my life took place.

I was three weeks past my due date when I entered the hospital. The nurses detected fetal distress and immediately called the doctor. When he arrived, he ordered an emergency C-section. After what seemed like an eternity, he pulled Casey out of me and whispered to the nurse, "The umbilical cord was wrapped around his neck." I lifted my head to see what was going on, but the darn blue sheet covering my overinflated belly blocked my view. The doctor's eyes caught mine. "Your boy is going to be just fine."

I breathed a sigh of relief. But I didn't take my eyes off the nurse, not for one second. Finally, she placed Casey in my hands. I kissed his head, his lips, counted his fingers and toes, and whispered, "I love you, sweet boy."

Lingering with my thoughts this afternoon, I think about how Casey's birth parallels his birthday today; both times he's in the hospital and has struggled to live.

Just as I'm about to rouse Casey and share my thoughts with him, the unmistakable strains of "Happy Birthday" float into his room. Four nurses step through the doorway. One is carrying a chocolate cake. A single candle sits on top, flickering.

The nurse closest to the bottom of the bed squeezes Casey's toe. "Make a wish."

He closes his eyes, takes a breath, and blows.

"It really sucks turning twenty in the hospital."

"It could be worse. You're one lucky boy. You need to say thank you."

"You're right." He glides his finger along the base of the plate, gathering icing, and sticks it in his mouth. "It still sucks."

Does Casey realize how far he's come? I don't talk to him about his first few weeks in ICU—in and out of comas, high ICPs, fevers, ice baths, and infections in his lungs. I'm not sure he would understand or if explaining would do much good. Maybe it's best to leave the past behind and focus on today's miracle.

The nurses leave and Casey stares out the window into nightfall. "When's everyone coming to my party?"

I'm about to utter, "Soon," when family and friends start barging through the door. The first one to arrive is Bo. As he's bending down to give me a kiss, I feel a tap on my shoulder. I turn and give Annie a hug. Maggie's on Annie's heels, holding a cake in her hand. We exchange a sideways peck. Behind her are Casey's college roommates, Ryan and John. We hug. Then Grace shuffles by and smiles. From the look on Casey's face, you'd think the sun just squeezed through the doorframe. Grace bends down, gives him a kiss, and sits on the bed.

For the next couple of hours, the kids joke, laugh, and tell stories. For the first time since Casey moved upstairs, Room 721 is alive in a different way.

As I take it all in, I'm reminded of the kids' birthdays through the years.

After I had prepared the birthday child's favorite meal and baked the child's cake of choice, I would decorate the kitchen with multicolored streamers, balloons, and a happy birthday sign. Next, I ornamented the table with a honeycomb birthday cake centerpiece, added decorative plates and cups, and topped it off with hats and blowers.

The kitchen would fill with familiar faces. We'd eat, laugh, celebrate, and end the night singing "Happy Birthday" just like we did today.

The room grows quiet as family and friends begin to leave. All that exists is the world I now know: a world of uncertainty, a world filled with hope.

Casey calls his high school buddies in Charlotte.

He talks, I listen. He laughs, I smile. He's quiet, I'm tense. He cries, I shudder.

"You know what my friend said, Mom? He said he was scared when he saw the sadness in your eyes. He freaked when he saw my head the size of a basketball. Afraid that his life was heading in the wrong direction, he cried for two days."

Casey pauses.

"When I get out of here, I'm going to get my life together. Help people. Do some good."

I want to tell Casey that's what I've prayed for and hoped for. I could say that I've always seen the good in him, even when he got off course. I could explain that a mother believes in her child, even when he doesn't believe in himself. Does he understand that a mother never gives up? I'll go to the moon and back for him. I'll sacrifice all I have and more, because that's what a mother does.

But I'm not sure he would grasp all of this, until he has children. I only hope that someday my unspoken words will ring in his heart.

"I'm tired, Mom. Thanks for everything. Love you." He hugs the covers and closes his eyes.

"Love you too, Casey, forever and always."

The dull light over Casey's bed bathes my boy in a soft, golden glow.

My cell phone rings.

"Hey, Mare. I've missed you."

"Sorry I didn't get back to you yesterday. I played tennis and went to lunch with the girls. Probably had too much fun, because I was on the couch by seven o'clock. Casey still awake? Wanted to wish him a happy birthday."

"I think he's down for the count, Mare. But I'll pass your message on."

"So, catch me up. What's been going on?"

"I had a chat with Dr. Bailey. He's going to operate on Casey's skull at the end of the week. If all goes well, Casey will move on to rehab shortly thereafter."

"What's wrong?"

Sisters come with built-in radar and can detect interference at any range. So it's no surprise Mary senses my concern.

"He'll only be at the rehab center for two weeks. Then he'll come home, where there's no around-the-clock care, no nurses, and no therapists. Help is not just a hospital button away. The only button I'll have to push is mine."

"You can do it, sis."

"Yeah. But when I think about the hats I'll be wearing—parent, employee, nurse, chauffer—I get overwhelmed."

"Wait. Are you saying you have to take Casey to and from outpatient rehab? What if his schedule is different than your work schedule?"

"No. Bobby has great insurance. It covers a driver and someone to sit with him until I get home from work."

"That's good. At least that's one thing off your plate. So, did Casey have a great birthday?"

"I think he did. He had two parties, two cakes, and was surrounded by people who love him. He laughed and cried."

"Is he okay?"

"Probably better than ever." I tell Mary about Casey's conversation with his friend. "It was as if he had an 'aha' moment, and something inside him shifted. I'm clinging to that moment, Mare, and hoping he'll have the opportunity to be a man of his words."

CHAPTER FIFTEEN

November 9

Emergency!

At five o'clock in the morning, my cell phone rings. I reach for my phone.

"Hello."

"This is the nurse from the hospital." Her voice is in a panic.

I press the phone to my ear, swing my legs onto the floor, and grab my jeans off the other bed.

"Early this morning, Casey broke loose from his bed restraints. He crashed against the wall, banged his head, and fell to the floor."

"What? Ma'am. Slow down. Is Casey okay?" Images of my boy lying in a pool of blood flash through my mind.

"Hospital orderlies got him back into bed. He's calmed down. But he keeps asking for you. How soon can you get here?"

"Fifteen minutes. Tell Casey I'm on my way."

I toss the phone on the bed and rush to the bathroom. I wash my face, brush my teeth, and comb my hair, all the time avoiding my reflection in the mirror.

Within minutes, I'm riding the elevator to the seventh floor. Feeling like my body's been squeezed through a hand wringer, I murmur out loud, "How did this happen? What if Casey reinjured his head? Dammit. I should never leave his side."

Before the doors completely open, I'm in the hallway, racing to Casey's room.

"Mom. What took you so long?" Casey says, agitated.

"Case. The nurse just called me fifteen minutes ago. You okay?"

"No," he screams. "I fell and hit my head. I was scared."

"It's okay. I'm here now." I press the call button, and the nurse arrives immediately. "Please give him a sedative. He's going out of his mind. I can't stand seeing him like this."

"We gave him one earlier. It should be taking effect shortly."

Finally, Casey's breath slows, and after a short while he is sound asleep. I walk down to the nurses' station, fuming.

"Excuse me." My fingers rap on the counter. "When was the last time someone checked on Casey?"

"Around 4 a.m."

"And at that time he was fine?"

"Yes."

"And at what time did you notice he was no longer in his bed?" My arms stretch upward.

"About a half hour later. One of the nurses saw him moving across the room. Then she heard a thud."

I can feel my blood pressure rising as I try to digest the awful news. "And how do you explain my son freeing himself from his restraints?"

"He must have wiggled himself free." The nurse takes a few steps back, as if my cloud of anger invades her space.

"Ladies, I inspected those belts last night before I left. Unless my son has taken on the powers of Houdini during his stay, there is no way he could have wiggled out of his straps. Are you sure one of the nurses didn't take him to the bathroom and forgot to refasten the restraints?"

"Not that we know of," the nurse says sheepishly.

Of course not.

"No one heard any sounds coming from his room during that time?"

"No."

"All of you know Casey by now, and nothing that boy does is quiet. There had to be moans or groans coming from his room before he fell."

"We didn't hear anything."

I almost live here and am quite aware of the sounds coming from the rooms. Was everyone wearing earplugs?

"Well, I would like to talk to your supervisor when she gets in." I take a few steps forward then turn back. "And you can tell her I'm really not happy with how things went down this morning."

Shock waves run through my body, as if my feet are plugged, wet, into an electrical socket. I wrap my pulsing fingers around the mustard seed inside my pocket. As my heartbeat slows, fear bubbles inside. What if Casey falls when he gets home?

A nurse I'm not.

When the kids were little, the sight of blood nauseated me. It wasn't for lack of wanting to help; I just didn't have the stomach for it. I would kiss Casey's boo-boos, drag a chair over to the sink, and teach him how to clean his wounds. "First, stick your finger under the water and rinse the dirt out. Good," I would say, hoping he didn't notice I only had one eye open. "Now grab the soap and rub it into the wound so you don't leave any dirt behind. That's it." I'd pull a washcloth out of the drawer and hand it to him. "Dab your wound until it's dry. Very good." Next, I'd squirt antibiotic ointment on his sore and apply the Band-Aid. He'd jump off the chair, go back to playing, as I stood there still feeling queasy, just like I do now.

God, help me.

With breakfast and lunch behind us, Casey nods off until the therapists arrive in the late afternoon.

The marching band walks into Casey's room. Each one pushes him harder than the day before. Casey eats chunks of food, tosses balls, stands while he brushes his teeth and washes his face. But when Casey heads down the final stretch of the day, sheer jubilation sets in. Casey walks. My son walks! He walks on his own, like he did for the first time nineteen years ago.

It was a beautiful day in California. The earthy, musty smell of falling leaves filled the air. Bo and Casey had just awakened from their naps and were ready to play. Bo straddled his legs over his Little Tike wagon, dug his tennis shoes into the cement, careened out of the garage, and ended on the back patio. As Casey watched his brother with envy, he tried to free himself from my hold, forcing us both to the ground. Bobby, a few feet away, stretched open his arms. I loosened my grip around Casey's waist. He moved one tiny bare foot in front of the other until he landed in his daddy's arms. We cheered.

Now, as then, I'm one proud mama.

Exhausted from today's triumph, Casey falls into a deep sleep. The church bells ring six times in the distance. I close my journal and gaze out the window into twilight.

A tall lady dressed in a business suit walks through the doorway.

"I'm the head nurse of this floor. I understand there was a problem before daybreak."

"Yes, ma'am, there was. And it would have taken a wild animal pumped on steroids to execute this morning's feat."

"I'm sorry you're upset."

"I am upset. Casey's motion is limited. He has a defunct left arm. His muscles are atrophied and his balance is still unstable. Yet, according to the nurses, he somehow managed to break free from the straps. For Christ's sake, Casey has an open skull wound. What if he landed on his brain's soft matter? What kind of situation would we be facing now?"

"I'm not sure." She clears her throat. Then she clears it again. "Going forward, we will be taking every precaution possible to make sure this doesn't happen again. The hospital hired a nurse to sit with Casey when you are not in the room. That's 11 p.m. to 7 a.m., correct?"

I nod. The blaze inside me dwindles to a flicker.

"Thank you. I apologize for my tone. The nurses have taken excellent care of Casey during his stay. I appreciate you stepping into my shoes. Casey has come too far to have a setback, and this one could have been fatal."

The nurse leaves, and I'm alone with my thoughts.

People are human.

Mistakes happen.

Choices are made.

Lessons are learned.
Forgiveness comes.
And life goes on.

I take a deep breath and exhale, realizing that today I was caught up in the never-ending circle of life. Now, like so many times in my past, I choose to forgive so life can carry on.

I think I inherited that trait from Dad and Mom. Whenever Dad was watching a football game and one of us kids made too much noise, he would blow. Shortly after, he would apologize.

As for Mom, she was also quick to forgive. I remember one time in particular: the older four children were just about ready to walk out the door and catch the bus for grade school when Mary strolled out of the bathroom and reported her find in the trashcan.

"Mom, someone threw their jelly sandwich away."

Mom, who couldn't stand for her children to lie, looked at each of us with fire in her eyes. "Which one of you tossed your sandwich in the trash?"

"Wasn't me, Mom," Mary replied. The rest of us copied her.

The bus horn honked. Mom ushered us out the door and said, "I'll get to the bottom of this when you get home."

At 3 p.m., we walked into the house. Mom was waiting. She lined us up and asked three times who the culprit was. Twice I lied. The third time I fessed up.

"Go to your room and say a rosary. I'll be right up."

When Mom came into my room, I was hiding under the covers, shaking, saying one Hail Mary after another. She pulled back the covers and asked, "Honey, why did you throw your jelly sandwich in the trash?"

"'Cause it tastes like mush after it bakes in the closet at school."

"You should have told me that when I asked the first time. If you had, you wouldn't be paying the consequences for your actions now."

"I know, Mom. But I was scared I was going to get in trouble."

Mom brushed the wet hairs off my face. "And you did. I hope you learned your lesson. Now, finish your rosary then come downstairs." She bent down, kissed me, and whispered, "I love you, sweetie."

I can't remember Dad or Mom ever holding the past over me. They got their point across and moved on.

Life is about choices—every minute, every second of each day. I've lived long enough to know that I've made choices that I regret, especially spending more time cleaning my house than playing with my kids when they were little. And it saddens me that I missed an opportunity to listen to what was on their minds and in their hearts when one of the kids said, "Mom," and I replied, "Not now." Some choices I don't regret: keeping Bo in jail when he got a DUI, leaving a marriage that no longer served Bobby or me (realizing we both deserved to find happiness again), and giving the nurse a piece of my mind.

Through it all, I've come to understand that sometimes we make a choice, and sometimes a choice makes us. Right now, just like Dad and Mom, I'm choosing to leave the past behind.

Chapter Sixteen

November 11

After thirty-seven days, Casey is undergoing his final operation.

"They're taking me into the operating room. You need to get to the hospital now!" Casey screams into the phone.

"Calm down, Casey. It's still dark outside. Your operation isn't until 11 a.m."

"No, Mom. The nurses are getting me ready now." He says it with angst, sounding as if he's spitting between each word.

"Honey, that's hospital protocol just in case the doctor finishes . . ." The phone goes dead.

Thirty minutes later, I arrive at the hospital. Casey's face is flushed. His arms are flapping. He's screaming profanities to everyone within range.

"Mom. I'm hungry. I need food. The nurses won't feed me."

"Doctor's orders say ice chips only. He doesn't want you to get sick during the procedure." The nurse tries to reason with him, but she does not succeed.

"The only way I'm going to get sick is if I don't get something to eat. Soon." Bulging purple roadmaps stretch across his forehead.

I want to say to Casey, "Be polite, watch your mouth, show some compassion and respect." But my emotions somersault, and my mind plays the "what if" game. *What if something goes wrong while he's in surgery? What if he reverts backward? What if—*

The phone in Casey's room rings at 10:45 a.m.

I answer, say "thank you," hang up, and tell Casey they're on their way.

The orderlies wheel a gurney into Room 721.

"'Bout time you guys got here," Casey blurts. "I've been waiting all morning to get this thing over with. Let's go."

The attendants gently lift Casey on the gurney and start out the door.

"Mom, aren't you coming?"

"Yes, sweetie. I'm just grabbing my purse." I can feel my nerves splintering one by one.

At the surgery center door, the orderlies pause. One of them turns to me and says, "Ma'am, you can't go any further. Dr. Bailey will come speak to you after the operation. You'll have to say your goodbyes now."

"Nope. No goodbyes."

"I understand."

"Casey, love you. You know that, right?"

"Yes, Mom. Love you."

"Case, I'll fill the operating room with angels. You are going to do fine. I love you." My voice trails down the corridor and then evaporates as the gurney disappears around the corner.

That's when it hits me. My boy is undergoing brain surgery. Again. I need to get to the chapel. I need to be alone. Pray. Meditate. Something.

My cell phone starts vibrating as the elevator rises. The phone stops, then vibrates again. I check the number. It's Mom. She's probably worried about Casey.

Worrying has become Mom's second nature. I'm not sure if it's a word synonymous with "mother," or if it's a characteristic she was born with.

In grade school, she would tell the older kids to watch over the younger ones. In high school, if one of the girls arrived home five minutes after curfew, she'd be waiting at the door. When the boys played football, the lines doubled on her face. When her girls went into labor, she prayed one rosary after another. As her children got older, she worried about everything and everyone. She just worried.

So, I'm not shocked that she's the first person to call.

"Hi, Mom."

"Honey, how ya doin'? How's Casey?"

"They took him into surgery a couple minutes ago. Just can't . . ." I stop at the end of the hallway and press my shoulder blades into the picture window ". . . believe that over a month ago he was operated on, and no one was here for him. I don't think I'll ever get over that."

"I know, honey. But you're there today. That's all that matters. Just wish I were with you. Are you alone? Any of the kids coming to sit with you?" I hear Mom sniffle.

"Annie's in class. She'll stop by later. Bo called last night. Said he'd be here this afternoon."

"And Bobby?"

"Not sure, Mom. He could be traveling. I can't keep everyone's schedule straight. I'm so focused on Casey that nothing else matters. Not now, anyway."

"I understand, sweetie. Promise you'll call me the minute you speak to the doctor. I'll be waiting by the phone, praying."

Time, measured in the agony of minutes and hours, crawls. Nervously, I pace in Casey's room, my feet pounding against the tile floor as my fingers clap against my palms.

A professional cleaning service employee arrives. My stride breaks.

"You need me to go?" she asks.

"No. Please." I wave her in.

For the next thirty minutes, I share every detail of Casey's accident and recovery. I check my watch again. "It's already afternoon. I thought the operation would be over."

"You're worried, aren't you honey?"

"I am." The six-foot, robust woman wraps her arm around my shoulder. I bury my head into her softness, welcoming her tender embrace.

"My husband's a pastor. After I finish here, I'm going to give him a call. He'll start a prayer group for your boy. But right now you need to go to a happy place." She tightens her grip. "There has to be a story about your son buried inside you; one that makes you proud to be his mama."

"There is." I feel my eyes glass over, remembering.

Spring had just sprung in Huntington, New York. The curved walkways leading to St. Patrick's Church were lined with daffodils, and the budding ancient oaks and maple trees stood like giants on the velvet grass. Once inside the magnificent stone structure, shaped in the design of a cross, we scooted into the wooden pew. Casey (a.k.a. Mr. Socialite, age 10) had a hard time settling down, constantly turning around, waving to his friends, or making comments to Bo and Annie, who erupted into bouts of muffled laughter. Finally, Mass ended. As we exited the pew, I was mentally rehearsing my lecture. But before I had a chance to pull Casey aside, he stopped in front of the box that read, "Offerings for the Poor." He dug into his pants pocket and retrieved a couple of dimes, some quarters, and pennies and dropped them in the box. That's when I quickly revised my speech.

Casey might be full of piss and vinegar, but his heart is made of gold. And in that fleeting moment, I felt like a lioness standing on the edge of a rock with my upper body puffed, proud of my cub.

I open my eyes and feel myself smiling.

"Better, child?"

"Much better. Thank you."

A short time later, I hear footsteps approaching Casey's room. Dr. Bailey walks through the door.

"The operation was successful. We'll need to watch his wound closely. It's susceptible to infection at this point. But I believe all will be fine."

"Did you feel the presence of angels in the operating room? I sent an entire legion, just in case you needed some assistance."

"I did see something flying around." The suggestion of a smirk plays at the corners of his mouth.

I love Dr. Bailey. I don't know whether he believes in angels or not, but he has hung in there with me. And when the road looked rocky for

Casey, he listened to me talk about the power of a mustard seed. He could have told the nurses and resident doctors to look out for the crazy woman in ICU Room 1, and on the seventh floor, Room 721. Instead, his attitude, one of acceptance and open-mindedness, set the tone for his team. That's something.

Profanities blast through the hallway. I recognize the voice immediately.

"He's in a lot of pain and will be for a while. The nurse will sedate him once he gets settled. Any questions?"

"Maybe later. I can't think." I press my fingers into my ears.

"I'll check in later."

"Dr. Bailey." Pressure builds in my tear ducts, as if the dam is ready to break. "Thank you for everything."

The operating staff wheels Casey's bed into the room. He continues to shout every curse word I know and then some. Bo enters. We make eye contact but don't speak. He can tell I'm coming unglued.

I bend down and give Casey a kiss.

"You're going to be fine, sweetie."

"It hurts like hell, Mom. What are you talking about?"

Bo chimes in. "Mom. Why don't you let me take it from here? You look exhausted."

"Thanks, Bo."

I take the elevator down to the chapel. It smells of burnt wax, furniture polish, and disinfectant. I sit in a chair in the back row, talking out loud to God.

"You know, God, I think you'd better pull up a chair. I need to talk. I've held so much inside for the past thirty-seven days. I can't do it anymore. I feel like a rug has been pulled out from underneath me, and my fall left scars that may never heal. I am mad as hell. That's right. Mad that Casey wasn't wearing a helmet. Angry that he made a stupid choice—drinking and then driving his souped-up moped. Frustrated that he can't comprehend how his actions affected everyone in his path. Furious that he almost died.

"Will he understand and appreciate the sacrifices everyone has made?

Will he know we did it all out of love? Will his experience change his direction in life? I don't know. I can only hope and pray that one day he puts it all in perspective.

"I'm so tired and afraid. I don't know what's around the next corner. Or, what portion of my son I'm bringing home. What are his challenges ahead? What are mine? I'm hurtin' here, real bad, God."

I start to stand then kneel back down.

"Oh and, by the way, don't get me wrong. I am so thankful you saved my boy and gave me faith, courage, and strength to greet each day. Please don't stop. I can't make it on my own. I need you. We need you. Amen."

Chapter Seventeen

November 12

The smell of breakfast lures me into the Marriott's dining room this morning.

"We missed you at breakfast yesterday. How was Casey's operation?" Connie asks. Several waitresses stand in an arc around her.

"I had to scoot out before the birds started chirping. But the doc said it went well."

"See, child, we told you, no prayers go unanswered." In rapid succession, their arms lift. "Praise the Lord."

My head moves like an oscillating fan on slow as I make eye contact with each woman, each blessed soul who prayed unfailingly and with complete confidence for my boy. These strong women, once complete strangers, came into my life and changed it forever.

"Ladies, I just don't know what I would have done without you."

Connie, built like a fire hydrant with black eyes that match her skin and hair, steps forward.

"The Good Book says that we should love our neighbors as we love ourselves. That's what we did." She claps her hands. "Now, let's fix your boy a real meal. He's earned it."

Within a matter of minutes, I'm holding to-go boxes filled with bacon, toast, waffles, and scrambled eggs. A feast fit for a king.

Smells of the harbor drift through the open windows on the ride to the hospital. The trees, once freckled in yellow and red, are naked.

"Stand by Me," plays on the radio. I smile, thinking about the angels in aprons.

I tiptoe into Casey's room. "You're awake. How you feelin' today?"

"Better." His facial features are soft and sweet, as if his spirits have been lifted.

My eyes lock onto the ghastly sight of his enlarged skull, covered in thick white tape sticking to his partially shaved head. Struggling not to let my voice break, I ask, "On a scale of one to ten, with ten being the best, how would you rank your pain?"

"Five. What ya got?"

"The sweet ladies at the Marriott thought you might be hungry."

"They got that right." He rubs his hands together.

Small waves of steam rise, encircling his face. Casey digs the fork into the scrambled eggs and shovels them into his mouth. Remnants cling under his nostrils and pimple his face. He keeps spooning.

What happened to his manners? The constant shifting between Casey's highs and lows, from excitement to terror, chisels at my heart.

There's a rap at the door. It's Dr. Bailey.

"Can I come in? Feeling better, Casey?"

Casey nods without looking up. In one hand he's holding bacon, the other toast. He moves his head from right to left, taking bites of each without swallowing.

"Looks like you're enjoying your breakfast," Dr. Bailey says.

Casey laughs through his words. "Mmm. Really good, Doc."

Dr. Bailey scans the notes on his pad. "Casey, if all goes according to plan, you should be leaving in a few days."

Panic sets in. A few days? I'm not sure if he's ready. If I'm ready.

"Your scars should heal well over time. Right now, the stitching resembles the lines on a baseball."

"A baseball? That's funny." Casey rubs the right side of his head.

Funny? I wonder, as the doc leaves. I'm not seeing humor in any of this. None at all.

The therapists make their rounds, fine-tuning all they have taught Casey up to this point: strengthening his left arm, helping him walk on his own, testing his cognitive skills by telling simple stories, making sure he can chew, swallow, and take care of his bodily needs.

As I watch Casey, it occurs to me that his healing is separate from mine. We're heading for the same destination. He's taking the back roads. I'm wanting to drive up the interstate. It doesn't matter who gets there first. What's important is that we eventually get there together.

Chapter Eighteen

November 15

The day of departure is here. I can hardly believe it. I'm ecstatic and terrified, all at the same time.

I stop in the Marriott dining room and say goodbye to the prayer angels. Connie does the talking. The others listen.

"Big day. Are you nervous about driving your son back to Charlotte?"

"His father arranged for Air Ambulance to pick him up."

Bobby may not be physically present on a daily basis, but when it comes to the fine details, he always comes through. And for that, I'm sincerely grateful.

"Air Ambulance. What's that?"

"It's an aircraft used for emergency medical assistance when a patient has to be transported long distances or can't reach a destination easily. With Casey's brain injury, we didn't want to chance driving."

"Of course. I'm assuming there's a nurse or paramedic onboard."

"Both."

"Medical equipment?"

"It's my understanding that the planes come equipped with medication, ventilators, ECG and monitoring units, stretchers and CPR equipment, the whole works."

"How does Air Ambulance work?"

"The crew arrives at MUSC, puts Casey on a gurney, then loads him into an ambulance. After driving him to the airport, the crew loads him into a private aircraft, gurney and all."

"Oh, child, you must be relieved you don't have to transport him."

"I am. Thank God his dad has good health insurance, or I wouldn't be smiling now."

Together, we wrap our emotions into one big bear hug. There's not a dry eye among us.

As I walk to the car, I feel like a lost puppy, dragging my tail behind. I toss my bag in the car. For a second, I scan the garage in hopes of seeing my guardian angel, but he's nowhere in sight. My mind travels back to our brief encounter and the promise he made to me—"I'm here for you"—which he has been, every step of the way.

I'm not bothered by the traffic or beeping horns on my final ride to MUSC. Instead, I'm consumed with my thoughts. How many days has Casey been in the hospital? I do the math in my head. It's been forty days and nights. I look through the windshield and glimpse a pale rainbow forming to the west, and I'm reminded of the biblical story of Noah's Ark. After forty days of rain, Noah released a dove, which returned because there wasn't any dry land. A week later, Noah released the same dove, and the bird came back with an olive branch, a sign of hope. Once the earth dried, Noah built an altar to thank God for keeping them safe. Honored, God created a rainbow as a promise to his people that He would never destroy the earth and its inhabitants by flood again.

I pull into the parking lot and get out of the car. When I search for the rainbow, I find it has grown even more brilliant.

I bow my head, humbled by the sign. It's as if God is saying, "I promise you and your loved ones will never have to go through this again."

When I arrive in Casey's room, people are everywhere, each with their own agenda.

"We have orders to transport Casey to Charlotte. Is he ready to go?" says one of the two young men from Air Ambulance. I point toward the bed. With assistance, Casey climbs on the gurney.

"You need to sign Casey's release forms," says another nurse, shoving papers into my hand.

"Here are Casey's belongings." A nurse hands me a plastic bag.

"Mom, I need to thank the nurses and doctors," Casey shouts.

I hand the nurse the paperwork. The therapists start arriving to say their farewells. Each one gives me sheets with instructions for his subsequent care. I place his belongings on the side of the gurney and stuff my "homework" inside my bag.

"Safe travels, Casey. Keep giving it your best. We're going to miss you," say the therapists.

"Gonna miss you guys, too. But I'm not going to miss being in the hospital. I can't wait to go home."

I wonder if Casey resents leaving his old life behind. I never asked him how he feels about going into rehab, leaving Charleston, missing his college buds and months of school or longer. Why haven't I thought about that? All he talks about is connecting with his old friends and going home.

Home to what? Fear shivers through my body. Concerned that my emotions are painted across my face, I turn away from the therapists. Dr. Bailey, dressed in his white lab coat and blue scrubs, stands just outside Casey's room, talking with his team of doctors.

As I approach him, my demeanor shifts, and a smile stretches from ear to ear. "Is there anything I can do to show my appreciation?"

Dr. Bailey pushes his wire-rimmed glasses up his nose. "Do you have any more of those little bottles of miracle water you've been spritzing on Casey?"

"Of course."

Dr. Bailey wants holy water? I pull a bottle from my purse and place it in his hands. All the while I'm thinking, "Does he want this for his patients or himself . . . just in case?"

"Here you go. Anything else?"

"No. This should do it."

"Again, thank you for saving my boy's life," I say, patting my chest. "He really is a miracle, isn't he?"

Dr. Bailey doesn't answer, but his mustache moves, revealing his smile.

The two Air Ambulance employees begin rolling the gurney toward the door. Dr. Bailey grasps hold of Casey's hand. "You take care, now. Keep working hard. I'll see you when you get back in town."

"Thanks for everything, Doc." He raps his knuckles on his bandaged head. "You did a good job."

Oh my God, he's going to lapse into another coma if he doesn't stop knocking on his head.

Casey tilts his head back, searching for me. "Love you, Mom. See ya tonight."

"Love you too, Case." I kiss his forehead then his lips. "Be safe, sweetie."

Once the gurney disappears down the hallway, I step back into Room 721 to gather my belongings.

Alone, I inhale the fresh scent of cleaning products. I stare at the bare closet door, photographs packed away. I run my hand along the cool, clean sheets, the perfectly fluffed pillow. I close my eyes, wishing this had all been a dream.

The elevator door opens. I press the button for four and get off on the ICU floor. Inside the waiting room, I write my final prayer—"Thank you for moving the mountain. And if it's not too much trouble, can you follow me home? I think there's another mountain waiting for us"—and stuff it inside the God box.

Soft chatter sounds from behind. I turn. New people gather in clusters, consoling one another. A stranger pats another stranger's leg. Their heartaches appear to merge. It seems as if time stops. Within that tiny sliver of time (time that has no beginning and no end), the room fills with love and compassion.

My heart shudders knowing their journey ahead: one filled with uncertainty, confusion, sorrow, and surrender, sprinkled with hope, and held together through the power of faith and love.

I walk toward the door, look over my shoulder, and grin. Judging by the expressions on their faces, I believe that they, like the thousands that came before them, have become family.

As I merge onto the dual highway, separated by tall pine and live oak trees, the city dissolves into my rearview mirror, yet the memories live on.

Some memories I wish I could erase—Casey's accident, his dance with death, his struggles to walk, talk, and eat again on his own—and some memories I'll hold on to for a lifetime. I will always cherish Casey's encounters with his angels and Mother Mary. Unforgettable too is my connection with earth angels at the Marriott: prayer and laundry, along with the mysterious gentleman who appeared in the parking lot garage claiming to be my guardian angel. Then there's Maggie and Drace, who had my back. Undeniably helpful was Dr. Bailey and his professional team of doctors and nurses at MUSC. Last but not least, I will always recall the support from my family and Mary who showed up when I needed her most.

Even though a part of me would like to turn back the hands of time, a part of me knows that everything happens for a reason. There's always a lesson to be learned. Life's challenges offer people an opportunity to grow. I don't have all the answers right now, but I plan on pushing through the pain, pushing through the tears, and never giving up until I do.

Maybe, just maybe, within the mystery of life lies the beauty of the mystery.

Three hours later, I drag my suitcase into the house. The dogs are barking and jumping.

"I sure have missed you guys. Looks like the dog sitter took good care of you." They lick my face. I rub their bellies. "Guess what? Casey's coming home soon."

Duke tilts his head left, as if he understands. C.D. (Children's Dog) growls. That's what he does best.

I give the dog sitter a quick call. I offer to pay her. She refuses to take a cent.

I throw in a couple loads of laundry. I drive to the grocery store and pick up a few staples. Two hours later, I'm back on the road, driving to the rehabilitation center, stomach in knots.

In the trunk lays a small suitcase filled with Casey's extras: boxers, T-shirts, and pajama pants. Next to me sits a folder: notes from the therapists, recommendations, and my own endless questions.

I pull into a parking space, grab my belongings, and walk inside.

The receptionist takes my information and hands me another stack of papers. She walks me down the empty, sparsely lit corridor to a set of double doors and scans her card. "We have tight security here. Some of the patients get very confused and try to leave."

Confused? This isn't a prison. It's a rehab.

Click. The door opens.

"Casey's room is the first door on the right. Let me know if you need anything."

Once in his room, I sing out, "How's my boy?" I pick up the remote and press the volume button down.

"Good. It took you long enough to get here."

I switch the subject, sensing Casey's unease.

"How was the airplane ride?"

"Nice. Smell that?" His nose twitches like a rabbit. "I think its hamburgers and french fries. Go find out how much longer, Mom." Casey waves his hand as if he's a policeman directing traffic. "I'm starved."

The nurse walks through the door with the dinner tray in hand.

Casey bites into the sloppy joe. Sticks green beans into his mouth. Shovels mashed potatoes into the mix. Grabs the milk carton. Slurps from the straw. Food drips down his chin. I hand him a napkin. He uses his sleeve.

I want to cry.

He tugs at the crotch of his pants. "I have to go."

I slide the walker in place. He shuffles into the bathroom then out.

"Let's walk, Mom."

At a snail's pace, we stroll down the poorly lit hallways, glimpsing commercials, MTV, and sports coming from the patients' televisions, interspersed with their cries summoning a nurse. I'm not sure what to do, so I run my fingers through my hair, tuck my shirt into my blue jeans, put my hands in my pants pockets, and pull them out again.

"So, how was your day, Case?"

"Had a smoke with the guy in Room 4."

"Nice guy?"

"Yeah."

Silence. The awkward kind, as if both of us are searching for something to say.

"Told Duke and C.D. you were coming home soon."

"And what did they say?" Casey says, mocking me.

"Well, C.D. did his characteristic '*grrrr*', and Duke tilted his head."

"Bring Duke tomorrow."

"Honey, I can't. Dogs aren't allowed."

"What the f**k?"

"Case, do you have to use that kind of language?"

"Sorry, Mom. That's the way I talk."

"But it's really not appropriate to speak like that in front of your mother. You know better."

Or does he? I'm not so sure anymore.

As the rehab doors close behind me, I'm frantically dialing Drace.

"I'm taking you up on your previous offer to call if I wanted to rant, rave, or cry. In fact, I'm about to do all three simultaneously. Lord, help me."

"Girl, what's wrong?"

"Casey's manners are gone. I mean gone, kaput, out the window. He curses like a sailor. I know that's a cliché, but I'm trying to spare you the lewd language that rolled off his tongue. I think I'm spent. No, I know I'm spent."

"Girl, breathe. That's it. Do me a favor, and get in your car. I don't want you standing in that dark parking lot alone."

"I'm in. Key is in the ignition. Pulling out of the driveway."

"Good. Can you talk to the doctor or Casey's therapist tomorrow?"

"It's the weekend. Don't think they're in."

"Okay. Then call first thing Monday."

"But I'll be at work. Never mind. I'll figure it out. Drace, even the rehab center is dark, dreary, and depressing. I wasn't prepared for this. What if I can't do this?"

"Yes you can. You got through the first phase, and you'll get through the next and the next. If you get stuck and you need me, I'll jump on a plane."

During our almost-lifelong friendship, Drace has been there for me. Just when she probably thought I was getting my life together after the divorce . . . wham, another damn storm strikes. Rather than running for cover, she sits next to me on the wet pavement, one arm around my waist and the other holding the umbrella, and she listens as I pour my guts out.

Drace continues, "You're drained, friend. Get some sleep. Things will be better with Casey tomorrow."

Not only is Casey rebuilding himself, I'm rebuilding me. He's returning to his life as I'm returning to mine. Yet both of us are working without a net.

CHAPTER NINETEEN

November 16

"Mary, you up?"

"Yeah. Going to Jazzercise at ten. Have about fifteen minutes. What's up?"

"I took the dogs out this morning and noticed pumpkins lining my neighbors' steps. That's when it hit me. Thanksgiving is just around the corner, and Casey will still be in rehab. He's going to be *so* upset."

"Maybe you can make dinner and take it to rehab? I'm sure Bo and Annie wouldn't mind a change of scenery."

"They go to their dad's this year. I had wanted this Thanksgiving to be so perfect, like—"

"Like the first year Dad, Ginny, and our family spent the holidays with you guys in Charlotte? And you forgot to buy the onions for the dressing?"

"Okay, well that wasn't exactly what I had in mind," I say, startled Mary has thrown me a curveball. "Dad was a bit perturbed, wasn't he?"

"Ya think? That's when stores were closed on major holidays. Dad made our kids knock on every neighbor's door, begging for onions." Mary titters. "All they wanted to do was ride Casey's go-kart."

"That's right. Bobby ended up driving to McDonald's, buying quarts of chopped onions, while Dad fretted at home. 'For God's sake, how can I make dressing without onions?'"

Mary laughs. I join in, welcoming her diversion.

"Well, Thanksgiving dinner has always been Dad's signature meal.

Nothing gives him more pleasure than getting up at the crack of dawn, making the dressing, and stuffing the bird."

I envision Pop standing in the kitchen, pots and pans everywhere, the room in complete disarray.

"Sis, you worked through that glitch, and you'll work through this one. Sometimes perfect is what you make it."

"Thanks, Mare. Listen, gotta go, 'cause Annie's buzzing in. Talk tomorrow."

I press the flash button.

"Hey, sweetie. How's it going?"

"Studying. Got exams next week. Ick. Wanted to let you know about Thanksgiving weekend."

"Can't wait to spend time with my girl."

I step out on the deck and stare below at my once-pristine flower garden—sunflowers, daisies, veronica, and purple vinca scattered under the peach tree—strangled by weeds, stripped of their radiance.

"That's what I wanted to talk to you about. I'm going to Dad's for Thanksgiving. Want to catch up with my friends in Charlotte. So . . ."

Feeling like my flowers, I'm crushed, and then some, but I try to bury my disappointment.

"Maybe we can sneak away for a couple hours and go out to lunch and shop, which you know is my favorite pastime. What do you think?"

Since Annie was a child, she's been the intuitive observer—energetically picking up vibes from people and her surroundings—never making a move until she felt comfortable. She wouldn't even spend the night at a friend's house until the family passed the test.

Now, even at a distance, Annie's tuning into my feelings.

"Sounds wonderful."

"We'll figure out the details when I get home. How's Case?"

"Nothing new since the last time we spoke."

"That's good. Gotta run, Mom. Need to hit the books."

"Sweetie, try not to stress over your exams. I know, easier said than done."

Even though Annie has always been diligent about her studies, when it comes to tests, she has a hard time focusing. Frustrated, she asked to be tested for ADD in high school. The results indicated she scored average in three categories and genius in Perceptual Reasoning—nonverbal concept formation, visual perception, and organization—which didn't surprise me. Early on, she had a good sense of direction. Annie loved sketching furniture placement for her bedroom and planning her birthday parties down to the finest details. Who knows, maybe she'll choose a career as an architect or an event planner. Too early to tell. But whatever path she chooses, I'm confident her strong work ethic will ensure success.

After spending hours putzing around the house, going through stacks of bills and vacuuming the dust bunnies that populated after months of neglect, I'm back on the road to rehab.

As I slip the gear into park, the streetlights in front of the building blink on, casting a soft light onto the sidewalk.

Belly laughter bounces off the walls in Casey's room.

I haven't heard him laugh that hard since Bo pranced around Room 721 in diapers.

"Hey, what's going on in here?"

"Hi, Mom. Dad was telling me a funny story. Look what he brought me." Casey waves a boating magazine in front of my face. "I found the boat I'm going to buy someday, too. Want to see?"

"Sure."

While Casey flips through the pages, I turn to Bobby. "How did it go today?"

Without looking up from his book, he answers. "Not bad. We watched football, ate, and I told Case a few stories."

That's it? Casey never had an outburst? Never used profane language? All was normal? Really?

Casey pulls on my sleeve. "Look, Mom. Look. Here it is."

"Just a second, Casey. Need to talk to your dad."

"You coming back tomorrow? Same time?"

Bobby tosses his Coke can and empty Frito bag in the trash bin.

He opts to answer me indirectly, which has been his strategy since the divorce; he fixes his eyes on Casey. "Work for you, Son?"

We aren't one of those couples that split and the two parties remain amicable. Most times we can't even stand being in the same room together. I believe Bobby still harbors resentment that I left him. I'm still angry at myself for giving my power away for most of our married years.

It's not that realizing our power imbalance was a conscious thought. It's something I became aware of at Nar-Anon meetings, which I began to attend after Bo went into treatment. Inside those trailer walls, I discovered that I had taken on the role of the enabler, just like Mom had with Dad, losing my identity, wanting peace and harmony, no matter what the cost. My big wake-up call came when the group leader recited the definition of insanity: "doing the same thing over and over again, expecting different results." Then and there, I decided to change my behavior and step into my power.

I sought support through Nar-Anon, counseling, and self-help books. I learned that if I didn't love, respect, and value the person I was, no one else would. Gradually, I stood up for myself, expressed my feelings, learned to love me and all my quirkiness, and took back my power. Those changes, I believe, fueled the demise of our marriage.

Yet, here I stand in this moment stuck in the past, struggling to find my voice again.

Bobby picks up his briefcase, kisses Casey, and walks out the door, saying goodbye to me over his shoulder.

His childish behavior grates on my nerves. But I have learned that change isn't about him and me, it's about me and me. That I'm responsible for how I act and react. Obviously, my inner work must be ongoing, because healing is like chiseling away at blocks of stone, one chunk at a time.

"So, let's see that boat, Casey."

Casey's glides his finger across a yacht sailing on the ocean. "I'm going to do that, Mom."

"Do what, Casey?"

He taps his finger on the man behind the wheel, repeatedly. "Be a captain of my own ship."

"How about school? Don't you want to get your degree someday?"

"I don't care about school. I've always wanted to be the captain of a ship."

Captain of a ship? No further schooling? Are either of these an option? I can't hear myself breathe. This isn't fair.

Dinner comes, and I can barely watch. Casey's cheeks, puffed like a chipmunk's, are filled with bites of a grilled cheese sandwich, peas, and pasta. I want to gag.

He finishes.

"Ready to walk?"

I roll the walker to the bed.

"I'm not using that stupid thing."

He stands. He wobbles. I offer my hand. He waves me away. He takes ten steps. Stops. He leans against the wall and breathes. "I'm tired, Mom."

I am, too. You step. I step. You stop. I stop. You lean. I lean. You breathe. I breathe, kind of.

CHAPTER TWENTY

November 17

Patience is not my strong suit. When I want something done, I want it done now.

I'm up and out of the house early this morning to purchase a mattress and box spring for Casey. But after I pay for the merchandise, the clerk informs me that Sam's Club doesn't deliver.

My body freezes. I stare at the clerk. She calls for assistance.

A middle-aged man appears at the counter. I explain my dilemma. He offers to help.

The gentleman ties the mattress and box spring to the roof of the car. "How far do you have to go, ma'am?"

"A few miles. Why?"

"I think you can make it."

Think? You have doubts?

I drive home under the speed limit. Everyone is honking, swearing, and flashing the bird. I'm crying one minute and praying the next.

I pull into the driveway. Grab scissors from the garage. Step onto the running board. Cut the rope. Push the box springs to the ground. Shove it inside and listen as it bangs against the wall.

"Damn."

I stand in the hallway for several minutes, scratching my head as I try to figure out my next move.

I lift the back end of the springs up the stairwell, rest it on the third step, walk around to the front, grab hold of fabric, and tug, and pull, and sweat, and swear until it clears the doorway.

I go through the process twice. Finally, the box spring and mattress are in place.

With my adrenaline still pumping, I put the finishing touches on Casey's bed: sheets, navy comforter, and khaki pillows that blend with the walls. Once the furniture is dusted and the carpet vacuumed, I stand in the doorway and take in each section of the room from right to left. Casey's newly appointed bed faces the window. His desk, lined with vintage model cars and books, rests against the center wall. Angled in the left corner sits a black leather chair, floor lamp, and end table. Dave Matthews and Bob Marley posters decorate the walls. I smile, admiring my day's work.

It's hard to say where my strong work ethic came from. Maybe it came from watching Mom, who was always in motion: cooking, cleaning, washing and folding laundry, painting, stripping furniture, and sewing clothes for her kids and their dolls into the wee hours of the morning. Maybe it came from observing Dad, who not only worked hard at the family business when he was younger, but also held down several part-time jobs—cutting grass and selling oil for furnaces—in order to make ends meet. Then later, he'd switched his career to real estate and worked around the clock to make a deal. But, in all honesty, I believe my stamina came from both.

An hour later, I'm driving across town to rehab. My phone rings. It's Bo.

"Hi, sweetie. Haven't heard from you lately. How's school going?"

"School is school. NC State won their football game this weekend. The crowd went crazy. Everyone from the stands went down on the field and tried to knock down the goalpost," Bo laughs. "It was nuts, Mom."

"Glad you're having fun, sweetie. I hope you're putting as much energy into your grades as you are partying."

"Grades are good, Mom. I promise."

Bo is smart, kind, funny, and prone to not keeping his promises.

After the divorce, I asked for only one present at Christmas: a letter on the tree. Bo's habitual pattern over the past three years has been showing up empty-handed. His response is always the same. "Shoot, Mom. I wrote you the best letter and left it sitting on my desk at Dad's. I'll bring it by tomorrow. Promise."

Disappointed? A little, but I understand Bo. His priorities get a bit askew at times, but I love him anyway. I believe one day he will keep his promise about the letter. But his grades? That's debatable.

Bo quickly changes the subject.

"What you been up to?"

I fill him in on my latest projects.

"Mom. You should be doing something for yourself."

"Can't right now. Casey's coming home soon."

"That's my point. You're not going to have time to have fun once he gets home."

Even as a toddler, Bo's motto was to have fun. One afternoon while I was cleaning the bedroom closet, he strolled in with my pink paisley purse strung over his shoulder and said, "Bye. Bye. Fun."

Today his motto hasn't changed.

"Ah, Bo, you know your Mom, externally organized, internally organized."

"Whatever. How's Case?"

"Pulling into the parking lot as we speak."

"Tell him I said 'hi' and that I'll call later. See you for Thanksgiving, Mom."

When I step into Casey's room, I hear the toilet flush. The bathroom door opens and out steps Bobby. He nods, acknowledging my presence.

"Guess it's time for me to head out, Casey."

"When you coming back, Dad?"

"I'm back at work tomorrow and then I'm traveling. But I'll bring Bo and Annie by Thanksgiving morning."

"What? I'm stuck in this place on Thanksgiving? Not fair."

"Sweetie. I'm going to make dinner at home and bring it here. I'll make our day special." Feeling his pain, I tenderly glide my hand over his arm.

"It won't be the same. Dammit, I want to go home." Casey tosses his magazine across the room.

I look at Bobby. His brows elevate and his forehead looks like rungs on a ladder. "Now, Casey. It will be—"

"What, Dad? Fine? How do you know how I feel? You're not the one stuck in this stupid rehab." He covers his ears with his hands. "I don't want to hear it."

Bobby leans over to kiss his son. Casey flicks him away. "I'll call you." Bobby walks into the hallway, mumbling under his breath.

"Casey, can you turn the TV down for a few seconds?"

"What, Mom? I don't want to talk about Thanksgiving."

"I was just wondering how you feel about being back in Charlotte."

His mood softens. "Okay."

"Just okay?"

He pulls his legs up, drops them then pulls them up again.

"What, honey? Do you miss Charleston, school, your friends?" I feel like I'm pulling teeth.

"Kind of. But as soon as I get out of here, I'm gonna hang out with my old friends."

"You have to take it slow, Case. You just had a major operation. The doctor and therapists stressed on your release forms that your brain needs sleep to heal."

"My brain's fine. Listen." He raps his knuckles on his skull.

I slump back in the chair.

"Tomorrow is my first day at work, Casey. And—"

He turns up the volume.

I miss the old Casey. When he called from college, he'd say, "Hi, Mom. What's going on with you?" When he came home from school, he'd give me a hug for no reason. When he told a story, interspersed with his sarcastic remarks, we'd laugh.

Now all of that is gone. I feel like I've jumped out of a plane without a parachute.

Chapter Twenty-One

Still November

At six forty five in the morning, I pull into Barnes & Noble's parking lot in Huntersville.

Seconds later, a car swings into the row in front of me. A man, small in stature, emerges. The soft golden light filtering from the lamppost illuminates his silver-white hair.

I roll down the window. "Danny. It's me."

"Give me a sec." With his briefcase wedged under his arm, he walks to my car. "Ready for your first day?"

"Sure am. Can't wait to get started." I grab my purse, and we walk toward the store. "How's Casey?"

Oh, please don't make me cry. Not now. Not on my first day of work. How can I explain to my new boss that my nerves are shot? I'm sleep-deprived. I'm anxious about today, tomorrow, and beyond.

"Okay. We're getting through it, moment by moment. I'm sure you've heard plenty of brain injury stories from your friend who works in neurology," I say, remembering that's how I got the recommendation for the rehab in Charlotte.

"Yes. I often wonder how the patients' loved ones get though each day." He pats my shoulder tenderly. "I'm here for you, if you ever need to talk."

"Thanks."

He doesn't even know me, yet he's offered to be my friend.

Danny resets the store's alarm.

"Come on in. I'll show you around."

Danny points out the genre sections as we pass the customer service station and make our way to the café, located in the back of the store.

"This is where our Monday meetings are held. There are six managers." He checks his watch. "They should be arriving any time now. Let me show you to your office so you can get settled in before the meeting starts."

Danny pushes open one of the double doors. "Please, after you." We walk through the break room: message board on one side, kitchen on the other. Just beyond is my room on the left.

"Here you go. There's no window but plenty of work space." His hand sweeps through the air, directing my attention to the white Formica top that wraps three walls. "That's your computer, printer, phone, supplies, and file cabinet. There's a key inside the first drawer if you'd like to lock up your purse. I'm right across the hall if you have questions. Right now, I need to get a few things in order before our meeting starts."

"Wait." I grab Danny's hand. "Sorry I missed the Grand Opening. Just can't thank you enough for holding this position for me."

"Glad it worked out for all of us. See you in the café in a few."

At the meeting, Danny introduces the managers then gets down to business. He reads the past week's sales statistics, alerts us on the store's incentives, and gives each manager a few minutes to report on their departments. The managers' faces begin to blend together, and all I see are lips moving. I'm overwhelmed.

The meeting ends. Managers shoot off like spokes of a wheel. I bundle the community relations and store policy binders under my arm and walk to my room.

Minutes later, Danny pops his head into my office.

"So, what do you think?"

"Great. Great." My head moves like a bobblehead doll.

"Oh, and before I forget, the community relations manager from our sister store will be working with you next week. She'll go over your duties and answer your questions."

"Fantastic. Where should I start today? I could line up media connections, contact schools for potential book drives, book Storytime characters for the children's weekly reading hour, or create the monthly calendar."

"Calendar. It's due the first of December. There's a template on your computer. Feel free to call one of the other CRMs. They'll guide you through the process." Danny starts to walk out the door then turns, as if my wave of panic nudged him back to the room. "Oh, and this calendar can be general. By next month, you'll have a list of events to mention."

I bury myself in the CRM manual, reading chapter after chapter and making notes.

The phone rings.

"Community Relations Manager."

A woman on the other end of the conversation identifies herself as the principal of a local school. She's looking to collaborate on a book drive. Before I can look up book drive in the manual, a voice sounds over the loudspeaker.

"Community Relations Manager to the floor, please. Community Relations Manager to the floor."

I promise the principal I'll get right back to her with the details.

At the information desk, the employee makes a formal introduction. "This gentleman is from *Lake Norman News*. He'd like to talk to you."

I extend my hand and welcome him to the store.

"What can I do for you?"

"I'd like to do a story about the store's upcoming events."

Upcoming events?

The employee behind the information booth taps me on the shoulder.

"Excuse me. I'm sorry to interrupt, but there's an urgent call for you on line one."

I raise my finger to the journalist.

"Community Relations Manager. How can I help you?"

"Mom, Mom! Why aren't you answering your phone? I called you six times, and you didn't pick up."

I turn my back and whisper into the phone. "Casey, is everything okay?"

"Yeah. But I need to talk to you."

"Case, I'm busy right now. I'll call you when I'm back in my office."

"How long?"

"As soon as I can, sweetie."

I turn around and face the journalist.

"Can you and I set up an appointment for sometime next week?"

"Sure."

I walk into my room and call a sister store. I ask to speak to the CRM. She briefs me on book drives, Storytime characters, and the local newspapers in the area. Just as we are about to review the calendar template, the loud speaker sounds again.

"Call for Community Relations Manager on line two. Line two. Please."

I hang up with the CRM and press line two.

"Mom. Why didn't you call me back? I've been waiting for hours. I'm bored."

"I know this isn't easy for you, Casey. Can we talk tonight?" I swallow my angst.

"When will you be here?"

"Around five. Just a minute, Casey. An employee is knocking on my door."

"There's an author out front who would like to speak to you."

"Thanks. Be right there."

"Casey, I have to go. See you in a few hours."

I speak to the author and cover for one of the employees at the register. Back in my office, the phone blinks, emails fill my inbox, and manuals are still waiting to be read.

The phone rings. It's Casey. Again.

"Mom, haven't you left yet?"

"I'll be there in an hour, Casey."

"I hate this place. It really sucks."

"I hear you. Just hang in there, okay sweetie?"

This week is only his first in rehab. Is this how it's going to be until he's discharged? I hang up the phone and bury my face in a soggy tissue. Hearing footsteps, I turn and see Danny in the doorway.

"You okay?"

"Sorry, Danny. This," I say, rolling my fingers around my face, "has nothing to do with work. It's—"

"Casey?"

"Yes. But I'm better now. I was just having an emotional moment."

"I'm a good listener, if you want to talk." He smiles gently. "Okay?"

By the time I get to rehab, I'm as fragile as a wounded bird.

I pull a chair up to Casey's bed.

"Case, can we talk?"

"Now what?"

"Sweetie, you can't call me all day at work. I have a job. As much as I'd love to chat with you, I have to work."

He fidgets in his bed, grabs the remote then puts it down.

"Sweetie, do you hear me? So, you won't call me at work unless it's an emergency?"

He picks up the remote again. "I'll try. Dammit. The thing is broken."

"Maybe it's just stuck, Case."

"No it's not. See? See!" He waves it in front of my face.

"Case, you're shouting."

"No, I'm not."

"You know, Case. I'm tired. Maybe we can just be still for a few minutes. What do you say?"

I make a promise to myself to call the doctor first thing in the morning.

If yesterday's pandemonium is an indication of my daily routine, I realize I need to create a more peaceful setting at work. I place on the desk the corrugated box filled with plants, pictures of the kids, and decorations. I unroll the ocean print and affix it to the wall above my computer. Through my mind's eye, I step into the picture: the white, frothy surf laps at my feet; the sweet, salty breeze fills my lungs; and the sun's rays warm my body. I can feel my spirit recharging, washing away my worries, carrying them off to sea. "Perfect," I say aloud.

At eight o'clock, I dial the doctor. After five rings, his answering machine comes on. I leave a message: "This is Casey's mother. I have a few questions about his recovery. Please give me a call at your convenience. Look forward to speaking with you."

I turn on the computer, sign in, and respond to my emails. Out of the corner of my eye, I notice my private line is blinking. I answer.

"Good morning. This is Casey's doctor. You called earlier?"

"Yes, Doctor. I appreciate you getting back to me. Can you hang on a minute? I need to shut my door."

"Sure."

I write "Do Not Disturb" on a piece of paper and tape it to the door.

"Sorry about that, Doctor. I have so many questions that I'm not even sure where to begin."

"Initially, I want to say that even though Casey has had a brain injury, he is a person first."

"I know."

My lungs deflate. My shoulders curl forward. I envision me holding Casey as a tiny babe and making a promise to love, protect, and guide him forever and always. I feel as if I haven't kept my promise.

I should have been there when his bike collided with the truck, holding and rocking him in my arms, telling him "everything is going to be okay." When the paramedics arrived, I should have been there to jump on the ambulance with my boy. I should have been sitting outside the operating room, praying. I should have been with him in recovery. But I wasn't. No one was. There has to be something I can do now.

"As you probably heard from Dr. Bailey, no two brain injuries are exactly the same. The brain is divided into two hemispheres, left and right. The left side controls a person's language centers, the right side controls cognitive functioning. In Casey's case, he suffered damage to the right side of his brain."

"So thinking, reasoning, attention—"

"And much more. Casey's challenges can be visual-spatial impairment, memory, organization, problem solving, social communication, and left-side neglect. His speech pathologist will be working with him to strengthen these skills."

"Doc, I feel at a loss trying to communicate with Casey. I need help."

"Ask him questions, avoid sarcasm, provide a routine, break down instructions into small steps—"

"Wait, Doc, I can't write that fast . . . small steps. Okay?"

"Decrease distractions. Use calendars, clocks, notepads to remind him of important information, until he's able to do that for himself."

"Got it."

I glance over my notes. One issue is hard enough, but I'm finding this laundry list completely onerous. Before I can stop reeling, he's adding more information.

"The right temporal lobe also deals with hearing. It helps to process musical information and identify noises."

"What if it's damaged?"

"He probably won't appreciate music or be able to sing."

I gasp, dumbstruck by the doctor's response.

"That's *so* weird."

"What?"

"Well, Casey used to have a great singing voice. The other day he was watching MTV and started singing. When he heard himself, he blurted, 'What the f**k . . . " Pardon my French. " . . . happened to my voice?'"

"Sorry to say that happens."

Not as sorry as I am. Singing is everything to Casey. I can't stand listening to him clear his throat, sing a few lines then clear his throat again, hoping for the impossible: that his voice will return.

"What about his sudden outbursts? Can you explain that?"

"Ah yes, controlling his emotions. The frontal lobes not only manage planning and organizing, but also play an important role in managing emotions, such as . . . dealing with hunger, aggression, and sexual drive."

"Interesting. Casey's eating habits are atrocious. His anger and foul mouth are over the top."

"The frontal lobe plays an important role in the areas you mentioned. Inside the brain are sections that control those primitive emotions. It has a 'stop' button that prevents people from doing something inappropriate. But for Casey . . . let's say he's starved. He's going to chow down without thinking about his manners. The 'stop' button isn't working."

"Will his manners ever come back?" Even though his manners are insignificant in the bigger scheme of things, I can't help but think how others will judge him when he's eating in a restaurant. The mumbling, the finger pointing, would cripple me.

"The therapists will be working with that issue also."

"And how about his aggression?"

"It goes back to what I just said. Casey doesn't have a filter. So, the slightest thing—something someone said or did, loud noises, screaming, yelling—can send Casey into overload. Before he knows it, he acts out."

"Is he aware of his short temper?"

"Usually not until it's too late. But if you learn to read his body language, you can spot it being triggered. Some of the signs are clenched fists, a tightened jaw, or he may start tapping his foot."

The doctor pauses then continues.

"Anger and depression are common. But with a brain injury, anger is more intensified. It's like flipping a coin. One minute it's resting on your thumb, the next it's spinning in the air, out of control."

"So, are anger and depression located in the middle sections of the brain, the primitive area you spoke about?"

"Yes. Dealing with Casey's instantaneous changes can be challenging for family members."

But for how long? I hear myself thinking.

"What can I do?"

"Casey will learn more about this in Outpatient. But the tool we teach them is Time-Out. Let's say Casey is so angry, he wants to throw or hit something. He needs to get out of the environment that is angering him and walk away. He can go for a walk or sit in a room with a door closed. Whatever works best for him."

"For five or ten minutes?"

"We recommend a minimum of fifteen, preferably thirty."

"So, during that time, he shouldn't have any contact with the person who angered him?"

"Right. The worst thing for Casey, which will only keep him in overload mode, is to continue antagonizing him. The other party needs to 'shut up,' to put it bluntly."

Finally I summon up the courage to ask the question I'm terrified to know the answer to. "Will he be like this forever?"

"Casey's in the early stages of his brain injury, and right now it's hard to predict the road ahead. It may take years before we know the final outcome." He pauses and takes a deep breath. "Have I answered all your questions?"

Years? He can't mean it.

"Just one more—for now, anyway. Why does the center keep the lights turned down low? I find it depressing."

"Bright lights can cause an overload for people with a brain injury, as can loud music and voices, crowded settings, and processing too much information at one time. Some people become so irritable they develop headaches. It really is in the best interest of the patients. Listen, I have to run. If you have any further questions, give me a call."

I lean back in my chair with my notebook in hand, scan my notes, and stop at "controlling his emotions."

As a mother, I feel my primary job has been to teach and guide my children. As a child, if Casey got mad at his brother, sister, or friend, I trained him to reason and problem-solve. If that didn't work, time-out provided a period to think. I showed him how to tell time, use a calendar, and organize his belongings—toys, closet, and schoolwork.

I flip the paper, and the word "overload" catches my attention. Since Casey was little, he's hated arguments. He would retreat inside. Now, he's on the giving end.

I feel like I'm back to square one, raising my boy all over again, only this time he's a grown man.

There's a knock on the door. "Storytime in fifteen minutes."

"Coming."

I grab the box of art supplies—multicolored construction paper, markers, glue, and scissors—for the art project. I have three books about Thanksgiving to read to the children. An hour later, I'm back in my office.

I work on the December calendar, read the CRM manual, and set up my first in-store book fair. Just when I feel like I'm in control of my universe, all hell breaks loose.

The intercom blares. "Community Relations Manager to the information counter," followed by, "All available employees to the checkout counter." Before I finish dialing the help desk's exchange to say I'm on my way, another announcement comes over the loudspeaker: "Community Relations Manager—call on line one . . . call on line one." I pick up the phone.

"Mom, this is Casey. When are you coming to see me?"

I respond. Casey pushes harder. I get nauseous.

An hour later, I walk into Casey's room.

"What took you so long? You're late."

Mentally, I affix an imaginary muzzle over my mouth. Fifteen minutes. God, help me.

We go for a walk.

"So, Case, how was your day?"

"Fine."

"Just fine? Learn anything new?"

"Not really. One gal kept telling stories and having me repeat them. Really dumb. The other one made me do exercises to strengthen my muscles."

"You're walking better than yesterday. That's good."

"I guess." Then he surprises me with, "How was your day?"

I stop, tilt my head toward Casey, and smile.

"Good. Thanks for asking. I talked to the—"

"Mom, I'm ready to go back."

I can sense Casey's frustration, and I'm right there with him.

As I walk down the darkened hallways, I think about the doctor's words. "Bright lights can cause an overload for people with a brain injury."

A little education goes a long way.

CHAPTER TWENTY-TWO

Thanksgiving

Dawn hides its head below the horizon, and the cold northern winds whirl through the cracked window, singing a voiceless song. Suddenly it hits me: today is Thanksgiving.

I jump out of bed and meditate, repeating the mantra that came to me at the close of last night's meditation—*In nothingness, there is greatness.*

An hour later, I'm in the kitchen, my hands submerged in soapy water. The phone rings. It's Annie.

"Hey sweetie, Happy Thanksgiving."

"You too, Mom. What are you doing?"

"Cleaning the dishes. Just finished getting the turkey in the oven."

"Mmm, save some for me."

"I will. When are you going to see Casey?"

"Soon. He's already called a couple of times asking when we'll be there." Annie bursts. "He really needs to work on his patience."

"Put yourself in his place, Annie. Can't be easy not being with the family."

"I know. So, here's how the night is going to play out: dinner at Dad's, hooking up with friends, then over to your place."

"Sounds good, sweetie."

"Bo wants to talk to you. See ya later."

"Mom?"

"Hey, Bo, Happy Thanksgiving."

"You too. You making a turkey and Grandpa's dressing?"

"Sure am."

"Put some aside for me. Not sure if Dad is cooking or ordering out. He mentioned picking up dinner at the grocery store. Sounds good, huh?" Bo laughs.

"Just enjoy, sweetie. Are you going to stay here?"

"No. Think I'll bunk at Dad's. I'll be by tomorrow to see you. Thought I might bring some of my friends by. They want you to do their numerology."

"Really?" I chuckle.

For years, the kids have made fun of my interests in age-old wisdom. In fact, one year they bought me a sign that said, "I live in another dimension, but I have a summer home in reality." Now they want to bring their friends over? I'm tickled.

"Bring them by, Bo. Can't wait to see you, honey. Bo, Grandpa's buzzing in."

"Tell him I say 'hi.'"

"Pop. Just hung up with Bo. He says 'hi.' And Happy Thanksgiving from me."

"You too. Got your turkey in the oven?"

"Sure do. Going to see Case this afternoon with dinner in hand."

"How's our boy?"

"Doin' okay."

"You sound a little down. Wanna talk?"

"It's just—"

"Honey, it's a miracle he's alive. You have so much to be grateful for. Just think what today would be like if he wasn't here."

My throat tightens. "You're right, Pop. Lately I'm feeling like a yo-yo. One minute I'm up, filled with gratitude; the next I'm down, hanging onto my fears."

"Just remember what I said, okay? Got to call my other kiddos. Have a great day, honey."

I hang up the phone, look to the heavens, and whisper. "Please forgive me, God, for being so selfish. For wanting things better than they are. For not focusing on my many blessings. You carried me and the family this far, and I know you will not let us down. Thank you for the opportunity to make me . . . us . . . stronger through adversity."

I empty the dishwasher and call Mom. The phone rings four times.

"Mom, I almost hung up. I wasn't sure if you were—"

"Bud and I just got home from church. Happy Thanksgiving, honey. How's Casey?"

"He's walking pretty good." I want to say more, but I bite my tongue.

"Good. Have I told you how proud I am of you? You've been so strong through all of this. When you make up your mind to do something, nothing stops you."

"Not so sure about that, Mom. I can fall with the best of them."

"Well, it's true. I still think about you graduating from high school and the comment I made, saying that I would understand if you didn't want to go to college."

Wow, that brings back a memory. At first I'd been stunned by Mom's comment. Not go to college? Not fulfill my dream of becoming a teacher? Really? But how would Mom know that? Back then I was an introvert, at least around my family. My lifelong dream was hidden inside the pages of my locked diary.

Charlie and Mary came before me and were both outstanding, straight-*A* students. I was average, pulling in *C*'s.

"Oh yeah. I remember that day well, Mom. You were standing in front of the stove making pork chops, decked out in your white slacks and red-and-white polka dot shirt. I was next to you, dressed like a geek in bell-bottom jeans and a plaid shirt."

"Do you remember what you said to me? You said, 'Mom, that's not an option. I'm going to college to get my teacher's degree.' And you did. You even graduated with honors. Honey, I was so proud of you. I just hope you know that I never meant to minimize your goal. I just wanted to present another option."

"Mom. It's okay. I know your intentions came from love. Really, I've moved on."

"That's good. When you get older, you start reflecting back on everything you did and said. The last thing I ever want to do is hurt my kids. The seven of you are my everything."

"Okay stop, Mom. Now I'm crying. You could never hurt my feelings. Listen, I still need to call the sibs before I go to see Case. Happy Thanksgiving."

At five o'clock, I walk into Casey's room with a turkey feast. He's sitting up in bed with a napkin on his lap, licking his lips. I remove the foil. Steam rises. Casey picks up his fork.

"Nope. First we have to pray."

"Really, Mom. I'm starved."

"Casey, please. We have so much to be thankful for. Listen to me." I cup his hand. "When I see you sit, watch you walk, hear you speak, and feel your touch, I can't help but think about your first day in ICU. I wasn't sure if this day would ever come." My body vibrates, feeling the aftershocks of the earthquake.

"Mom. It's okay. I'm here now. Can we eat? I think you already prayed."

Casey makes several attempts to cut his food, but his left hand won't cooperate. He slides his plate over to me.

"Mom, can you . . .?"

I nod. "Sweetie, you tried. Gonna take some time to gain strength back in your left hand."

"Feel like a baby, having you cut my food."

While slicing the turkey into bite-size pieces, I think, *These are the cards we've been dealt; and together we will make the best of them, one step at a time.*

Casey piles the dressing on top of the turkey and starts his shoveling act again, until his plate is clean.

"Mmm. Really good, Mom."

While we are walking down the corridor, Casey stops.

"Mom, can't you talk to the doctor and get me out of this place? I'm fine. I don't belong here."

Casey's medication must be working. His voice is relaxed, his demeanor soothing.

"I can. He'll also need to get the therapist's input to see if your legs are strong enough to manage the stairs at home."

"Tomorrow then?"

"I'll see what I can do. But sweetie, I am a bit worried about—"

"You need to stop worrying, Mom. I'm fine."

How can I? I'm your mother, and you're my son. Every hurt, pain, accomplishment, and joy you feel is mine, too.

I unravel the covers from the bottom of the bed and blanket Casey's body.

"Thanks for bringing dinner, Mom. I love you."

"Love you too, Case, more than you'll ever know."

On the ride home, waves of gratitude expand outward from my core like ripples in a pond.

Expecting nothing, I found greatness.

FAMILY STRONG

Annie and Casey, MUSC Room 721.
October 2002

Maggie and Casey, MUSC Room 721.
October 2002

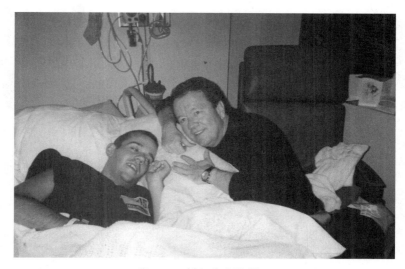

Casey and his dad, Bobby.
November 2002

Bo in diapers, MUSC Room 721.
October 2002

Casey's 20th birthday in the hospital with Maggie and Annie.
November 2002

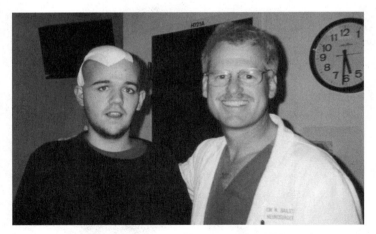

Casey and Dr. Bailey, neurosurgeon, prior to Casey's release from MUSC.
November 2002

Mary and Pattie.

Drace and Pattie at the Marriott Courtyard, Charleston.

The Lemon Drops at Kiel Auditorium, St. Louis, Missouri, 1960.
Left to right: Mary, Pattie, Rita, Geri, Margie.

Growing up! Christmas in Grantwood, St. Louis, Missouri, 1961.
Left to right: Rita, Pattie, Margie, Johnny, Geri, Mary, Charlie.

Best Mom in the world! 1985.

Best Dad in the world, preparing Thanksgiving feast! 1996.

Annie brings home the gold in North/South Swim meet, Long Island, 1993.

Pattie visiting Bo at an alcohol/drug rehabilitation center in North Carolina, 1998.

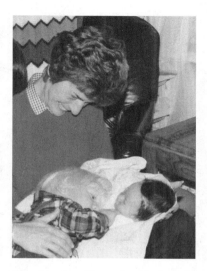

Big brother, Bo, meets baby brother, Casey, for the first time with Grammy, 1982.

"The Bo and Casey Show" in full swing! 1985.

Pattie tangles with the 200 pound Christmas tree, 2003.

One of the last three photos of Pattie and her three children taken outside a
New York hotel, Christmas, 2003. Left to right: Casey, Annie, Bo, and Mom.

Twin Towers, Christmas, 2003. Left to right: Bo, Annie, and Casey.

Casey, Bo, and Annie at Strawberry Fields in Central Park West, Christmas, 2003.

Fairy tales do come true! Lyly and Casey's wedding, September 2011.

Pattie caught up in the miracle . . . the dance of her lifetime . . . this dance with
her son Casey at his wedding, 2011. He's not only walking . . . and talking
. . . he's dancing . . . *we're dancing*.

PART THREE

FULL CIRCLE

Chapter Twenty-Three

End of November

> *Now I am going to reveal to you something which is very*
> *pure, a totally white thought.*
> *It is always in my heart; it blooms at each of my steps . . .*
> *The Dance is love, it is only love, it alone,*
> *and that is enough . . .*
>   ~ Isadora Duncan

The dogs bark. Jump on the couch. Stare out the window. Bark again.

I look through the shutter slats and see Bobby's car parked outside. Casey's closing the passenger door.

My boy is finally home.

The dogs rush to the front door and start scratching, wanting out, wanting a piece of what's on the other side.

I open the door several inches and stick my arm out.

"Bobby, can you hand me Casey's bag? The dogs might bolt if I—"

"Mom, just hold the dogs and let me in," Casey says, impatiently.

I grab the dogs' collars. Casey and Bobby step in. Within seconds, Casey's on the floor with Duke and C.D. The dogs swipe wet kisses across his face. He returns their affection, rubbing their tummies.

I turn to Bobby.

"Thanks for bringing him home. So, the driver will be taking Casey to and from rehab and staying with him until I get home from work?"

He nods.

"I'm going to head out, Case."

After Casey gives his dad a hug, Bobby leaves.

I turn to Casey.

"Got one of those hugs for your Mama?"

He gives me a sideways grin and wraps his arms around me. We rock. I don't want to let go.

"Glad I'm home, Mom."

"Me too, Son." Yet I sense something's different about Casey, foreign in some way. I can't put my finger on it. For the most part, his face looks the same—pointed chin, full lips, broad nose, thick brows, and bronze skin—yet his hazel eyes are glassy and distant.

I tuck my inner thoughts into an imaginary box, close the lid, and stuff them inside.

"So, Case, when did you start wearing your hat cocked to the side?"

"I've always worn it like this."

No, you haven't.

"I'm tired, Mom. Can the dogs sleep with me?"

He shuffles over to the stairs, the dogs on his heels. He reaches for the banister, wobbles then tightens his grip.

"Here, lean on me." I offer, not wanting him to fall and reinjure his head.

"I'm fine, Mom. I can do this."

Minutes later, Casey reaches the bottom of the stairs. His Birkenstocks clap across the tile floor. Barely breathing, I follow with opened arms. He grabs for the doorframe. I exhale.

This process was much easier when Casey was a toddler. If he was going up the stairs, I'd spot him from behind. If he was coming the down the steps, I'd be in front of him to catch his fall.

But today, my hands are shaking.

"Mom. My room looks different."

"I bought you a new bed. I didn't want you sleeping on that hard futon with your head injury. Like it?"

"Yeah, but—"

"But what, honey?"

"I don't know."

Again, an eerie feeling washes through me like rain gushing down a gutter.

"Duke, C.D., up," he commands.

Casey pockets himself between the sheets. C.D. settles on his pillow. Duke snuggles by his side. I bend down and kiss my boy.

"I'm putting your cell phone right here on the nightstand. See? Call the house number if you need me. I don't want you coming upstairs on your own until you're strong enough."

He doesn't answer.

While climbing the three flights of stairs to my bedroom, my stomach knots, and the little box of thoughts I stuffed earlier opens.

My son is home. Finally home. But something's not right. I feel like a stranger just walked inside my front door. Even though he looks like my son, walks like my son, his energy doesn't feel like my son's.

Inside my bedroom, my knees crumble. My body convulses. My tears gush. And guttural sounds emerge. I pound my fist on the carpet and talk to God.

"I want my son back. Do you hear me? Back. Now!"

The phone rings, drowning out my cries. I answer. "Hi, Mom."

"What's wrong, sweetie?"

"How did you know?"

"I can hear it in your voice."

I share my feelings with Mom.

"Do you have someone you can talk to?"

"I don't know, Mom. I think everyone will think I've flipped my lid. Wait. A friend told me about a new spiritual church that opened. Maybe I can go there."

Over the years, Mom, who is very Catholic, has accepted that my spirituality is different from hers. It didn't happen overnight. She asked a lot of questions. I gave answers. But when I told her I hadn't turned my back on God, that meditation was about seeking God at a deeper level, she listened. She understood.

"Good idea. Let me know what you find out."

"Mom, I keep thinking about the families of the soldiers who have returned from Iraq and Afghanistan. Do you think they feel the same way I do? That the person they said goodbye to, isn't the same person who came home?"

"I don't know, but maybe so. I think you're tired. You've been through a lot. Get some rest. Things may look different when you wake up."

I crawl into bed at 4 p.m. to get a couple hours of shut-eye before Casey awakens.

Three hours later, I wake up to the smell of smoke. The house is pitch-black.

I turn on the lights and rush down the stairs to the kitchen. Fanning my way through the white clouds, I see flames blazing from the range. I turn the knob to Off. A scorched pan sits on the burner. I toss it into the sink. *Casey.* I sprint down the stairs and throw open his door. He's sleeping. On his nightstand sits a plate with dried egg yolks. A bent Coke can lies in a pool of ketchup.

I can hear my heart pound against my ribs.

Oh my God! This house could have gone up in flames. And Casey and me with it.

CHAPTER TWENTY-FOUR

Early December

Casey's been home for a week. It's been one hell of a ride.

I'm standing in the kitchen washing dried blood and crusted ice cream off my hands when Casey walks upstairs.

"Case, you and I need to talk."

"Hear that, Mom? Dad's honking. We're going out to lunch." He slams the door on his words.

The phone rings.

"Hey, Drace."

"Sorry I haven't called. Work has been nuts. How's it going?"

"Where would you like me to start? That Casey spends the majority of his day sleeping? That he almost set the house on fire? Better yet, that he left the freezer door open last night, and the meat and ice cream thawed."

"Really?"

"Really. And I'm doing everything in my power to hold it together. To understand."

"Have you talked to the doctor about any of this?"

"We spoke yesterday about Casey's fatigue. He said the simple process of walking and being alert zaps Casey's energy. Mentally, he's okay for short periods; but then his brain shuts down."

"I can relate to that. It's like the time I was overtaxed with work deadlines and went to the store, shopped, then left my cart filled with unpaid items behind."

Reliving Drace's theatrics, I snicker.

"Oh, enough about me. How long does it last?"

"According to the doctor, physical fatigue can linger for six months or more. But mental fatigue never completely goes away."

"Hmmm. How's his memory?"

"Obviously, not so good. He couldn't remember leaving the stove on. I'm sure he won't remember leaving the freezer door open."

"You can't fault him. He just doesn't remember."

"God, no. The doc mentioned that Casey's immediate and short-term memory was affected by the brain injury. That I should get him a notebook so he can write things down. But a lot of good that will do when he sleepwalks. Wish I could be in two places at the same time."

"Oh, girl." Drace switches the subject, probably hoping to lift my spirits. "So, you ready for Casey's party tomorrow night?"

"I am."

Drace and I continue talking and laughing. By the time we hang up, I'm in a much better place than when the day started.

Clank. Bang. Crash.

"Mom, what are you doing down there?"

"Getting out my spaghetti pot. Need it for your party tonight."

Casey opens the fridge. Takes out the orange juice. Gulps from the carton.

I hand him a glass. "No one wants to drink your backwash."

"I'm starved. Can you make me breakfast?"

Casey lines the counter with eggs, bacon, cheese, and bread. "What party?"

"Your homecoming party. Bo, Annie, and your friends are coming. Remember?"

He tilts his head and looks at me, squinting. "Kind of. Got any strawberry jelly?"

"It's on the third shelf down on the door."

"Where?"

Why is it that men have such difficulty locating objects smack dab in front of their faces? Does it have something to do with their primordial hunting skills: good for tracking down prey but downright pathetic for finding things within close range?

I push the toaster button down. Put my left arm inside the fridge and pull out the jelly.

"Oh. There it is."

"How 'bout that, Case. Right in front of your nose."

I slide the omelet onto the plate and skirt it with toast and bacon. Casey grabs the dish and walks in the family room.

"Case, in here." I point to the table.

"But I can't see the TV from there."

I give him "the look." That's the point.

He sets his breakfast on the table. Walks back into the family room, grabs the remote, presses the on button, and turns up the volume.

Behind me, I can hear the crystal glasses chiming and the plates clanking in the china cabinet. If he doesn't lower the volume, everything is going to shatter, including me.

"Casey, turn that thing off. I can't hear myself think. Plus, you'll wake Annie."

Casey places the remote next to his spoon, as if it's a part of the table setting. He grabs the ketchup and squeezes it over his omelet.

Really? "So, how's rehab going?"

He raises his finger. "They're all nuts."

"Who's nuts?"

"Mom. Mom. The phone is ringing." He taps my arms.

Before I can even say hello, Casey shouts, "Who is it? Is it for me?"

My hand flies into the air.

Bo shouts into the phone.

"Mom. MOM."

"Hi, Bo. Sorry about that. Casey and I were having a discussion."

Casey shouts again. "Yeah. And I have nothing else to say."

"Hang on, Bo. Casey, sit back in that chair. Now."

Why can't he sit still? I need to talk to the doctor about his meds.

"Mom. Won't keep you. Sounds chaotic there. What time is dinner tonight?"

"Around six. But come earlier, hon—"

Casey interrupts again. "Mom. Hurry up. There's a good movie coming on."

I hang up the phone and pull my chair next to Casey's.

"You were rude. Down right rude. You hear me? Life isn't always about you. Got that?"

Casey freezes. His chin dips. I shudder.

I can't believe I just yelled at my brain-injured son. It feels like I drove a knife into my heart. I take a deep breath, then another, move my chair back, and apologize.

"Now. Who's nuts?"

"All the people in rehab." Casey's eyes move rapidly from left to right as if he's speed-reading. "Fred's okay. But the rest of them are different. Some of them can barely talk."

I want to shake Casey and say that those other people could be you. *You!* But I know my words would fall on deaf ears.

"Can I go now?"

I close my eyes and yearn for one normal moment in this less-than-normal life.

Fingers feather my shoulder.

"What you doing, Mom?"

"Annie. I didn't know you were up."

"Just going to grab a bagel. You just keep doing . . . whatever." She walks into the kitchen.

I want to ask Annie if she slept well. If she wants me to make her an omelet. If she needs a hug, like I do. But my sadness buries my words.

I take a few deep breaths and collect myself. Soon the table is cleared, and the dips and side dishes are underway.

At dusk, the front door slams.

"Mom. Where are you?"

"In the kitchen, Bo."

Bo picks me up and swings me in circles.

"Bo. Put me down." I giggle, not meaning a word I'm saying. He laughs. Tightens his grip. Lifts me higher. My feet dangle in midair.

I love being in my boy's arms, being a part of his playfulness.

"Where's Casey and Annie?" He asks, as my feet touch the ground.

"Casey's sleeping. Annie's showering. Bo, I wish you would stay here like Annie does when she comes home from school. Isn't the same without you."

"I know, Mom. But I don't want Dad to live alone. He needs one of us to stay with him."

I can't help but wonder if Bo has shared his feelings with his dad. Even though their relationship can be rocky at times, I believe hearing Bo's words would move Bobby to tears.

I rub Bo's shoulder.

"You're a good son, Bo. Your heart is in the right place. I'm so proud of you."

"Aw, Mom. You get me." He fingers the corner of his eye. "You see what others don't."

Annie strolls into the kitchen.

"Like your hair, sis. New do?" Bo smirks.

"Get your fingers out of my hair." She slaps Bo's hand. "And no, it's not a new do. This is what my hair looks like when I don't straighten it."

Bo is a pro at antagonizing his sister and brother. I can tell that sometimes they don't mind and other times, he drives them crazy. He has more energy than the whole family combined, and at times it can be draining.

There's a knock on the door. Bo answers. The eleven guests start filing in. Laughter and banter fill the air. Everyone talks over everyone else, trying to get their two cents in. Standing in the midst of all the excitement, I think about how much I love having company over and celebrating the good times. For the first time in months, we have something to celebrate.

Casey makes his way up the stairs wearing a long-sleeved, white cotton shirt, jeans, and a black toboggan, cocked to the side.

Bo takes one look at Casey and rather than saying, "Hi, bro," and sharing their fancy handshake, which used to be their normal "M.O.", he tries to straighten Casey's hat.

"What the hell are you doing?" Casey swats Bo's hand as if he just smacked an annoying fly.

"Your hat. It's cattywampus on your head."

"I like my hat this way." Casey pushes his cap back in place.

As far back as I can remember, Bo and Casey's relationship has resembled two children perched on a teeter-totter. Sometimes it's a carefree game filled with fun and laughter. Other times, it becomes one of power—each one fighting for control. Early on, the family dubbed them "The Bo and Casey Show."

Casey brushes Bo's shoulder. High-fives the guys. Hugs Megan, Annie and Casey's mutual friend. He smiles at his sister.

"Off to a good start, don't you think?" I mumble under my breath as I return to the kitchen to fill drink orders. No wine or beer on the menu tonight. After Bo went into treatment, I set my boundaries: no alcohol in this house.

The troops gather around the table. We pray then I lift my water glass and make a toast. "Here's to Casey, our miracle boy. Welcome home, sweetie."

The clanking of glasses is soon muffled by laughter and prattle. Then there's a pause. Sometimes a pause is good. Other times, like now, it means trouble.

Bo, who talks nonstop, decides to make a few snide comments to those sitting next to him. "Did you see the way Casey wears his hat? He looks so goofy. Like he's not all there." Then . . . he has the audacity to laugh, and so do some of the others.

Bo doesn't let up. Casey's head moves from side to side, listening to his brother and his friends as they berate him. He slouches in his chair and doesn't say a word. Yet, he smiles.

Who are you? Casey? The stranger? And why are you smiling? Speak up. Take your power back. You don't need to pretend you are okay with these spiteful comments. I think this, and more, but Casey remains still, which is not like him at all. I throw up my hand.

"Enough, Bo. ENOUGH."

He wipes his face with his napkin and avoids making eye contact with me, which is good. Because right now my eyes are on fire and adrenaline is racing through my veins. I seal my lips. Now is not the time to address this matter.

After pie, everyone moves into the family room. I clear the dishes, happy to have a few moments to myself.

What the heck got into Bo? Why did he slam his brother with all those insensitive comments? It's as if he moved through dinner in blissful ignorance, unable to see what was happening around him. Is this his way of coping with the new Casey? Choked by his fears? Treating him as he would have if Casey had not been injured?

Since I was a child, I could sense other people's subtle energies. Even though they'd try to disguise their feelings, telling jokes or using laughter as their defense, I could tune into their underlying currents of energy. Right now I feel like my clairsentience is kicking into gear, big time.

Annie walks into the kitchen. Sinks her chin into my shoulder.

"That sucked, didn't it, Mom?"

"Mmm . . . hmm."

"I can tell Casey's feelings are really hurt. He's just sitting in the wingback chair, not saying a word. Mom—"

"It's okay, honey." I feel Annie's tears.

"Casey *is* a little different though, isn't he, Mom?"

"In some ways, he is. In others, he's the same. But heck, he's still a person. A person with feelings."

"I know, Mom. You going to talk to Bo?"

"I am. Later."

After the guests leave, Bo and I sit on the couch. His arms rest on his legs. His head is lowered. I rub his knee.

"You know what I want to talk about, don't you, Bo?"

"Yeah." He glances at me then looks away. "But I didn't mean what I said."

"I'm sure you didn't, sweetie. But your words were harsh and hurtful."

"I'll talk to Casey. I'll make everything right. I promise."

"Good idea."

"But, Mom. You have to admit . . ." Bo rubs his shoe on the carpet. "Casey's different. Just look at the way he wears his hat. What's with that?"

"I have my thoughts on that subject, but I'll save those for another time. Right now, I want to help you identify your feelings."

"It just sucks, Mom. I want my brother back. Do you think that will happen?"

"I don't know. But one thing I do know is we're his family, and we need to stand strong behind him. He needs our support right now, more than ever. Can you do that, sweetie?"

"Yeah. I'll try not to be so sarcastic. But it's my—"

"I know: Your way of avoiding the truth. But, Bo, you have a gentle heart. It's really okay for others to see that side of you."

"But this is the way I've always been. My friends will think I'm nuts if I start getting all sappy."

"Maybe. Maybe not. And I'm not saying you have to be sappy all the time, just when it's appropriate."

"I hear you. It's just that I always want my friends to have a good time." Bo leans his head back on the cushion. "I guess that gets in my way, right? I mean, making people laugh rather than tuning into their feelings."

Bo uses his shirtsleeve to wipe his eyes.

"Everything is going to be okay, Bo. None of us have ever walked through this storm before. Sometimes we just don't know what type of rain gear to wear or if the sun will shine along the way. We just don't know. All we can do, Bo, is to give it our best, rain or shine."

"I'll try to be better." Bo clears his throat. "I love Casey so much."

"Of course you do, sweetie. Of course. None of us are perfect, Bo. We slip and fall through life, making mistakes, picking ourselves up and dusting ourselves off. Then, we start all over again."

After Bo and I sit in silence for a few moments, he stands.

"Get on up here, Mom. I need to give you a big hug."

We hold on. Pat each other's backs. When space divides us, we simultaneously whisper, "I love you," while staring into each other's bloodshot eyes.

CHAPTER TWENTY-FIVE

Christmas

When I hear the word magic, I think of Christmas in my childhood home in Grantwood. Grantwood is an older neighborhood in south St. Louis, close to Grant's Farm. Most of the homes are almost a century or older, and none of them look alike. The majority of the houses sit on an acre of land, and their plush green lawns are filled with holly, sycamore, oak, and pine trees that stand far above the rooflines.

Each year at Christmas, the neighborhood association would hold a contest for the best-decorated yard. Pop, who never likes to lose at anything, was determined to win, which he did for the sixteen years we lived there.

He hung colored lights along the roofline on the front porch, attached strands to the gazebo gutter, nailed pine wreaths on the front and back door, and adorned them with fresh pine garland. But what won him first prize was the large wooden stable he erected on the side yard that faced the street. Inside the structure, he scattered bales of hay and topped it with a life-sized nativity set: Mary, Joseph, baby Jesus in his crib, a couple lambs, and the wise men. On the outside, he stuck a floodlight in the grass. The light came on at dusk, as did colored lights that he'd wrapped around the three sides. It was a sight to behold.

Inside, Mom placed a red runner with tassels on the ends in the center of the dining room table. Two white deer and a crystal bowl filled with multicolored ornaments sat on top. In the living room, seven red stockings, each with a kid's name stitched at the top, hung from the fireplace mantle. The Christmas tree, strung with hundreds of tiny white lights, sat to its left. A white porcelain nativity scene sat atop clouds of cotton on the coffee table. And all the other rooms on the first floor—bathroom, kitchen, and den—had some kind of Christmas decoration.

Mom made sure that Santa brought the seven of us a few items on our wish list. But it's not the gifts I remember most. It's the magic and spirit of Christmas that filled our home during the season.

No matter how old I get, those memories come alive during the holiday each year.

Caught up in the moment, I call Dad. "Hey, Pop. Good morning and Merry Christmas. Were you just singing, 'Chestnuts Roasting on an Open Fire'?"

"I was. Ginny has the music on, and I have a roaring fire blazing in the fireplace. Wish you were here."

"Me too, Pop."

"So, how's our boy? You mentioned earlier this week you were going to call the doctor about—"

"Casey's recovery time. He was so helpful."

"I'm sorry, honey. That's Geri buzzing in. Let me tell her I'll call her back."

Nostalgia fills my heart as Pop clicks over.

It seems like only yesterday when all seven of us lined up in birth order on the landing upstairs and waited for Pop to call us downstairs.

Once the Christmas tunes were playing and the movie camera was rolling, Pop gave us the go signal. We pushed and shoved one another, shouted "Hurry up," and waved our hands in front of the camera lens, as we trotted down the steps.

One by one, seven sets of bare feet gripped the cold tile floor. "Ohhhh . . . Wowwww" bounced off the walls and drowned out the music, "I'll Be Home for Christmas," playing in the background.

We scrambled to our designated seats—piano bench, step, couch, and covered radiator—and waited for Mom and Dad to distribute the gifts. I kept thinking "Hurry up!" but I didn't dare voice my thoughts, or

I would have been sent to my room. Finally, Mom took her place in the gold-silk ladies chair, and Dad in the flowered wingback chair.

Mom looked at Charlie, her oldest, and signaled with a nod that he could open a gift. We all watched and simultaneously chanted, "cu-u-u-u-te," as the paper fell to the floor. Mary was next in the pecking order. She opened. Again "cu-u-u-u-te" rolled off seven sets of lips. We continued in that fashion until Margie, the baby, had her turn. Then we started over.

With nine people in the family, our Christmas mornings stretched into early afternoon. Patience was the name of the game.

My priceless childhood memories fade as Pop comes back on the line.

"Sorry, sweetie. So, what were you saying? Damn, my phone is buzz—"

"Pop. You go. We'll catch up tomorrow. I have to get a few things done before the kids arrive. Merry Christmas. Love you."

I tuck the kids' letters I wrote last night between the tree branches and lean presents against the furniture, just like Mom and Dad did when I was a child.

Home sweet home.

As I'm setting the table for Christmas brunch, the phone rings.

"Merry Christmas, sweetie. Are the kids there?"

"Not yet, Mom. In about a half hour. Merry Christmas to you, too."

"Do you have a sec to fill me in on your latest conversation with the doctor?"

"Sure. The first question I asked was, 'Is there any way to measure Casey's strengths and weaknesses from the injury?'" I pull out the potatoes for tonight's dinner and start peeling.

"And?"

"He said that Casey's psychologist will eventually give him an I.Q. test to measure his abilities—complex thinking and subtle changes in behavior. In two years, Casey needs to take the test again."

"Why?"

"To compare scores and see if there's been any change. According to the doctor, a patient's numbers will improve over the first two years. But after that, there isn't much change, normally."

"I see."

"It's scary, Mom. What if the way Casey is today is as good as it gets? What if he attempts to return to college and fails? What if he can't hold down a job? Then what? I don't want him to go through his whole life feeling different. For God's sake, he's only twenty years old. He should have his whole life ahead of him. It's tearing me to pieces."

"I know, honey." Mom's voice cracks. "Do you know what the therapists will be working on?"

"They'll help him improve the skills he has and give him additional tools to work with, allowing him to progress on his own. But there are so many facets to his recovery, Mom. Mentally, physically, and emotionally."

"Of course. Did the doctor mention if it's possible for a patient to fully recover?"

"I asked the same question, Mom. He said that he's never met anyone who claimed to recover completely. Yet, it is possible for patients to regain 95 percent of their former abilities. It doesn't happen often. But it can. His final words were: 'We just need to ride out the storm.'"

As I drop the last peeled potato into the pot, I hear loud voices coming from outside.

"Mom, I hear the kids. I'll call you tomorrow. Merry Christmas. Love you."

Laughter, like a plume of smoke, drifts through the opened door.

"Ho. Ho. Ho. Merry Christmas."

I rip off my apron and rush into the family room. Bo pecks me on the cheek. Annie pushes him forward and gives me a sideways kiss. Casey follows, wearing a brown baseball cap that matches the color under his eyes.

"You okay, Casey?"

"Fine." He takes off his coat, tosses it on the chair, and joins Annie and Bo in the kitchen.

"When are we eating?" Bo asks in a muffled voice as his head sinks deeper into the fridge.

"I thought we'd open—"

"Bo, move!" Casey shouts as their shoulders collide.

"No. I was here first."

I place my hands on their backs.

"Boys. It's Christmas. No fighting. Let's put the "Bo and Casey Show" on hold for now."

I believe I hear the rumblings of swearwords coming from their mouths, but I pretend my ears are full of wax.

"Scoot, all of you. Go put your letters on the tree."

Casey strolls into the family room. Annie takes one step forward then steps back. She stares at Bo as if she's saying, "I'm not going to miss this one."

"Oh yeah, Mom. About your letter. You see, I wrote this really good one," Bo says, elbowing me, "and we were in such a hurry to leave that—"

"You left it at your dad's."

I glance at Annie. Together we both roll our eyes, probably having the same thought.

Déjà vu.

He glares at me with a puzzled look. "How did—"

"I know what you were going to say?" I tap my chin. "Wild guess, maybe."

Both Annie and I start laughing as Bo continues to dig himself deeper and deeper into his lie.

"Bo," I say while escorting him into the family room, "it's okay, honey. Really. You need to stop before you bury yourself alive. Let's enjoy our day."

Annie plops down on one blue-striped couch. Bo sits on the other one. Casey wedges his body into the corner pocket of the navy wingback chair, looking lost. I walk around the room, reading the tags then stack the gifts in front of the kids.

"Bo, you go first."

Bo grabs the smallest box, probably thinking that good things come in small packages. He yanks off the string and rips the paper.

"Thanks, Mom." He fans his hand in front of the Tiger Ornament, imitating Vanna White.

"You like it?" I laugh so hard that I snort.

"This isn't going to be another Eckerd's Drug Store Christmas, is it?" Bo laughs through his words.

The year before Bobby and I got divorced, I was so distraught that I ended up doing all my Christmas shopping at Eckerd's Drug Store. Really! I can't even remember the junk I gave the kids. But they were good sports. And at times, our laughter turned into tears. I'm sure when the day was over, each gift got stuffed in the back of a drawer or thrown in the trash.

"Casey, you're up!" He bends over, knocks down his pile, and cautiously studies the packages in front of him. "What are you doing?"

"Mom. I'm looking for something good and not my ornament."

He grabs a large rectangular box wrapped in snowmen paper and tries ripping off the ribbon. Frustrated, he hands me the package.

"Mom, can you take it off? My hand sucks."

I slide the ribbon off the box and tear a hole in the paper, giving him a head start. In a matter of minutes, the lid falls to the floor. Casey pulls out his gift and grunts with approval. He stands, drops the shirt on the chair, and starts to wiggle out of his sweater. His left arm gets stuck. The word "help" seeps through the opening. I tug on the sleeve. He breathes. He pulls the cotton, long-sleeve shirt over his head and struggles again. I try to help, but Casey shouts, "I can do this, Mom."

Bo chimes in. "Casey, don't yell at Mom."

I signal Bo to be still. I step back, clasp my hands, and wait. Finally, Casey's head crowns, and his fingertips peek through the cuffs. Using his right hand, he tugs on the bottom of the shirt and sits down.

Thank God I didn't give him shorts or we may have seen more than we wished for. This is going to be a long morning.

"Your turn, Annie."

She also avoids the small box and chooses a large square one wrapped in red-and-white striped paper. She pulls the robe free from layers of tissue paper, and her eyes dance with excitement.

"I love it, Mom. Blue. My favorite color." She bends over the coffee table to give me a kiss. "Thanks, Mom."

Since I can remember, Annie has always expressed gratitude for anything I gave her, whether she loved it or not. That's just her way.

The phone rings and rings.

"Mom, aren't you going to get that?"

"I'll call them back, Bo."

"But what if it's—"

"Bo, sit down." I know I'm asking the impossible because that boy can't sit still longer than five minutes without fidgeting or pacing the room. "Whoever it is, Bo, they'll call back. Okay? Your turn."

A couple hours later, my house looks like a cyclone just blew through. The kids stuff wrapping paper inside garbage bags and cram their presents under the tree. Cell phones buzz. The doorbell rings.

Friends come and go. We eat again. Finally the house grows still.

I crawl into bed with the kids' Christmas letters.

Casey's is on top. Gently, I open the envelope. In the top section, the words "Merry Christmas, Mom," are scribbled in large block letters. In the middle of the page, Casey writes, "I love you so much." At the bottom he signs, "Thank you for being my Mom. Love ya, Casey."

My sweet, sweet boy.

Next, I open Annie's letter and begin reading.

Mom,

Well, it's finally another Christmas, and you get your yearly letters that you love so much. You have always been there for me, no matter what. I never really thanked you for that, and I should. I also never thanked you for all those letters and the sayings you give me when I'm down. They really mean a lot.

This year has been really hard for me. But you are always there, no matter what.

I hope you never die, or at least not until I do, because I don't know what I would do without you. I really don't know what any of us kids would do. But I know God is watching over you.

I can't remember which one of my friends told me this. It might have been Megan. She said that you were the strongest person she knew.

Well, you are. You have been through so much and you are still so strong . . . and you are always reading your strong sayings. Even with all you've gone through, you still have a positive outlook on life. That is amazing to me. If I was you, I really don't know what I would do.

Mom, you are always there for me, to guide me in the right direction and help me to see things in a good way. You might not know this, but you have made me make some really good decisions. All those little notes you write me make me see the things I have trouble with . . . making what seems huge in my world, simple. That means so much to me.

Well Mom, I know I have told you this like a billion times, but everything you do for me means so much. All the stuff we have been through this last year, and it has been a lot, you still look at life like it's great. That's the gift you have—to always get right back up when you fall. That is so hard for me to do, but you have made me get up a little faster over this past year and made me see things from a whole different point of view.

Your faith in God is also soooo strong. I think that's what makes you who you are.

I just want to tell you how much you have affected me and others in this world with all the love you have in your heart.

I love you sooo much that even words can't describe how I feel. I know you are always there for me. I love you to death.

Love you,
Annie

Carefully, I dab the wet splotches off the paper, wanting (always wanting) to preserve my keepsake. I slip under the covers, clutch my letters to my heart, and think to myself . . . *What a wonderful world!*

CHAPTER TWENTY-SIX

January 2003

I'm free, at least for the next few hours. Casey, Bo, and Annie are off to lunch with their dad. I'm driving to Phoenix Rising, a New Age store, to participate in a spiritual service. I hope to meet *someone* who can answer all my questions about Casey's odd behavior. I sense that there's a stranger living inside him—one who likes wearing his hat cocked to the side.

I park, wrap my knit scarf around my neck, and walk across the parking lot. Peeking inside, I see rows of bookshelves. On the left is a small open space. People are gathered there, engaging in conversation. A semicircular counter is fastened along the same wall. A tall, lanky gentleman with silver-white hair and olive skin stands inside the space.

Bells, hanging on the front door, signal my arrival. The gentleman behind the counter looks up, smiles, and extends his hand.

"Welcome. You're new, right? Don't recall seeing you before. And I never forget a face. You here to shop? We have a huge selection of spiritual books, essential oils, and a sundry of other items. Or are you here for the service?"

"Yes. I mean, yes, I'm here for the service."

He lifts his arm, looks at his watch and squints. "It should start—"

A gong sounds, indicating the service is ready to begin. The group ambles down the hallway and into a small, candlelit room. Pictures of deities and angels decorate the walls. Smoke rises from the incense burner and the sweet scent of sandalwood permeates the room. Zen music plays, and a waterfall can be heard in the background. After everyone is seated, the lay minister stands, reads an inspirational passage, and guides the group in meditation.

For the next fifteen minutes, it's as if time stops. I drop deeper into my internal silence, deeper into my heart. It's a place where I feel comfortable. A place I call home.

The music stops. The minister clears her throat.

"Thank you all for coming today. Please join us next door for coffee and donuts."

People stand. Chairs *clank*. Feet patter toward the door. Intoxicated by the stillness running through my body, I'm slow to move.

I feel a tap on my shoulder.

"Hi, I'm Amy. Care to get a cup of coffee?"

"Sure. I'd like that."

Chatter, laughter, and the aroma of freshly brewed coffee fill the air. Amy walks ahead, stopping to greet friends along the way. We grab a cup of coffee and sit down.

"So tell me, what brought you here?"

"Uhm." I try to speak but nothing comes.

"It's okay. Your story is safe with me."

Am I that transparent, that even a complete stranger can read me?

I share Casey's story and then voice my concerns.

"I feel like there's a strange spirit sharing Casey's body, and it's like he comes and goes." My hands tremble.

"You should feel blessed."

What? Did she hear what I just said? Blessed?

Without blinking an eye, Amy continues.

"I believe your son has a walk-in."

Huh. The stranger has a name?

"I'm sorry. I don't understand. What's a walk-in?"

"It's an incoming soul who is an extension of the natal soul. It's like your son—Casey, right?—and the new soul are partners."

"Partners. This walk-in wants to come in, but why?"

"Walk-ins have a deep desire to complete their soul's mission by assisting others who are struggling to manage the changes they are facing."

"So, are you saying that Casey is the natal soul—the walk-out?"

"Right."

"And why would Casey want to walk out?"

"Maybe he's become discouraged with his life. It got too hard. He wants to go 'home.'"

Not Casey. Not my boy.

"Okay, Amy, let's say you're right. Then what?"

"The two spirits, the incoming and natal souls, do an exchange. This usually occurs during a near-death experience, which allows both of them to accomplish greater spiritual development in one earth lifetime."

As Amy continues to talk and educate me, the background noises die away.

"Wait. Slow down. How? I mean, when?"

"When a death is forthcoming, the soul is brought by his Guardians to a holding room on the other side and given a choice to exit or to have a walk-in experience."

Hearing Amy's words, the light switch turns on. Casey's twenty-four-hour period when the nurses and doctors weren't sure he was going to make it . . . and his extended coma.

"So this walk-in, seeking spiritual advancement, confronts Casey's soul while he's in this holding room, to see if he's open to the exchange? If he accepts, then his Guardians guide him through the decision-making process?" My fingertips dig into my temples.

"Exactly. Let's say your son reached a point in his lifetime where he needed to heal a part of his soul. Both the incoming and natal souls make an agreement prior to this incarnation, with each other's permission, to enter into a spiritual partnership to help one another evolve."

"So they just swap roles?"

"Basically, yes."

This is way too creepy. My mind engages in a mental game of ping-pong—*Bolt. Stay. You need to hear her out.*

"You okay? I know this is confusing. Just hang in there with me."

Amy raises the coffee cup to her lips, drinking deeply. She continues. "Once the agreement is put into play, the two souls have to learn how to test-drive their new planes. It's actually easier for the walk-out during this transition—like when he dies, and the soul leaves his body behind. But the incoming soul has to go through an adjustment period. He hasn't been in a physical form for some time. He needs to stabilize his emotions and familiarize himself with the natal soul's family and friends."

My thoughts flash back to Casey's homecoming party.

"You know, Amy, I had a party for my boy, and he was so quiet, not really his old self. Do you think—"

"Absolutely."

"Can that be why Casey is sweet one minute and short with me the next?"

Amy nods.

I release a long-winded gust of air, as I muster up the courage to ask the next question.

"How do I know the walk-in isn't some sort of discarnate spirit? I mean, you hear—"

"What people don't understand is a walk-in/walk-out is the transfer between two souls to move them forward in their spiritual evolution, bringing a purer vibration to earth. The walk-in is extremely focused on accomplishing his divine purpose."

"And how does he do that?"

"He brings in his healing abilities, accurate intuition, empathy, and spiritual gifts he's mastered through lifetimes of incarnations."

"So, let's say you're right, and Casey is a walk-out. Does that mean he leaves completely?" I ask, almost afraid to hear her answer.

"Sometimes. Or the spirit can hang out in the auric field of the body that it left and become the observer, learning lessons. Meanwhile the incoming soul picks up the pieces, healing the body and emotions, and any residual karma and limiting beliefs that caused the natal soul's desire to exit."

"Bottom line then, these walk-ins come—"

"In for spiritual advancement."

"And stay how long?" I cringe.

"Some incoming souls stay on. Mainly because the natal soul has decided it doesn't want to return. But in other cases, the natal soul does return. That can happen around three to six months, maybe longer, so I've read."

"Okay, Amy, let's say Casey's natal soul wants to return."

"When the timing is right, the incoming soul leaves and Casey's soul returns completely. Again, I'm not an expert. I'm just paraphrasing what I've learned."

We sit in silence for a few moments.

"You know, the occurrence of walk-ins was first clearly stated in ancient Hindu sacred scripture."

"Seriously, Amy?"

"Yes. In the 70s, people began to be interested in the subject again. Have you ever read *Seth Speaks* or *Strangers Amongst Us*?"

"No."

"You should someday. Both of them cover the subject. Interesting reads. Listen, gotta run. Hope to see you again."

As Amy walks out the door, I think, *If I tell any of my friends about this conversation, they are going to think I'm nuts.*

I walk into the house around three o'clock. The TV is blaring, intermingled with bouts of laughter from Bo, Casey, Annie, and others. As I round the top stair, I see the kids' friends sandwiched together on the couch. Karl, Ryan, and Travis get up to greet me.

"Boys, good to see you," I say to all three then follow up with a hug. "Can I get you guys anything?"

"We're good." Their replies overlap, sounding like an echo.

"I can see that." Every inch of the coffee table is covered with pizza boxes, potato chips, and soda cans. "I'll be upstairs if you need me."

No one answers.

Around six, I awaken to a knock at my door. I must have fallen asleep reading *The Four Agreements*.

"Come in," I say in a groggy voice.

"Mom, we're going to meet up with Robbie and grab some dinner. We'll be home early."

"Okay, Bo. Have fun. Casey going?"

"Yeah. Don't worry, I'll keep an eye on him."

I really wasn't worried. Should I be?

After I hear the last laugh disappear behind the closed door, I walk down the stairs. The coffee table is cleared, and the centerpiece is back in place. "Aw." I round the corner to the kitchen and see the dishes washed but sitting on the counter. Do they think the dishwasher bites?

Back in bed, I fold my book over my lap when I hear car doors close, followed by the front door. Voices sail to the second floor.

"Night, Case."

"Night, Annie."

The stairs creak louder as Annie approaches the top step.

"Night, sweetie. Sleep with the angels."

"Night, Mom."

I love having my girl home from college and sleeping under my roof again.

I glance at the time. It's nine o'clock. Good job, Bo. As my eyelids grow heavy, I have one final thought. *I wonder who's sleeping in Casey's bed tonight—the walk-in or the walk-out?*

As I'm driving home from work the next day, my thoughts are in sync with the traffic: speeding up, slowing down, shifting lanes, and getting boxed in. I grab my cell phone and call Mary.

"What's wrong? Something's wrong. I hear it in your voice. Is it work?"

"No. I love my job."

In the few short months I've been the CRM at Barnes & Noble, I've made great contacts at the local newspapers, arranged book signings for authors, and created two book discussion groups. Not bad for a newbie.

"Is it Casey?"

I make an attempt to switch lanes. A horn blares. I swerve back into the left lane and give my "so sorry" wave and get the finger in return.

"That's one concern gnawing at me. This is the first time I've left him alone when I went to work. He never gets up until two in the afternoon on the weekends."

"It's okay, sis. He'll be fine."

Ever since the kids were little, leaving them alone was never easy for me. After Bo was born in St. Louis, I returned to Saudi Arabia where Bobby's business had relocated us. When Bo was one year old, we returned to the States and settled in California, home base for Bobby's business. So, never having the luxury of family babysitters, I was a bit of a nervous Nellie when I left the kids with new sitters for a night or a weekend trip away. Even though I needed and longed for the breaks, I found myself missing them shortly after I had left.

"I know. But it's not just Casey."

"What then?"

"I need some alone time, Mare. I just wish when Bobby came into town, he would offer to take Casey for the entire weekend. Ya know, help me out a little here. He is Casey's father."

"So why not ask him?"

There's the question I've been asking myself for years. I've spent decades being the enabler, wanting to keep peace, trying to please everyone, and probably doing more harm to them, to me, than good. Yet, when it comes to asking my ex-husband to step up to the plate, I slip back into my old patterns.

"Why not? Because here's how I believe the conversation would go. I'd ask. He'd listen, sort of. Then he'd start telling me about all the things he's done for Casey: getting him a driver, calling him daily to check in on him, taking him to lunch when he's in town. When he was finished, he'd throw in his busy work and travel schedule."

"Well, sis, you need to tell him that you work, too. Not only eight hours a day, but round-the-clock caring for Casey. Your time is just as valuable as his."

"Mare, before I could even get all those words out of my mouth, he would start arguing. I think Bobby feels that I am the mom, therefore, taking care of Casey is my responsibility."

"What?"

"Think about it. That was my role in the marriage, and his was the provider."

"Wait a minute. You were a mom and then some. Not only did you hold down the fort while he was away, you made sure the kids' needs were met, and you almost lived in your car driving the kids to and from their extracurricular activities. Plus, you started your own design business. You worked as an independent sales rep for Market America. Okay, you were only with them for a year. But that wasn't your fault. You had a car accident and could barely walk. Don't get me started. Hey, got a call coming in. We'll talk later."

I pull into the driveway, grab my Tupperware container and the early release of *The Da Vinci Code* from the passenger seat, and walk inside. I give Casey's door a slight push. He's sleeping. A half-eaten bagel slathered in cream cheese is sitting on his nightstand. The dogs are curled up beside him. One knot in my stomach unwinds.

Later that afternoon, I hear the garage door open and shut. Ten minutes later, Duke and C.D. dash up the stairs. Casey follows them into the kitchen.

"Hey, Mom. What ya doin'? Making me a sandwich?"

"No, but I can. Grilled cheese okay?"

He doesn't answer. He walks into the family room and turns the TV on.

I slide his sandwich onto the plate, add chips and a few sliced oranges, grab a Mountain Dew from the fridge, and carry his lunch into the family room.

"Here you go, sweetie." I sit yoga-style on the couch. "So, Casey, how was rehab yesterday? You were sleeping when I came home from work, and you didn't feel like talking last night."

"I hate it."

"That's a powerful statement, Case."

"Like I said, 'I hate it.' I already told you, I don't belong there. You can tell that stupid driver she doesn't have to stay and babysit me. I'll be fine until you get home."

I can't even imagine how mortifying it must be to have a babysitter at his age. He hasn't fallen down the steps or started a fire lately. Maybe the driver can just drop him off. But I wish his tone of voice and mood swings weren't so harsh. Ever since Casey's brain injury, his actions feel like they've been magnified times ten.

Casey's cell phone rings. He stands and walks out on the deck, leaving the door open. I hear him say, "Hey, Dad. I'll be ready. No kidding? Cool. Okay, see you soon." He walks back in the room, grinning.

"What is it?"

He sits down on the couch and turns the volume down on the TV.

"Remember when we were talking last week, and I told you about my conversation with Dad?"

"Refresh my memory."

"Dad called, and he started yelling at me for something."

"Yeah." So what's new? "Go on."

"Well, I told him he sounded like he was having a temper tantrum. And I said it calmly."

"Really?" The two of them didn't get into a screaming match. Interesting.

I can feel Casey's energy growing softer.

"One of my counselors in rehab told me that I didn't have to take his yelling anymore because it overloads my senses. She said I needed to tell him how I feel, so I did."

Huh. I lean forward and look deep into Casey's eyes. Who is this person talking? Is this the stranger?

"How'd that work for you?"

"I guess Dad thought about it," Casey smiles.

"Why's that?"

"Well, my dream is to be a captain of a ship, right?"

"Right."

"Well, Dad just said he was going to buy me a boat."

"A boat?" What? Is the man nuts? His son just suffered a brain injury. Maybe Casey heard him wrong.

"Yeah, but I know he doesn't mean it. I think it's his way of saying he was sorry for yelling." Casey smirks.

I lean back and stare blankly ahead, wondering if Casey has worked out a good way to deal with his dad.

Casey's cell phone blares again. He flips it open.

"Yeah, Dad. But I like my cargo pants." His voice grows louder, and soon he's yelling. "Okay. I'll look nice when you pick me up."

This isn't the first time I've heard this discussion. Since the boys became teenagers, Bobby has been on them about dressing "properly." Truthfully, they always look nice, just not up to Bobby's standards.

Casey's feet clunk down the stairs, and he starts rattling off a litany of curse words, none of which I care to share. Then he slams the door on these words: "What the hell is his problem?"

The pictures hanging on the wall tilt sideways.

A horn blasts. I step out onto the front deck and look beyond the manicured lawn sprinkled with crepe myrtle trees, and I spot Bobby's gray Volvo at the curb.

"Casey. Your dad's here to take you out to dinner," I say, leaning over the banister.

Honk. Honk.

"Case."

"I'm coming."

As he's climbing the stairs, his cell phone rings. He answers.

"Yes, I hear you. The whole neighborhood hears you. I'm on my way."

Just being within earshot of Casey's conversation makes me realize how glad I am to be living alone.

Casey pecks me on the forehead and walks toward the door.

"Have fun, Casey."

"Yeah."

"When will you be home?"

"A few hours."

The door bangs closed. I flinch. Water splashes out of the fountain in the hallway. I clean it up and call Lili.

Lili's son, Nate, and Bo became good friends in grade school. Whenever I would drop Bo off at their house, prior to the boys getting their drivers' licenses, Lili and I would sit for hours at her kitchen table, talking and laughing. I took an instant liking to Lili; most people would. She's smart, compassionate, and funny.

"You up for company? Sure could use some girlfriend time."

"Come on over. Love to see you."

I stop at the market, pick up a bottle of wine, and within fifteen minutes I'm ringing Lili's doorbell.

She gives me a once-over. Born a Sagittarian, Lili never minces her words.

"Damn friend. You look like shit."

"Really?" I pat my face. "I even put on makeup."

"Then you must have forgotten the eye concealer for those bags. How about a glass of wine?"

"Love one. Thanks for letting me come on such short notice. Lili, I don't know what I would have done if I hadn't gotten out of that house. It's hard enough raising a teenager, much less a teenager with a brain injury. I think I'm going nuts."

"Slow down. Breathe."

Lili fills two rounded crystal goblets with wine, hands one to me, sits down at the island bar with hers, and continues.

"So, what's going on?"

I swirl and sniff, savoring the medium-fruity body of the Sonoma Merlot.

"It's all so complicated," I begin, fumbling for the right words.

"What is? Getting sleep? Cuz, girl, judging from your appearance, you could use some."

"I know. I don't sleep well. All night long I toss and turn, listening for unfamiliar sounds that signal danger."

"I presume you're talking about Casey, right?"

"Right. Anyway, that's a portion of the problem. Then there's—"

"What?"

"I've only had three days to myself since Casey's accident. Three damn days. And that was just before Christmas when Bobby took the kids to St. Louis. I need a couple weekends to be with my friends and have some fun."

Lili lifts her glass and *clanks* mine.

"Well, I second that. So how do you think Casey's doing on the whole?"

"Better. In one respect, so am I, especially because I have an understanding about his walk-in."

Lili spits her wine across the counter.

"What? A walk-in?"

I spend the next forty-five minutes rehashing my conversation with Amy. Lili's eyes widen. She gulps. Refills her glass. Then gulps again.

My cell phone buzzes. Stops. Buzzes again. I check caller ID. It's Casey.

"Lili, would you think I was a terrible mother if I didn't answer? I just don't want to go home yet."

"What do you think Bobby will do? He won't just drop him off and leave him alone in your house, will he?"

"No. Even though Casey would probably do fine, I don't think he'd risk it. Maybe he'll take Casey to his condo to spend the night."

Swallowing my guilt, I close the phone and let the message go to voice mail. Casey will call back. That's his M.O. By then, I'll know what I want to do.

"Stay here. You need a good night's rest. More wine?"

I nod.

Lili tops off my glass and continues. "So, let me ask you something. Doesn't all this talk about walk-ins give you the heebeegeebees?"

"At first it did. Heck, I didn't even know walk-ins existed. But I needed something to hold on to. Something that could explain Casey's erratic behavior. Actually, the more I think about it, I think it's beautiful."

"Beautiful?"

"Yeah. The incoming soul, walk-in, has come out of compassion. He's here to evolve spiritually and assist Casey on his journey. Truthfully, Lili, just knowing that helps me to be more tolerant of Casey's mood swings."

"If you say so. You hungry?"

Lili sets a plate of cheese, grapes, and crackers on the kitchen island.

My cell phone buzzes. Stops. Buzzes again. I stare at it, wondering if I should answer. The ringing ends. I flip open the phone, press in my voice mail code, and put the phone on speaker.

"Mom. Where are you? Dad and I have been driving around your condo for an hour. What, Dad? Okay, he's taking me back to his place. I'll talk to you tomorrow."

Another pang of guilt rushes through my body. Maybe I should have gone home? But don't I deserve to have a life, too?

"For an hour? You got to be kidding me," Lili sneers. "So, let me get this straight in my head. This is a lot to digest. This walk-in came in to help Casey—"

"Spiritually evolve."

"So, honestly, you believe all this?"

I shrug. "But Amy's theory may just explain another dilemma."

"Which is?"

"Why Casey all of a sudden wears his hat cocked to the side, looking like a rapper. I believe the incoming soul is using it as a compass."

"A compass?" Lili's eyes blink closed.

"Yeah. Here's how I see it. When the bill moves front and center, I believe the walk-in will go back to the other side, and Casey will step back in completely."

"I don't know about any of this. It's all very bizarre."

Lili and I gab and laugh into the wee hours of the night until exhaustion sets in.

"Here you go, friend." Lili opens the door to the bedroom. "Enjoy the quiet. And, friend, a mere suggestion: If I were you, I wouldn't share your concept about walk-ins with too many people. You know they might think . . ." She spins her finger above her brow. "But not me. I know you're looking for something to hold on to. Something that will give the insanity of your life meaning."

CHAPTER TWENTY-SEVEN

February

The idiosyncrasies of life are leveling out. Casey's time at rehab is approaching the finish line, only two months to go, and my new job is a godsend. I love meeting authors, organizing events, and stepping back into my creativity.

I'm rushing around the house changing beds, doing laundry, and enjoying my alone time while Casey's at rehab. The phone rings. It's Drace.

"How did your reading go with the psychic? Was she any good?"

"Not as good as the first gal we saw in East St. Louis. Remember when you talked me into going to that psychic?"

"I do."

I had never been to a psychic. Didn't know the first thing about one. But one day, back in the '70s, Drace handed me a card. Embossed in black letters was a lady's name. Underneath it, in bold letters, it said "Clairvoyant."

"What the heck is a clairvoyant, Drace?"

"She reads the future. Want to give her a try? It's cheaper than going to therapy. Plus we can have some laughs."

"Okay. I'll do it. But if she answers the door wearing a turban and sits in front of a crystal ball, I'm out of there. Got it?"

The clairvoyant called me into her room and motioned for me to sit down. After putting a tape in the recorder, she handed me paper and a pencil to take notes. Five minutes into my reading, the skeptic in me flew out the window. I couldn't write fast enough.

When Drace's session was over, we drove back to Clayton, a suburb in St. Louis where we lived, and we stopped at a neighborhood restaurant. Drace ordered a beer. I ordered a glass of wine. For the next hour, we shared our notes, shared our "oohs" and "ahs," and laughed so hard tears streamed down our faces.

Over the years, Drace and I have gone to more psychics and mediums (who have the ability to connect with the afterlife) than I can count. When we got word of a good psychic out of town, we booked a telephone reading, knowing that there are no boundaries with intuition.

Then, like now, we love to share the feedback from our reading. It's a girlfriend thing.

"So, girl. What did she say?"

"She sees me moving to upstate New York. Someone's going to dangle a carrot in front of me, offering me a job."

"Girl. Maybe your cousin Jim is going to ask you to work for him."

"Maybe." I turn the page and find Casey's name, underlined. "Now listen to this. She saw Casey on the other side holding a teddy bear. A teddy bear. It gave me chills."

"Isn't Teddy your nickname for Casey?"

"It is. You know that. I know that. Casey knows that. But how in the heck did she know that?"

I started calling Casey "Teddy" after he was born, for two reasons— his round belly and his sweet, loving nature.

Drace laughs. "Keep going."

"She saw Casey with his guardian angel. Mentioned something about him taking time off to smell the roses so he could get back on his path again."

"Girl. I just got goose bumps. Maybe there's truth to the conversation you had with Amy at the spiritual church. That Casey's soul is waiting on the other side, and his walk-in is standing in his stead."

"I thought the same thing. But the next part gets a bit confusing. She saw Casey getting a job in the springtime."

"Which Casey is she talking about now? The familiar one or the stranger? One minute he's on the other side holding a teddy bear. Then he's back on earth working."

"Welcome to my world, Drace. Since Casey arrived home from rehab, I've been trying to make sense of this walk-in concept, trying to keep track of the different Caseys. Believe me, it's taxing."

"I know, girl. But overall, she nailed your life."

"She did. What I loved most was that Casey and I weren't going to be stuck in quicksand forever. Drace, I just heard the front door close. Casey's home. Call you tomorrow."

"Bye, girlfriend."

"Mom, you upstairs?"

"Coming, sweetie."

Casey turns when he hears my footsteps.

"You look like you just saw a ghost."

"I do?" *Maybe I have.*

"So, what's for dinner?" Casey asks while lifting the lid on the Crock-Pot. "Mmm. Chili. I'm starved."

We sit down to dinner, and Casey tells me about his day.

"You know, Mom, Fred is quite a character."

"How so?"

"Oh, I don't know. We just have fun together. When we get a break, the two of us go outside, smoke, and shoot the shit."

I can sense there are layers to their conversation, ones I may never be able to peel back. But for now, listening as Casey reminisces about his day and hearing his laughter reminds me of days gone by.

"So, what does Fred think about rehab?"

"He can't wait to be finished. He needs to get back to work to support his family."

"Aw. It can't be easy having that kind of pressure when he still has healing to do."

"No, Mom. He's good, like me," Casey says calmly.

What happened to his anxiety? His foul mouth? Raging moods?

"So, how's Grace? Haven't heard much about her lately."

"Doing good. Misses me at school. She's going back home, D.C., over spring break. She wants me to visit."

Casey wipes his bowl clean with the garlic bread and shoves the whole piece in his mouth, chews twice, then gulps.

"Oh, and when's that?" I ask with a forced smile, trying to conceal my worries.

"Soon, I think."

"How will you get there?" I ask, knowing Casey has to pass the driver's test before they will put him behind the wheel. That's months away.

"Amtrak."

The train is safe. Time with his girl is good. Maybe it's time to give Casey some rope.

Given Casey's situation, it's not easy to let go. But I need to release my fears. Need to quit playing the "what if" game. Need to give him back his wings.

He may fly east instead of west, getting off course. He may dive straight into a storm and plummet into the sea. Or the winds may rise up to meet him, and he'll soar above the mountaintops.

But I need to remember that this is *his* journey, and the choices he makes belong to *him*.

CHAPTER TWENTY-EIGHT

Still February

Casey's been refusing to take the prescribed medication for his fluctuating moods, and it's showing. I feel like I'm riding a roller coaster and the gears keep locking mid-ride, jolting me forward then back without any warning.

"Hey, Casey, did you take your pills?" I shout from the kitchen as he's leaving for rehab.

"I'm not taking them anymore. They make me feel strange. I'm quitting rehab, too. It sucks. I'm not like the rest of the dudes."

Before I can come back with a rebuttal, the door closes.

I get busy cleaning the house, a ritual on my day off. When I tackle Casey's room, I find a pad of paper covered in scribbles of his handwriting. I sit on the floor and start reading.

> *This world is really messed up.*
> *This last year I've really gone through some shit.*
> *People are really weird.*
> *Why do they think I'm a loser?*
> *I'm not some kind of weirdo.*

My hand quivers against my pursed lips as I feel my boy's anguish snake through my veins, sending a distress signal to the trillion cells in my body. Slowly, my hand traces my boy's words, and I hear myself whisper aloud, "You're not a loser, sweetie. You're beautiful inside and out. God, I wish you knew that." There's no date. No title. Did he write this after his homecoming party? Why didn't he come to me? I would have listened. I would have told him about my talk with Bo. I could have eased his pain.

Then I recall one of my conversations with the doctor when he shared a common statement made by patients of head injury, "I just feel different."

Oh, honey.

I turn the page and read the next entry.

Take me to the place where I can find peace again.
You are my strength that keeps me walking.
You are the hope that keeps me trusting.
You are my heart, my soul.
You are my everything.
You are the one.
You are my purpose.

The pad falls between my legs.

Did Casey write this or did the walk-in, not knowing how to cope in the body? I wish I knew.

I lean back and hear a *ping* come from under the bed. I lift up the bed skirt and pull out not one, but a six-pack of empty beer cans. My mood shifts, and I feel like a steamroller leveled me to the ground.

He's drinking again? Is this how he's dealing with the pain?

The clock can't tick fast enough for me. Finally, at four o'clock, Casey walks into the house. I'm there to greet him. Not with my normal, "Hi. How was your day, sweetie?" Instead, "I was cleaning your room today. Do you have anything you want to talk to me about?"

"About what, Mom?" Casey strolls toward the kitchen.

"The beer cans I found in your room. Where did you get the beer?"

"A friend."

No matter how hard I try, I know I can't make his choices for him. But I won't go down without a fight. As his mother, it's my duty to guide him in the right direction.

"Good friend he is, Case. Doesn't he know what you've been through? That drinking will only make matters worse!"

Casey stares at me without saying a word.

Concerned, worried, and afraid that Casey will slip back into his old patterns, I can hear my voice growing louder.

"For God's sake, Casey, use your brain before you have no brain cells left. This is not the way to cope with your problems or what you perceive as your failures. It's a Band-Aid, honey, and the Band-Aid will fall off. Sooner or later you are going to have to—"

"What Mom? What? Like what happened to me? It sucks. I hate it. I want things to go back to the way they were."

So do I.

Feeling like someone released the valve on the pressure cooker, I lower my voice.

"I'm worried about you, Case. I want to help. Sweetie, listen," I say, grabbing hold of his forearm. "Drinking at this stage of your healing process is so destructive. It can impair your memory, along with . . ."

I see a tear form in the corner of Casey's eye. He looks in the opposite direction.

"I'm okay, Mom. Really."

I want to say, "No you're not. I read your poetry and felt your gut-wrenching pain." Why won't he talk to me? I drive the nail deeper into the wood.

"Casey, you won't take the pills that will help you. But you'll drink beer, which only hinders your healing. Am I missing something here? Help me to understand what's going on inside that head of yours."

He walks toward the steps.

"I don't want to talk anymore. I'm done."

"Honey."

I close my mouth, locking my thoughts inside the cave, remembering my conversation with the doctor. "When the patient goes into overload, the best way to handle it is with a time-out." Right now, I'm thinking we both need one.

Days later, Casey and I talk.

I thought he was going to say that he thought about our conversation. That going forward, he'll take his pills. That he'll stop drinking. But no. Instead, he throws me a ball from the outfield while I'm standing at home plate without a mitt.

"Been thinking. I'm finished with rehab. I want to go back to school. I already talked to Dad. He's okay with it."

But your dad doesn't spend his nights and days with you.

Yes, Casey's improved, but school would be a giant leap for him. How about the walk-in? He still comes and goes. Plus, his hat is still cocked to the side.

"I contacted an old friend, and he's looking for a roommate. He wants me to move in with him in two weeks. I've decided to get a job waiting tables and go back to school."

"Slow down, Case. I haven't even digested the job, and now you're talking about school." I put a lasso around my thoughts and pull them in slowly. "Okay. So let's say you go back to school. What are you considering? Taking one class then—"

"Dad said I need to take twelve hours to be considered a student."

"What? And set yourself up to fail?"

School never came easy for Casey. As he grew, so did his frustrations. His guidance counselor in high school suggested having him tested, and the results revealed that his mind processed information differently than others. A school with a smaller teacher-to-student ratio was recommended. Casey changed schools and graduated.

"Sweetie, when you're the big fish in the little pond, you do well. But the class sizes are larger at Trident. You'll need to get assistance with studying, which will take a huge chunk out of your day. Throw in waiting tables and late nights. Something is going to suffer."

I can already hear our future phone conversation. "Mom. I lost my job and had to drop three courses. It was too much."

I take a deep breath. I exhale and try to reason with Casey.

"How are you going to get around town? You can't drive until you pass your driver's test."

"I'll take the bus. They go all over Charleston."

"Casey, I need to sleep on this. Right now I just can't think."

"Okay. Oh, and can I take Duke with me? My roommate has a dog, and the two of them would have so much fun."

Even though that's the best idea so far, and I would feel more comfortable if Duke was by his side, I need time to ruminate on the subject. As I lower my head, I catch a glimpse of C.D. curled at my feet and point.

"How about the little guy? He'll be so lonely."

"He'll probably miss growling at Duke, but other than that he'll be fine." Casey laughs. I join in, welcoming a break in the tension.

The following day I call rehab from work and talk to Casey's instructor.

"Do you have a minute? Casey and I chatted yesterday, and he is insistent on returning to Charleston."

"Yes. Casey told us he missed his girlfriend and wanted to go back to school."

"Do you think he's ready? Yes, he's making progress. But a job? School?"

"Believe me, I understand where you're coming from, but we can't force a patient to stay. Casey's only one month away from his dismissal date. Could he benefit from the extra time? Absolutely. But he's not committed. Sooner or later, he's going to have to test the waters."

"Mmm—hmm."

"He needs to come back in a month for his neuropsychological evaluation."

"That's right," I say, vaguely remembering our previous conversation. "Remind me again what the evaluation will look for."

"It will determine Casey's current levels of cognitive and emotional functioning. With the results, we can establish goals and treatment plans for vocational rehabilitation."

"Getting a job and returning to school?"

"Exactly." There's a pause. "He may get some added benefits at school—extra time taking tests, assistance with efficient note-taking, tape recording classes, outlines of each class lecture, multiple choice testing, and other special student services."

"That would be beneficial."

"Yes. It's a great help to the patients when they go back to school. But until he is tested, our hands are tied."

Returning to school at this point feels a bit premature, just like it did when he moved from ICU to the step-down floor, on to rehab and home.

Yet, fourteen days later, I'm driving down the highway, taking Casey back to Charleston.

Casey sits in the passenger seat, listening to music with earphones, his eyes closed. Duke's lying in the backseat behind his master. His doggie bed, favorite blanket, treats, and play toys are stacked next to him. Stuffed on the floor is a two-month supply of dog food, a couple of plastic gallons of water, and his metal bowl. Piled high in the back of the 4Runner are bags and boxes of newly purchased supplies—dishes, glasses, silverware, sheets, comforter, pillows, clothes, shoes, and knick-knacks—and Casey's suitcase.

Suddenly, the move hits me. Thoughts roll through my mind, sounding like steel balls hitting their targets in a pinball machine, ricocheting off one another. *What if Casey doesn't take his pills? What if he hooks up with his old buddies? What if he starts drinking and returns to his old habits prior to his accident?* The final metal ball falls into the hole, echoing *. . . what if . . . what if?*

Wanting to dislodge my negative thoughts, I shake them from my mind like a dog shakes water off his fur, and I return to the beauty surrounding me.

A breeze whips through the open window and fills the car with the sweet smell of lilacs and freshly cut grass. Wildflowers are scattered in patches along the highway divide. Hawks soar overhead, weaving through the tips of pine trees, and then flying back into wide-open space. The sight of them jars my memory, and I'm sucked back in time to the moment these spectacular birds first appeared in my life.

After the divorce, I was driving on a backstreet in Charlotte, my thoughts fixated on my kids and how they would adapt to yet another change in their lives. A huge red-tailed hawk caught my eye in the open field. She flapped her wings and soared in front of my car. I slammed on my brakes, almost crashing into the vehicle in front of me. Sucked into her energy, I pulled into an empty parking lot ahead, jumped out of the car, and glanced upward. As she circled overhead, riding the currents of the wind against the backdrop of a cloudless sky, I sensed her spirit communicating with me telepathically. Intuitively, I knew she and I had danced this dance before, possibly in another lifetime. With the old imprint activated, my soul longed to uncover her hidden message.

At home, I grabbed Ted Andrews' *Animal-Speak* off the shelf and started reading about the magical power of the hawk: "spiritual messengers, protectors, and visionaries of the air." Their presence indicates the power of mental, physical, emotional, and spiritual forces. Raptors call for us to be open to the new, and they show us how we can teach others to do the same. Speechless, I sat in gratitude, understanding why she had appeared.

But what took my breath away was when a kettle of hawks appeared on the highway the day that I was stuck in traffic on my way to MUSC. They soared above the left lane, which had become congested with vehicles. Watching as the cars in the left lane converged right, creating a seamless path to the hospital, I thanked the universe for sending their spiritual messengers again.

Now, like before, these remarkable birds have appeared to remind me of those enigmatic moments formerly shared and the messages left behind. Mindfully, I breathe in the new, trusting all is in divine right order. On the exhale, I once again surrender my "what ifs," knowing

I'm not responsible for Casey's actions. Duke starts barking at a passing motorcyclist, waking Casey.

"Mom. You need to stop."

"Why?"

"I have to go to the bathroom. Now. Pull over."

"Honey, you'll have to wait until I can get over in the right lane. There's a line of—"

"Just pull out. There's a space," he says anxiously, looking over his shoulder. "Go."

I gun it and slip between two cars, my heart palpitating.

"Case, the sign says there's a gas station one mile ahead."

"One mile. I can't wait." He wiggles in his seat.

I understand he needs to empty his bladder. He drank a couple glasses of orange juice and downed two cans of soda before we got into the car. Trust me, I'm empathetic. After drinking several cups of coffee, I, too, feel that same urgency to clear my bladder. But he can't hold it for one mile?

I put on my blinker and swing into the emergency lane. I'm not even at a complete stop when Casey opens the door and jumps out. Duke leaps into the front seat. I grab his leash. He sits down.

Casey turns, sees Duke sitting up front, and smiles.

"Need to go, boy? Mom, let him go. He'll be fine."

I release my hold, and Duke springs into the air, looking like a deer leaping through an open field. He stops at Casey's side and walks with him deeper into a patch of shrubs. A moment later, both relieved, Case and his loyal companion strut back to the car. Casey tells Duke to sit as he retrieves his metal bowl and fills it with water.

"Drink, Duke. Good boy. Up." Casey points to the backseat. Duke obeys. Casey pats Duke on the head and closes the door. He slides into the passenger seat. Puts his earphones back on. Presses the green button on his CD player, and closes his eyes.

As we're coming down the homestretch, Casey yawns and removes his earplugs.

"We almost there?" he asks, his eyes still shut.

"About thirty minutes away. Sleep good?"

"Yeah. I'm hungry, Mom. Can we get something to eat before you drop me off?" He sits up, surveying our location. "There's a Burger King ahead."

Not wanting to leave Duke alone, we eat in the car.

"Casey, I am really going to miss you," I say, setting my burger down.

"Mom, don't cry."

"Sweetie, we've been to hell and back together, and I'm so proud of how far you've come. Oh, how I've cherished our conversations—you opening up, asking for advice, working through our issues. But—"

"What, Mom?" Casey looks at me, smiling softly.

All the things I wanted to say on the ride to Charleston surface.

"Don't take on more than you can. Don't forget to call Dr. Bailey. You need to get your prescription refilled soon. Do you still have his number?"

"Right here." He slaps his back pocket.

"How about school? Did you ever contact Trident to see if you can take courses in the middle of the semester? Or do you have to wait until the summer session begins?"

"I forgot to call. I'll contact them after I get settled. Oh, and I'm going to check into getting my captain's license."

Captain's license? I thought he'd put this thought to bed. It hasn't come up in our most recent conversations.

"And if that doesn't pan out?"

"I'll go to school. Really, Mom. We've talked about most of this."

"Just trying to keep the facts straight in my head, sweetie."

Casey gathers the trash and drops it in the bin. We get back on the road.

For some reason, I'm not feeling Casey is taking this move and his commitments seriously. If the job or school doesn't get underway immediately, what is he going to do with all his free time? My gut clenches.

Casey's admitted he's downed a few beers. Bo, on the other hand swears he seldom drinks, yet his behavior tells a different story. Consumed with worry, I can feel myself slip backward for the second time today.

"So, where do you plan on waiting tables?"

"Not sure. But with all the restaurants in Charleston, I know it won't be a problem getting a job."

I nod. "But if you feel inundated, I want you to call me, okay?"

"Okay. Take a left, Mom. The house is . . . here." He points. "Stop."

I parallel park. Casey opens the back door. Duke joins Casey's roommate's dog on the side yard.

"Hey, man, can you watch Duke? We need to unload the car."

He waves. We fill our arms with boxes and walk a few feet. Casey introduces his roommate.

"Mom. This is Tom. Tom, my mom."

"Nice to meet you, Tom," I say, shifting the boxes and extending my arm. "Been here long?"

"Few months."

"Casey mentioned that you go to Trident."

"Yes, ma'am. Trying to get my basic classes out of the way. Much cheaper."

"Come on, Mom." Casey holds the door open. "Tom, my bedroom is—"

"At the top of the stairs on the right."

"Thanks, man."

Tom had emailed Casey pictures of the apartment and his room prior to our arrival.

As the screen door closes behind me, my thigh grazes the end table. Casey's eyes are on me.

"What do you think, Mom?"

Two tattered couches butt up against the walls. A wooden coffee table—filled with food-crusted plates, overflowing ashtrays, bent soda and beer cans—rests on a throw rug in front of the couches. Posters of musicians hang from the wall, their corners curling forward. Metal ginger jar lamps hatted in smoke-stained shades sit on the two end tables.

"Definitely has a masculine feel."

"Come on upstairs, and I'll show you my room."

We climb the wooden steps, navigating past piles of dirty clothes and schoolbooks, and turn right into Casey's room. Draped above the futon bed are dark-navy curtains; the sunlight filters through the scattered holes. Against the wall stands a five-foot maple dresser with words and phone numbers carved into the wood.

Casey points to the two-foot space between the bed and the dresser.

"I thought I could put my stereo here."

"Great idea," I say with enthusiasm while thinking, *The only other possibility is hanging it from the ceiling.*

"Case, should we vacuum before we bring in any more boxes?"

"Why?"

"It's filled with dog hair, food crumbs, and a myriad of other unidentifiable things."

"It's fine."

Ick.

After we bring the last load into the house, I turn to Casey.

"You're really okay with me driving back to Charlotte now? If I didn't have to work first thing in the morning and if C.D. wasn't home alone, I'd stay and help you unpack."

"I'm good, Mom. Hey, I wonder if C.D. is marking his spot since Duke is gone."

"I need to get on the road."

After I say my goodbyes to Tom, Casey walks me to the car. We hug. Then we hug again.

"Case, you take care of yourself, okay? Call me if you need anything. Promise?"

I bend down, grab hold of Duke's yellow fur and kiss him between his ears, one up and one down.

"Now, don't forget to call Annie if you need something," I say while starting the car. "She's only a few blocks away."

"I will, Mom. I have her on speed dial." Casey holds up his phone.

"Thanks for driving me back to Charleston. I'll call you later to make sure you got home okay."

Casey sticks his head inside the window, gives me a kiss, and then slaps the car door twice.

"Be safe, Mom. Love you."

"Love you too, Case."

On the ride home, I feel empty inside. Then I remember something Mom said: "I raised you kids so that someday you would have wings to fly on your own."

As I'm uttering, "Mom, I just hope Casey's ready," I sight hawks soaring above.

CHAPTER TWENTY-NINE

March 15–16

My heart skips a beat when I get time with my children, whether by phone or in person. Preferably the latter, but I'll take what I can get.

Every couple of days, I call Casey to see how he's getting along. It's difficult not checking in daily, even hourly. But he's in my thoughts constantly since I took him back to Charleston. It's hard to believe he's been there a month.

I'm out in the garden, dressed in a tattered cotton shirt and workout shorts, pulling weeds, when I hear a car racing down the street. Loud music vibrates off the interior panels; a hand waves out the window. I squint into the sunlight and drop a fistful of dandelions from my muddy hands, recognizing the navy Jeep.

The car screeches to a halt, and the door flies open. Out jumps my six-foot gorgeous hunk of a son, Bo, dressed in jeans and a NC State T-shirt. He lifts his shades, revealing his ocean-blue eyes, and smiles. I melt.

"Surprise!"

"I thought you decided to stay in Raleigh for your birthday," I say as Bo picks me up, swings me in circles, and whispers, "Missed you, Mom."

"Sweetie, I put your cake in the mail yesterday. You won't be there when it arrives."

"Don't worry, Mom. It'll be fine."

Growing up, birthdays in our home were extraordinary. Mom made a point of making sure her birthday child felt special.

She'd let us pick our dinner of choice. Decorated the kitchen with streamers. Baked our favorite cake. Placed a small present in front of our plate. Turned our water glass into a card easel.

Freshman year in college was the first time I was away for my birthday. Even though my dorm buddies and I had plans to celebrate that night, I missed my family and the hoopla. After class, I stopped by the mailroom and handed the mail lady a slip from my box.

"Wait here, honey. You have a package."

A package?

She handed me a large, square, corrugated box, with a return address of Missouri. My pigtails bounced off my shoulders as I double-trotted across campus, galloped up four flights of stairs almost ripping the seams in my skin-tight yellow slacks, and rushed down the hallway to my room. I grabbed a ballpoint pen off the desk, punctured the tape, and ripped open the box. Staring back at me was an angel food cake, a can of frosting, and a box of candles. On the side was a card.

"Happy birthday to my girl. Love, Mom."

That was the best present I ever received on my birthday. Ever.

I made a vow to myself then and there that when my kids went away to college, I'd send them their "birthday in a box"—filled with their favorite cake, frosting, candles, party hats, and streamers to brighten their day.

So far I've kept my promise.

Bo opens the trunk and pulls out a duffle bag that stretches from his torso to his calf then tosses it over his shoulder.

"How long are you staying, Bo?"

"Oh, this," he chuckles, glancing back at the green canvas bag bulging at the seams. "It's my dirty laundry."

"What the heck have you been wearing? Everything you own must be stuffed inside that bag."

"Pretty much. Got anything to eat? I'm starved."

While Bo unloads the car, I make him a turkey sandwich on cracked wheat bread topped with tomatoes, provolone cheese, and sprouts. As I'm setting his plate on the breakfast bar, I shout, "Lunch is ready, sweetie," hoping my voice will carry to the second floor.

He sprints down the steps with an armful of dirty laundry, leaving a trail of socks and boxers on the stairs.

"Be right there. Just need to throw in a load."

We barely sit down to eat when Bo's phone starts ringing. He flips it open.

"Hey, dude. Yeah, I'm home. My mom's house." He turns and asks, "Okay if I take this?"

I nod. He strolls out on the deck. I can hear him chortling through the door.

Just hearing him cackle takes me back to our miraculous nine-month journey together.

When I got pregnant with Bo, I didn't only grow a fat belly, but also a new laugh. It was so contagious that even the most solemn person in the room would burst into laughter. I was so disappointed that my newborn chuckle died after I gave birth.

What I lost, Bo gained.

Bo opens the door, slides his cell phone into his pants, and grabs his sandwich off the plate.

"I'm going to meet up with the guys, and I need to shower. Okay if we visit later? Oh, and thanks for the sandwich, Mom."

Around five o'clock, the front door squeaks open and closes.

"In here, Bo."

"Mom, close your eyes and keep them closed," he says, while standing outside the kitchen.

He pulls my hands away from my face and wraps them around crinkly cellophane.

"Okay . . . open."

Stuck between the palms of my hands are six long-stemmed yellow roses.

"Oh, sweetie, they're beautiful. But it's your birthday, not mine."

Bo places his hands on my shoulders and looks past my eyes, into my soul.

"This is my thanks to you, for birthing me and being my mom."

I cup my mouth. The warmth of my tears glides over my hand.

"It was and always will be my honor, Son, to be your mama."

We dance around the kitchen in our hug, a hug that neither time nor space can ever erase.

Twenty minutes later, Bo and I sit down to his birthday feast: steak, asparagus, baked potatoes, and cake.

After sticking a couple bites of meat in his mouth, mumbling "mmm" under his breath, he says, "You need to come see my new apartment, Mom. The khaki suede couches and wooden coffee table we picked out at Rooms To Go look awesome.

"Tell me."

He gets up from the table, grabs a pencil and paper from the kitchen counter, and starts drawing. He sketches the two couches, sitting in an L formation with the coffee table in the center.

"Like this. Well, actually it looks a lot better than this. But you get the idea." He snorts.

"The walls?"

"Oh, yeah. I bought this really cool plaster picture from Bed Bath & Beyond. It's a copy of a famous Michelangelo painting. Really cool. It weighs a ton. It's on the mantle."

"So, you have quite the flair for decorating?"

He shrugs.

Since Bo was a child, he loved to draw. It was as if his mind and pencil fused as they flowed across a blank canvas, creating images of his visions. One day I got in a pinch and turned to Bo.

"Annie's assignment for her religion class is to dress up as her patron saint using either her first or middle name. Annie wants to be Veronica, which means I have to paint Jesus' face on a cloth."

"Uh-huh."

"Can you help me out? I'll paint it. I just need a guide."

With pencil and paper in hand, Bo sat down and sketched. Within seconds, Jesus' face came alive. Alive!

"How—?"

"I just see it in my mind, Mom."

"Like those cartoon characters you drew when you were in middle school?"

He nodded.

The ring of Bo's phone pulls me back to the present. Bo pushes the paper aside.

"Hey. Listen, I'm having dinner with my mom. I'll call you back." He hangs up. "Sorry, Mom."

"It's fine. So, what else has been going on in your life, Bo? Still having those prophetic dreams?"

Bo rattles off his latest.

"You know, Mom, I see things and feel them, too."

"Does that scare you, sweetie?"

"Mmm. Not really. Yeah, sometimes."

Born a Pisces, Bo's nature exhibits the sign's positive personality traits—spiritual, creative, artistic, imaginative, with enhanced intuitive abilities—along with some of the not so positive: emotionally conflicted and escapist.

I want to dig deeper, but Bo changes the subject.

"How's Annie and Casey? Really love my bro and sis."

"How sweet." Just as the words—"Where did that come from?"—are about to roll off my tongue, Bo swipes a tear from the corner of his eye and looks away. I don't push.

"Hey, I'm going to meet up with the guys shortly. You mind?"

I do mind. I don't want this moment to end, now or ever.

I shake my head, and we continue talking.

An hour later, the house has gone empty again. Walking out of the laundry room with a handful of Bo's clothes stuffed under my arm, I stop at the dining room table and sniff the roses from my boy.

How sweet was that! I climb the stairs, put a stack of fresh, clean towels and folded jeans next to Bo's suitcase. The phone rings.

"Annie. How are you sweetie?"

"Good. And you?"

I fill her in on the details of Bo's surprise and how we spent the day.

"You know, Annie, Bo got quite sentimental at dinner talking about you and Casey."

"He did. Why?"

"Not sure what triggered his comment or the single tear that broke free from the corner of his eye. I just wanted you to know how much your brother loves you and Casey. Then Bo and I kept talking for, gosh, I don't know how long. I lost track of time."

"Aw. That's nice. Well, I have to run. Want to call Bo and wish him a happy birthday before I go out with the girls. Just wanted to check in on you, Mom, and tell you I love you."

Long conversations on the phone have never been Annie's thing. Yet there's always been a depth to our relationship, something I could never put my finger on.

With the phone still pressed against my chest, I travel back in time.

Annie, age two, had just woken up from her nap. She was stuffed inside her soft, white-footed jammies. I scooped her little body into my arms and carried her down the stairs. As I kissed her lips, her little fingers brushed my cheek. "Mom. Waited for you so long. Never let you go."

I'm not sure where that statement came from. But I've read that a child retains memories from past lifetimes until the age of five. Maybe Annie and I had been together before and for some unforeseen reason had been separated. Longing to pick up where we had left off, we made a pact to return together again, this time as mother and child. I believe Annie's spirit grew anxious as she waited to come.

The shrieking sound of a phone off the hook startles me back to the moment. I whisper into the phone, "And I will never let you go."

Around nine, I crawl into bed and read *The Seven Spiritual Laws of Success* until my eyes grow tired. The phone rings again.

"Mom. It's Casey. You sleeping?"

"I'm good. What's up?"

"Thought you'd like to know I got my pills today."

"Really? Aw, Casey. That's great news. How's the apartment? Duke?"

"Great and great. Think I might have a job."

"Doing what?"

"Waiting tables. I'll hear in a couple of days. The manager asked if I had black pants and white shirts, so I think it's a done deal."

Thank you. I've been so worried about Casey returning to Charleston, unsure if he made the move too soon. But everything is falling into place.

"I'm so proud of you, Case. Any idea when you might start?"

"Probably next week. Well, wanted to share the news. Go back to sleep, Mom. Call you in a few days."

I lie awake, thinking about how blessed I am to have three beautiful children, each unique in their own way, filled with personality and a heart of gold. I imagine I'm just about the richest woman alive.

Around two thirty in the morning, the front door closes. Voices and giggles, male and female, sweep up the stairs. Then suddenly they stop.

Maybe I was dreaming? I sit up and listen. All is quiet. Yet my gut tells me something isn't right. I throw back the covers and tiptoe across the room. Slowly, I crack open the door, stretch my neck and envision my ear telescoping down the steps, stopping at the landing. What's that smacking sound?

I grab my robe off the hook, walk into the hallway, and hear footsteps clump down the stairs. In one second flat, I arrive on the main floor, feeling like I flew down on a broom.

Bo is standing, barely, in the entryway.

"What's going on, Bo? I thought I heard a girl's voice."

"Nothing, Mom." His breath smells like the inside of a beer barrel.

"Bo. You're lying."

"No, I'm not." He hiccups through his words. "See," he says, opening his arms and almost falling face forward on the tile. "No girl here."

"Uh-huh."

I open the hall closet door. Stuffed between all the winter coats is a blond bombshell, looking like cream filling sandwiched between chocolate wafers.

"Seriously, Bo? So who might this be?"

She waves. She actually waves at me.

"Oh, her. She didn't have anywhere to stay tonight so—"

"You thought you'd bring her home to sleep with you? How

thoughtful of you! Well, this is my house, and there will be no you-know-what under my roof."

"Okay." Bo hiccups a few more times.

I grab his arm and nudge him toward the steps.

"You go sleep in the spare bedroom. And you, whatever your name is, come with me," I say, tugging on her arm.

"Wait." She squeaks. "My ear . . ."

I look over my shoulder and see her earring hooked on a metal hanger. I almost want to laugh. Almost.

Bo falls several times on the way up the stairs. Laughs. Pulls himself up. Falls again. Laughs again.

Drunks—they can't talk and they can't walk. They giggle, laugh, and have no clue why. I wonder if they have any idea how obnoxious they are? Probably not.

We finally make it to the top landing. The girl starts following Bo.

"Wait a minute, sweetie. Where do you think you're going?" I grab her arm and nudge her toward my room. "You're in here with me."

"What? You're kidding, right?"

"Wrong."

I grab a sheet, blanket, and pillow from the closet and make a bed on the floor, underneath the bay window.

"That's your bed for the night—unless you can call a friend and have her pick you up."

With my heart still pounding, I crawl back in bed, my eyes glued on my unexpected guest.

For the next couple of hours, my new roomie keeps calling her friends. She tells each of them the same thing.

"You have to come get me. I don't know where I am. Oh, this guy at a bar brought me home with him. And get this, his mom caught us. Now I'm sleeping in her room. Yep, on the floor. Shit. You have to come and get me. This is a nightmare from hell."

Finally around five o'clock the room grows quiet. I fall asleep.

It was *almost* a perfect day.

Opening my eyes, I check the time. It's 9:05 in the morning. Suddenly, I remember last night's drama. I check the floor. Scattered across the carpet is a pile of blankets. My roomie is gone. Someone must have picked her up. Or?

I jump out of bed and rush down the hallway, the balls of my feet skim the carpet. I open Bo's door. He's snoring like a drunken sailor. The aftereffects of last night—stale beer and tobacco mixed with his sweat—fill the air. No roomie. We need to talk.

I shower, slip into my running clothes, and take C.D. outside. Five minutes into our run, C.D. tires, and we return home. After pouring myself a cup of coffee, I grab the bills and checkbook and sit down at the kitchen table. Three times I write the wrong amount on the check, my mind still replaying acts from last night's drama.

I press my fingers into my temples, but the pulsing persists. Even the light streaming through the shutters hurts my eyes. Slowly, I stand and softly walk over to the bay window and close the shutters. A garbage truck screeches to a stop outside the window. Trash cans roll and clunk across the asphalt. The driver flicks on the motor switch, and the rumbling, grinding sound thunders through the walls. My head throbs.

I snake through the dining room into the kitchen, grab the bottle of Aleve from the cabinet, and swallow three pills. Slowly, I amble into the den, sit, and blanket my eyes with my hands. Within minutes, I'm asleep.

I feel someone nudging my shoulder.

"Mom. I'm going."

"What?"

"I've got to get back to school."

"What time is it?" I mutter.

"It's two o'clock in the afternoon."

I don't get migraines regularly, but when I do, they kick my butt. My eyelids roll upward and stop at half-mast. I catch a glimpse of Bo. His hair is combed, but his beard is rough. I get a whiff of soap mixed with the smell of dirty clothes.

"Bo, we need to chat."

"Can't, Mom. I have to get back to Raleigh."

"Nope. First we talk. We're not brushing the blond bombshell and the drinking under the carpet. Plop your body in the chair now," I say, pointing to the matching blue-and-yellow-print club chair next to mine.

I take a few breaths and collect my thoughts.

"First, I'd like you to enlighten me on why you thought you had the right to bring a girl into my house with hopes of shacking up with her?"

"Sorry, Mom. I guess I had one drink too many."

"Really? I don't believe I noticed."

Bo looks at me as if he feels like he's divulged too much information. Can he possibly be thinking he looked sober?

"I'm having a hard time trying to wrap my brain around your decision-making. Damn, Bo, you've been in and out of how many treatment centers?"

"I don't remember." Bo stares at his shoes.

He doesn't remember or he chooses not to remember? Big difference.

Bo looks in my direction, avoids eye contact, and continues. "But that's the first time I've had a drink in months."

One thing I learned while sitting in Nar-Anon meetings, "You can tell alcoholics are lying when their lips are moving."

"Sweetie. Please listen to me once and for all. You can't keep doing the same old thing and expecting different results. You have a problem. A serious problem. I'm afraid if you don't get it under control . . ." I gasp for air.

"But, Mom—"

I extend my arm. "Let me finish. I'm afraid I'm going to lose you. I can't bear the thought of you not being in my life forever. I love you so much, the good and the ugly. You're my boy, my flesh and blood, the first miracle I ever held in my arms." I wipe my tears. "I love your wit, charm, sharp mind, laugh, sensitivity, and huge heart. Damn, I wish you could see what I see."

"I know." Bo rubs his hands on his jeans. "I messed up."

"You did. Look at what we just went through with Casey. How many times did we see him dance between life and death? My God, we almost lost him. Do you have any idea what I went through? The terror, the torment I endured daily? The thought of losing my boy, of his life ending too soon, almost did me in."

I can't talk. All those blocks of pain I stuffed and stacked neatly inside me come crashing down. My body sways.

Bo reaches out and touches my knee.

"I can't make your decisions for you, Bo. Damn, I wish I could. Do you have any idea how painful it is for a mother to watch her son destroy himself?"

"I'll do better, Mom. I promise."

I want to believe him.

"Bo, I'm so sorry you got the gene. It was a hard one to dodge. Both of your grandfathers carried it. Grandpa was in his fifties by the time he recognized his best friend—the bottle—was killing him. Did you know that?"

"Maybe. Can't remember."

"He was sitting in a hotel room one night watching TV when an advertisement for an AA treatment center appeared on the screen. He recalled the gentleman said, 'If you can answer yes to the majority of these questions, you are an alcoholic.' As Grandpa tells it, by the time the last question was asked, he had answered yes to every one of them. The next day, he checked himself into a rehab center and hasn't had a drink for decades. But by then, Bo, he had little left. He had divorced Grammy, lost his business and most of his friends. Do you get where I'm going with this? What if he never acknowledged he had a problem? Can you even imagine your life without your grandpa?"

Bo stands and walks in circles.

"I can't, Mom. I feel like I've let him down. He helped me so much when I was going through treatment. And look—"

"At you now? Oh, honey. There's always hope. You just have to want it. You need to control it, rather than allowing it to control you."

To someone not having the disease, these words come easy and appear to be a simple task. But I remember sitting in on an AA meeting and listening to heartbreaking stories of how these people hit rock bottom: losing their family, friends, their home, or their sanity; becoming homeless after holding top-notch positions in the corporate world; facing felony counts; and spending years in jail. For some, hitting rock bottom happened several times, and each time it was more devastating spiritually, physically, emotionally, and financially than the last. No two stories were the same. The only thread that held them together was the disease.

I've never walked in the shoes of an addict, but I've walked beside a couple: Bo and my dad. At this point in my life, I'm not sure whose pain is worse.

I can't help thinking about some of the most beautiful people God has put in my path. They, too, fought the disease but have conquered it. Or as they would say, "Just for today." I admire and respect their strength, courage, and tenacity to take control of their lives. Easy? No way, at least that's what I've been told. But being in the presence of these people is refreshing and enlightening. I believe that they've learned the only way to change one's surroundings is by changing the self; that mirrors are their teachers, not a means of pointing a finger. They realize that they don't proclaim to walk the walk like so many do. They just do it and with great humility, grace, and honesty. To me, they are my heroes. How I want this for my boy!

I stand and wrap my arms around Bo.

"You can do it. I believe in you."

"I know, Mom."

We rock back and forth, hugging and whimpering. Bo makes promises. I listen and hope.

"Bo, I just want you to know, there will be no repeat performances like last night, no alcoholic beverages in this house . . . and if you keep making the same mistakes, don't expect me to follow you around with a mattress, cushioning your blow."

The hardest lesson I had to learn in Nar-Anon was tough love. I was taught that Bo needed to take responsibility for his choices and to own his mistakes. I've had to watch the love of my life fall, bury himself, get up, only to fall again, harder. When he screamed for help, I learned not to come. Damn. That was tough. But I feel it's been my gift to him. I can only hope one day he realizes that. Practicing tough love doesn't mean I don't love my child. It means I *really do* love him.

"I know, Mom. I've seen you in action." He smiles then kisses the top of my head.

I walk Bo to his car. The streetlights are on, and the chirping of crickets hums through the air.

After Bo opens the car door, he turns and holds me tight.

"I love you, Mom. I'm so sorry about last night."

"I'm sorry too. but it's the past now." I pull my boy close and whisper in his ear, "Let's see what you can create for your future." I kiss him on the lips and give him another big squeeze.

Bo backs out of the driveway. I wave, sending love to my boy, my heart tied into knots.

CHAPTER THIRTY

June

All the managers are gathered in the Barnes & Noble café around two laminated tables butted together for our early Monday morning meeting. The main topic of discussion is the release of J. K. Rowling's newest Harry Potter book, *Order of the Phoenix*, fifth in the series, to go on sale at midnight on June 21 in the store.

Danny, the store manager, opens the meeting.

"Scholastic, Rowling's publisher, commissioned a record 8.5 million first printing. Amazon already pre-sold one million copies. I'd like to see us sell every book in stock, and when we're out, continue taking orders. By the way," Danny glances around the table, "good job on the pre-sale of the book." He scratches his head as he looks over his notes. "I'd like each of you to share what your department is doing to prepare for the Friday night madness."

After all the managers share their information, Danny turns to me.

"So, how many activities do you have planned for the kids?"

"There will be several hours of games and contests going on prior to midnight. I have a magician lined up in the Children's Department, along with employees who will be doing crafts. Kate, another employee, has volunteered to dress up like a wizard and ask Harry Potter trivia questions."

"Good. Media?"

"Spoke to my contacts at *The Charlotte Observer*, *The Huntersville*

Herald, and *The Lake Norman Times* and they couldn't commit to an exact time, but they will be showing up during the course of the evening."

"Great. Decorations?"

"I'm still painting the stone wall to go around the information booth. The posters—magician, lion, and snake—are finished. I just need a ladder to hang—"

"There's one in the stock room," says one of the managers.

"Thanks. I'll suspend them from the ceiling with fishing wire this week. Also, my son is coming into town tomorrow to paint the flying car. I'll get that up when it's completed."

"Perfect. Great meeting, everyone. Thanks for your tireless effort to make this upcoming event a huge success."

I spend Tuesday morning running from store to store, picking up the supplies Bo needs to paint the flying Ford. By noon, the car is unpacked and his project is in place: a large piece of cardboard is centered on a plastic tarp, bordered by paints and brushes. Bo pulls into the driveway, music blasting.

"Sweetie, you are going to damage your eardrums if you keep listening to your music blaring like that."

"I'll be fine, Mom. So, what you got?" Bo surveys the garage floor. "You want me to fill that whole board with the car?"

"Uh-huh. I want it to stand out. Can you do it?"

"I guess."

Having read the Harry Potter books, Bo drops to the floor and starts sketching the car. I sit at the crown of the board.

"So, Mom. Did you hear Casey lost his job?"

"Yeah. He came home to be tested, and when he returned to Charleston, they'd filled his position. But he called yesterday and said he was hired as a busboy."

"That's great. But what's the testing for?"

"Oh, for when he goes back to school. The neuropsychological evaluation helps to chart his progress since his head injury."

"Can you pass me the light-blue paint and that large brush? Thanks. So how did that turn out?"

I smile, recalling the day Casey and I attended the meeting at the rehabilitation center.

We took our place at the long pine table opposite the team of doctors and teachers assigned to Casey's case. The lead doctor welcomed us and began explaining the ranking of Casey's verbal and performance subtest.

"Test scores are presented in percentile rank. Average scores fall within the twenty-fifth to the seventy-fourth percentiles. Low-average scores fall within the sixteenth to twenty-fourth percentiles. High scores fall within the seventy-fifth to eighty-fourth percentiles. As you can see by Casey's intellectual functioning, WAIS-III in your booklets, he scored between mildly deficient and average."

The doctor proceeded to break down each category. When he finished, Casey spoke.

"I don't know why you guys are so upset. I was like this before I had the accident."

Everyone chuckled. Me especially, because it was partially true.

One of Casey's teachers gazed in our direction.

"Even though Casey continued to lack insight into deficits and showed problems with recall, he was pleasant and cooperative throughout rehab."

Casey smiled and winked at his teacher.

"Mom. Did you drift away somewhere?" Bo asks, breaking into my memory.

"Sorry, sweetie. I was just thinking. So, to answer your question, he has some deficits—memory, attention, reading fluency, calculation, and math. But with time, depending on how hard Casey is willing to work, those abilities can be strengthened."

"Interesting. Can you hand me the black and white paints for the tires? Thanks. Anything else?"

"They discouraged him from being a captain of a ship. Thank God. Recommended he stay on his meds. Suggested he take advantage of the added benefits through student services. And—"

I let out a long-winded sigh.

"What, Mom?"

"They feel if he returns to school, he just might have to take a course twice to fully retain the information."

C.D. barks at the door. I let him out. He curls up beside Bo.

"Bo, the car is really turning out good, honey. I wish you'd do something with that talent of yours."

"Thanks, Mom. Can you hand me the silver paint? So what did you think about Casey's encounter on the train? Wasn't that unbelievable?"

"It really was. If I close my eyes, Bo, I can picture that moment all over again."

Casey was on Amtrak en route to Washington, D.C., to see Grace, when my phone rang.

"Mom. Are you sitting down? You won't believe this. The most amazing thing just happened."

"Slow down, Casey. Take a breath. Start at the beginning."

"Okay. So I went to the smoking car to have a cigarette. While I was there, another dude joined me and we got talking. While we were shooting the shit, I told him about my motorcycle accident in Charleston back in October."

"Yeah." I said, wondering why Casey would share the details of his accident with a complete stranger.

"So he said to me, 'Where did the accident happen? I told him on the corner of Spring and President Street, and the guy just stared at me. So I said, 'What, dude?' And he smiled."

"Smiled? Why?" I asked.

"This was the best part, Mom. He told me he was right behind me that morning, and he's the person who called 911."

Shivers ran up and down my body.

"What?"

"Yep. That's what he said. So you know what I did? I hugged him and said, 'Dude, you saved my life. Thank you.' Then I hugged the guy again. Anyway, Mom, I know you're into all of this synchronicity or whatever you call it, and couldn't wait to tell you. Call you when I get back from Grace's. Gotta run."

After we hung up, I looked up and thanked the heavens and all the angels for watching over my boy.

"Mom. You finished reliving that moment?"

We both laugh.

"Look at your creation, Bo. A real Flying Ford Anglia. It's awesome, Son."

"Yeah, just have to finish painting the sky. Thought I'd add a full moon up in the corner. What do ya think?"

"Go for it."

"So, Mom. How do *you* think Casey's doing?"

"Better. Not one hundred percent, but better."

When Casey came home in April, I'd noticed the bill of his hat was moving toward the center. Not quite there yet, but it was inching its way to the front. It felt as if the walk-in was trying to show me that he was slowly transitioning out of Casey's body.

Bo finishes his masterpiece, and we sit on the cold cement floor. He tells me about his girlfriend and how much she adores him. A little humility would do him good. He showers, meets up with a couple of his friends, and gets back on the road to Raleigh around seven o'clock that evening.

CHAPTER THIRTY-ONE

August–October

Even though Bobby and I were legally divorced three years ago, today we reconciled our differences concerning the financial settlement.

While driving home from the lawyer's office, my mind fills with monkey chatter, and I can't turn it off. *What are you going to do now? You're finally free. The kids are away at school. You have your whole life in front of you. It's time to think about you.*

Emotionally it wears me down. All I want to do is go home and take a nap. I pull into the garage, insert the key into the basement door, and hear the phone ringing. I double-step up the stairs to the kitchen and grab the receiver. It's my favorite cousin, Jim, on the other line.

"Listen, I've been thinking. I would love for you to come and work here."

"New York? Seriously, Jim?"

"Listen to me. Northeast Parent & Child Society is a great agency dealing with abused, neglected, and poverty-stricken children. We need compassionate people like you working for us."

"Why now? You've been CEO for a year."

"Just doing some restructuring."

"I don't know, Jim. Casey's in Charleston with his sister now. Bo's at NC State, and I'm smack dab in the middle of them. New York is so far away."

I open the medicine cabinet and down two aspirin while musing over moving. That's when I decide to share with Jim how my day went down.

"Sounds like my proposal is coming at the perfect time."

"Let me sleep on it."

Even though I have thirty cousins, I am the closest to Jim, but our closeness didn't happen overnight.

Yes, we are the same age. Yes, we hung out in the same circle in high school and college. Yes, we engaged in small talk and laughed. But it never went deeper than that. Mostly because I was always afraid if I spoke my heart, Jim would laugh. Which was absurd, yet I'd formed my opinion of him at a young age when all I heard was, "Jim is brilliant." Back then I had self-esteem issues, so I figured I'd just keep things between us on a surface level.

But at the age of twenty-one, while slow dancing at a mutual friend's wedding in St. Louis, we reached a new depth in our relationship.

His words in that moment are still vivid in my memory: "You know, cuz, you and I have been through many lifetimes together."

I moved my head off Jim's shoulder and looked at him, my eyes curious.

What? Jim has a spiritual side? I thought he was just a party animal. In fact, he could have played John Belushi's role in *National Lampoon's Animal House*. At least that was the side of him I saw during our teenage years. But when he mentioned "other lifetimes," a topic that interested me, he had my attention.

He continued. "It's true. I knew it the first time I looked into your eyes when we were three years old."

I laughed, not because what Jim said was funny, but because I had finally found someone who had the same beliefs that I did.

"Yeah, and we probably had too much fun," I said, slapping him on the shoulder. "So, here we are back on Earth again trying to learn the lessons we missed in our last lifetime."

After that dance, there was no turning back for us. It's as if we picked up where we had left off hundreds of years ago. Our relationship continued to grow but on a more spiritual level. When times got tough, Jim appeared on the scene, as if he had an inner inkling of what my soul needed.

Like now.

Four weeks later, my plane lands at Albany International, an airport that could fit inside one terminal at Charlotte Douglas. I grab my belongings and follow the crowds to the baggage claim area. As I'm riding the escalator down, I notice Jim searching the crowds with his hands inside his navy shorts. He looks up, spots me, and begins waving and smiling, looking like Santa Claus sporting a black beard.

My feet glide onto the tile floor. Jim wraps his burly arms around me, and my feet dangle in midair.

"Good to see you, cuz."

Jim talks non-stop on our fifteen-minute excursion to Clifton Park.

"Ahead is Saratoga Springs. Southeast of us is Albany. Schenectady is to the west."

As my head moves from right to left, my eyes blink in rapid succession, as if I'm pushing the shutter button on a camera, capturing each scene—rolling hills, soaring trees, and lush countryside dotted with weather-beaten red barns and farmhouses.

Jim pulls into the driveway and carries my bag inside. Cathy, his wife, wraps me in her loving arms.

"Don't you look nice decked out in your white-collared shirt, navy striped sweater, flared jeans, and boots. Oh, and you still have your Dorothy Hamill haircut, just a tad longer." Cathy ruffles my hair. "Love it. I can't believe you're still tan."

Before I get to say anything, Jim breaks in. "Come on Pattie, Cathy and I would like to show you around the house."

After getting the grand tour, we sit down to dinner. Jim plots out our agenda for the next couple of days.

"Tomorrow I'll take you to Northeast Parent & Child Society and introduce you to your future coworkers in the development office. Then I've made arrangements for you to tour our facilities: Children's Home, School at Northeast, and the Children's Shelter. More wine?"

I slide my glass across the table.

"The following day, we'll explore areas where you might want to live. If this move feels right to you, we'll discuss how we'll move forward."

A month later, I land the job—giving me fourteen days to pack, set up a dinner with the kids to break the news, and find a home for C.D.

I call the kids and invite them to dinner on Saturday. It's vital that I see their facial expressions when I break the news. Their input is important to me.

First, I call Bo.

"Sure, Mom. Sounds great. Was planning on coming into town anyway on Saturday."

Next I dial Casey.

"Sweetie. Bo's coming into Charlotte this weekend, and I'm going to call Annie after we hang up. I'm really missing my kids. Like to take you all out to dinner. What do you say?"

"Sounds like fun. I'll catch a ride with Annie."

I punch in Annie's number and extend the invitation.

"Can't, Mom. I have two major tests Monday. You remember how sophomore year is? Or do you?" She laughs. "Why? What's up?"

I spring the news on Annie. At first there's silence. Then she says, "I'm happy for you, Mom."

Deep in my heart, I know this transition is going to be tough on her. Annie has always been my low-maintenance child, my rock. Even though our relationship has shifted over the years—from her being my appendage throughout grade school, to learning to fly on her own—she still needs her mama, as I need my little girl.

"Sweetie, I promise to call you every night or once a week, whatever works best for you. We can talk for hours. Okay? In a couple of months, we'll be together for Christmas," I say, trying to reassure her that the move won't put a damper on our relationship.

Annie and I continue to chat about school, her social life, and Carey, the new guy she has eyes for.

"Oh and, sweetie, Casey's going to call you for a ride. I'm not sure how he's going to get—"

"Don't worry, Mom. Casey can hitch a ride with one of his Charlotte buddies. Someone is always heading that way. Can't wait to see you in December. Call me after you have dinner with the boys."

Saturday night, the boys walk into the restaurant at seven, laughing and joking with each other. I'm already seated. They're late, of course, and full of excuses, as usual. But I don't care.

I jump out of the booth and hug Bo then Casey.

"Casey, look at your ball cap inching its way to the front." I slap the bill of his hat.

"What?" His brows furrow.

"Never mind."

Now is not the time to have a conversation with Casey about his walk-in. In the future? Maybe.

"Sit, guys."

The kids put their phones on vibrate. For the next hour, I feel like I'm sitting across the table from Pinocchio, as Bo's imagination kicks in and he shares one outlandish story after another. Finally he comes up for air. I speak.

"So, Casey, how are you doing taking twelve hours this semester?"

There's laughter. Bo nudges Casey as if he already has the inside scoop.

"Well—"

"Go ahead. Tell her Casey," Bo prompts. "You'll love this, Mom. Then again . . ."

"Bo, be quiet." Casey pipes in.

I look at Casey. He looks at me.

"So, what's going on, sweetie?"

"I had to drop two of my courses. It was too much, Mom," Casey says, looking at me with sorry, puppy dog eyes.

I reach across the table and grab his hand.

"Sweetie. It's okay. Really. The doctor said that many times when kids return to school after a brain injury, they end up taking courses over again. It just takes time."

"I know."

Bo interrupts.

"So, Mom. Why did you want us to meet you for dinner?"

I clear my throat.

"I was offered a new job."

"Really?" Casey says.

"That's great," Bo replies. "Where?"

"Upstate New York."

"New York? That's so far away," Casey mutters.

"I know, sweetie. That's why—"

"Doing what?" Bo asks.

I give the boys the details and watch Casey fidget with the silverware. Bo looks me square in the eyes.

"Mom, it's time you get a life. Go have some fun. We're only a phone call away." He laughs and adds, "Or a plane ticket, right Casey?"

Not for one second, one breath, did Bo think about himself. I'm moved.

"And, Casey, how about you?"

"I'm good, Mom. Happy for you."

But his eyes tell a different story. We've grown close over this past year, and even though we don't see each other that often, I believe he finds comfort knowing I'm close by.

We walk to the car, and I'm twisted like a pretzel in my boys' arms, smiling. Casey grabs his bag out of Bo's car.

"Case, you might want to stay at your dad's tonight. My condo is wall-to-wall boxes."

"Okay. Want to do breakfast?"

"Sounds like a plan. Give me a call when you two wake up."

We kiss and hug. I grab the boys again. But this time my head lingers on their shoulders. I inhale their Armani cologne, a scent I've grown to identify with my boys.

Two days later, the phone starts ringing off the hook. People are inquiring about the ad I put in the paper for a free Bijon.

Twice a family picked up C.D. then returned him the following day. That's when I realize I need to explain to C.D. why I'm giving him away. I cuddle him in my arms and speak.

"I'm going far, far away, C.D. And my new job requires long workdays. I just can't stomach you being alone for hours. I won't know a soul in New York who can take care of you. Oh, bud, I love you so much. You've brought so much happiness into our lives. I want you to spend the rest of your years with a loving family. Okay? I'll always carry you in my heart. Always."

C.D. licks my face as if he understands.

The following day, the phone rings.

"I'm calling about your ad. I'd really like to get a dog for my grandson. Is he still available?"

"He is."

"Can we come right over?"

It's love at first sight.

I tousle C.D.'s furry white curls and give him a kiss on his way out the door. "Remember what I told you."

The little boy tightens his grip around his new best friend and carries him to the car. C.D. never looks back. Never barks. Never yelps. The car pulls away, and I shout, "I love you, boy," knowing he won't return.

Moving day arrives. After I drag the last bag from my bedroom to the garage and cram it into the car, I go back inside and say my goodbyes to our home—the home that has provided safety and comfort from the darkness to the light.

I step into Casey's room. My eyes scan the empty walls and space. Casey's saga comes alive. Again.

It's a story of a boy who beat the odds, struggled to relearn the basics—talking, walking, eating, and thinking—fought to understand the complexities of life, endured the judgments of others, adapted to a new norm, and learned to rediscover himself. Perhaps with my help, perhaps with the help of this spiritual walk-in. Either way, he's moved on.

I visit each room in turn until, at last, there's no more stalling the inevitable.

After I merge onto I-77N, I look into my rearview mirror and say goodbye to Charlotte, thanking the city for eight years filled with my family's fair share of highs and lows. Without being yanked out of my comfort zone, I never would have had the chance to stretch myself and grow in ways I never imagined. It's as if, as a mother, I was finding myself at the same time the kids were finding themselves.

My eyes shift back to the windshield. I never look back.

Three days later, I meet the movers at my new condo. For six hours, they move furniture and boxes into the house. When there's no more room, they fill the garage. Finally, the truck pulls out of the driveway, and I call my kids.

"How's the rental?" Casey asks.

"Very cool. You're going to love it. It's a condo complex. I have the unit on the end with open space to the side yard and the backyard. There are three bedrooms, two baths, kitchen, and eat-in area, dining room, and a good-size family room with vaulted ceilings and a fireplace."

"Sounds big."

"Probably more room than I need, but the perfect size for when you kids visit. How's school, sweetie?"

"Tough. But I'm getting through it. Listen, Mom, I have another call coming in. Buzz you this week. Love you."

I was hoping to have a longer conversation with Casey. I didn't even get a chance to ask him about his job.

Next, I dial Annie.

"Hey, sweetie. I made it."

"Long trip?"

"Yeah, but I stopped outside of New York and spent the night. I wanted to make the trip in one day but—"

"Are you in downtown Albany?"

"No. In a little town called Voorheesville."

"Weird name."

"Yeah, I know. But, Annie, you will love how secluded it is. I've even seen deer in the backyard, and the neighborhood is filled with dogs," I add, knowing how Annie loves animals.

From the time Annie was in middle school, she talked about becoming a vet. Then senior year her dream was squelched. Her friends kept telling her, "You have to have a 3.8 and above to get into vet school." Lacking confidence in her ability, she gave their words credence, and her future career changed direction.

"Deer? Dogs? Sounds cool, Mom. Send me pictures. Meeting up with Carey. Love you."

First Casey has to run, now Annie. I was really hoping we could talk. I grab a health bar and a bottled water, step outside on the back porch, and breathe in the fall air. I call Bo.

"Hi, honey. I'm finally here."

"Do you love it, Mom?"

"I do. I live up on a hill. Albany Country Club is a street away. According to my landlord's son, who lives behind me, the vistas of Hudson Valley and the mountains are spectacular from there. Maybe we can sneak over there at Christmas."

"Cool. Did you start work yet?"

"No. Going to unpack tomorrow then head into the office the next day."

"You'll finish unpacking in one day?"

"No way, but I'm anxious to start my new job."

"You'll be great, Mom."

"Thanks, sweetie. How's life with you?"

"School's good. Having a blast with my friends. Hey, how far are you from New York City?"

"About three hours, depending on traffic. Why?"

"Was thinking we could check it out over Christmas. Ya know, get in the Christmas spirit like we did when we lived on Long Island."

The first winter after we arrived in Huntington, the family took the train into New York City. We visited Rockefeller Center, took a carriage ride around the park, and went to an off-Broadway show.

Maybe just the thought of me living so close to the city has stirred up a past memory for Bo.

After we finish talking, I move back inside. Standing in the family room, I spot the perfect corner for the Christmas tree.

Only two months away.

CHAPTER THIRTY-TWO

December

In less than three weeks, the kids' plane will arrive in Albany. So much to do!

I drive to the Christmas tree lot early this morning in hopes of beating the weekend crowd. I meander through the lot until I spot the tallest and fattest tree. An employee approaches.

"Can I help you, ma'am?"

"Yes, please." I point. "I'll take that one."

He calls for assistance. The two men strap the tree on top of the car.

"After you pay, ma'am, you're good to go. Do you have someone at home to help you unload the tree?"

"No. Why?"

"Ma'am, that tree weighs two hundred pounds."

I size it up. He's kidding, right? It looks like an ordinary tree.

I park the car in the driveway and grab a pair of scissors from the garage. With my feet on the running board, I cut the rope and give the tree a push. It doesn't budge. I step down, grab hold of the branches, and tug, and yank. The beast crashes on the ground.

I sigh, knowing our dance has just begun.

With my hands clutched around the eight-inch trunk, I shimmy the tree down the sidewalk and through the front door. The branches, twice the width of the doorway, get lodged in the doorframe. Determined to overcome the obstacle, I roll up my sleeves, grab the trunk again, and pull until the crown rests inside the door.

I step into the family room and drum my forefingers against my lips, evaluating the next steps of our dance.

Firmly, I grasp hold of the upper trunk and heave it into the air. The base of the tree slides into the stand. My hands climb down the trunk, and I hold it steady as I tighten the screws. I let go. It holds.

Panting like an overheated dog, I take off my sweatshirt and toss it on the chair, wanting nothing more than to take a time-out.

Instead, I grab the black garbage bag that sits under the tree and carefully drag the heavy cargo along the carpet until my backside smacks against the wall. As I slide from behind, I unfold the bent branches, hoping the damage is only temporary.

With awe and gratitude, I stand before the twelve-foot tree and admire its beauty in its nakedness. I bow, curtsy, and thank the tree for our dance.

"But, my lady," I say aloud, "no one goes to the Christmas ball without wearing her finest."

I grab the box of decorations, place them on the coffee table, and begin dressing the strong yet graceful lady. I layer her arms in bling. Scallop crimson beads over her fingertips. Adorn her in nostalgic family jewels. Attach red gingham bows to her limbs. And hat her with a porcelain angel wearing a white-and-gold evening gown.

Proud of my handiwork, I step back and admire my labor of love.

The next morning, the tree leans forward. I grab three books, crawl under the tree, and slide the books under the stand. It holds. Teeters. Crashes on top of me.

Immobilized by the weight of the tree, my eyes mist over as I struggle to set myself free. I tuck my arms under my ribs, press down on my elbows, and dig my toes into the carpet. As I slowly crawl backward, I can feel my jeans roll up to my knees, my T-shirt climb up to my neck, and my heart pound. Jagged limbs dig into my skin. Blood seeps through the open wounds. I keep moving.

Finally free, I hoist the tree and prop it against the wall.

Bling and beads dangle from stray branches and puddle to the floor. The family's nostalgic ornaments, mostly shattered, carpet the family room. The angel, sitting sideways, is wedged between the branches, her feathers bent and broken.

In a flash of a second, the tree dressed in her best was instantly disrobed, like she was years ago when the kids were young.

We lived in California, and our party guests were due to arrive in thirty minutes. I was in the kitchen creating a cheese platter when I heard a crash in the living room. I raced into the room. The Christmas tree was tilted forward. Ornaments and lights were strewn across the floor. The kids, dressed in their pajamas, sat on the step.

"What happened?" I asked Bobby as I wiped my hands on my apron.

"Annie pulled a candy cane off the tree, and it fell."

I grabbed Annie. Kissed her tears. Assured her everything was going to be okay. "Time for bed, sweetie," I said, putting her in Bobby's arms.

Tears raced down my cheeks as I leaned the tree against the wall, stuck the lights back on the limbs, and rehung the ornaments. That's when Bo, wise beyond his years, spoke up.

"Mom. I think it's beautiful just the way it is. Don't cry."

Bo's words ring in my ears as I catch my reflection in the mirror and notice that I'm wearing remnants of the tree. Ornament hooks and tinsel hang from my hair. Needles cling and stick to my T-shirt and pants.

Not wanting to lose sight of this bittersweet moment, I run into the bedroom and slip into my Christmas sweater. Back in the living room, I grab the camera and attach it to the tripod. Searching for props, I tuck the book *'Twas the Night Before Christmas* under the fat lady's dress and shove a Santa hat on my head. I hit the timer button, lean into the tree, and manage to smile.

The camera flashes. I get back up, pull the debris from my hair and clothes, and start all over again.

Two weeks later, I am rushing around the condo getting ready for the kids' arrival in the afternoon. I clean, blow up a mattress and put it in the third bedroom, stack presents under the tree, and tuck the kids' letters between the branches. Once everything is in place, I shower and drive to the airport.

My phone rings. It's Bo.

"Mom. Our plane landed at four instead of four thirty. You on your way?"

"Pulling into a parking space as we speak."

Inside the airport, I ride the escalator to the baggage claim area. My heart skips a beat as I spot the kids. The boys are engaged in another episode of the "Bo and Casey Show."

Bo kicks Casey's book bag.

Casey picks it up and puts in on his shoulder.

Bo taps Casey on the right shoulder, then the left, then the right again.

"Get off me, Bo." Casey slaps Bo's hand.

Bo pulls Casey's hat off his head and sticks it behind his back.

"Give it to me, Bo. Now."

With the hat clutched between his fingers, Bo stretches his hand. Casey tries to grab it. Bo tucks it behind his back again and laughs.

Annie shakes her head. Turns and looks my way. She waves. The boys mimic her.

I rush toward the kids and give them the biggest hug and kiss.

Casey pulls on the suitcase handle and walks toward the door.

"Let's go, Mom. I get front seat. There's no way I'm sitting next to Bo."

Annie walks beside me.

"Mom. Do you think it will snow while we're here?"

I look at the gray clouds hanging low in the sky and inhale.

"Looks like snow. Smells like snow. I'd say there's a pretty good chance it's on the way." I pull Annie close. "I missed you so much."

Ten minutes later, I drive into the neighborhood.

"Which one is yours, Mom?" Annie's voice rings with excitement.

"The cute yellow unit ahead."

I pull into the garage. Jump out of the car. Rush to the front of the condo. Unlock the door. The kids follow with their bags.

Prior to going to the airport, I'd plugged in the tree lights. I wanted the wonderment of Christmas to assail them the minute they stepped into the condo.

Once inside, I stand in the entryway, waiting to capture the kids' expressions.

"You like?"

"Really neat. Love the sunken family room and French doors in the dining room. Do they open to a deck?" Annie asks.

"Yes. I'll take you out there shortly."

"Holy shit, Mom. Where'd you get that tree?" Casey blurts as he wheels his bag inside.

"Better yet," Bo asks, following behind, "how'd you get that monstrosity through the door?"

"Long story and an adventure to boot."

Annie releases the handle on her suitcase. Steps into the family room. Fingers the familiar old ornaments. Her eyes light up as she moves around the tree.

"I love it, Mom."

I motion to the door to my left.

"Bo and Casey, you two are in—"

"I get the—"

"No, I get the bed. I'm the oldest."

Ignoring the bickering, I move toward Annie.

"Is this the tree that fell on top of you, Mom?"

"It is, sweetie."

"Looks better than it did in your Christmas card."

I smile, thinking about what the tree and I have gone through: joy to sorrow and back again.

Annie drags her bag down the hallway to her room.

Casey walks into the kitchen and steps out on the deck.

"Mom. Come quick. Deer." He points to the open field.

"Want to feed them?"

"Sure."

I pull a loaf of frozen bread from the freezer and hand Casey a couple of slices.

"What do you want me to do with this?"

"Toss it out on the lawn like a Frisbee. Trust me. They'll come."

Casey throws, and within a matter of minutes, the meadow is dotted with several bucks, does, and two fawns, fighting for the sailing bread.

"Aren't they beautiful, Case?"

He nods. "Do they come often?"

"Every morning. And they keep growing in numbers. I believe they trust me now. Know I'm not going to harm them. It's like we've become family. Want to hear a great story?"

"Sure."

"The other morning I was out on my run and came across eight or so deer. I knew it was just about feeding time, so I said aloud, 'I'm heading home. Meet you back at the house.' They didn't budge. They just stood there staring at me. Casey, stop rolling your eyes. So, I got home, walked out on the deck, and—"

"Let me guess. The deer were in the backyard."

"Yep."

"Really, Mom? You believe the deer understood what you were saying?"

I shrug.

"Whatever."

Casey and I linger for some time in silence. He's with his thoughts, and I'm with mine.

Over a year ago, I lost the son I once knew. When that happened, I lost a part of myself, and something inside me died. But I learned to push through the pain, push through the heartache, and push until I couldn't push anymore. It was at that point of no return—pure emotional exhaustion—that I surrendered and accepted life the way it was.

Casey is not the same person he used to be. But neither am I. Honestly, I'm okay with that.

At seven o'clock, we attend Christmas Eve Mass at St. Mary's, one of the oldest churches in Albany. After Mass, we eat dinner downtown. At ten o'clock, we arrive home, exhausted.

The following morning, I tiptoe out of my bedroom, turn the lights on in the kitchen, and plug in the coffee pot. As I'm pouring my second cup of coffee, the kids pile into the kitchen, rubbing their eyes.

"Merry Christmas. Sleep okay?"

They nod.

Casey talks through his yawn.

"Can we open presents now?"

The kids and I stroll into the family room and sit down—Casey and Annie take the wingback chairs facing the roaring fire, and Bo sits on the step facing the picture window.

"Mom, I can't believe you don't have a couch. Why didn't you bring one from Charlotte?"

"They were falling apart and not worth the cost to ship them. I'll get one eventually, Bo."

Casey taps his fingers on the end table.

"Mom. Can we get going?"

"Casey, I was talking to Mom."

"About nothing, Bo."

As I'm reprimanding the boys, Annie stands, grabs an armful of presents, and passes them out.

I get my camera and set it on the coffee table next to me.

"Okay, Bo, you can start."

One by one, the kids unwrap presents, and their excited voices push the music and crackling fire to the background. I snap one picture after another—Bo with his pinstripe men's dress shirt, gray silk tie, leather belt and wallet, toboggan, and plaid boxers; Annie with her cashmere scarf, robe, T-shirt, purse, picture frames, leather boots, and thank you notes; Casey with his ball caps, T-shirts, cargo pants, sweatshirt, striped boxers, and socks.

Hours later, the last present has been unwrapped. I grab a garbage bag and stuff the wrapping paper inside. Annie and Casey gather their gifts and take them to their bedrooms. Bo lingers.

"Mom, come sit next to me. Got a surprise for you." He hands me a card. "This is in place of my letter on the tree."

After all these years Bo remembered.

"Go ahead. Read it out loud."

I press my fingers into my eyes, blotting away teardrops filled with love.

> *Mom,*
>
> *I don't think that anyone can put into words a mother's love for her children.*
>
> *When I was little you were my world. As I grew, I came to realize that there was more. But the older I get, the more I see that without your strength, love, encouragement, understanding, joy, peacefulness, and tender touch, the world just wouldn't be anywhere near worth living in.*
>
> *I know you'll always be with me, everywhere I go.*
>
> *You're in my thoughts, my heart, and my prayers.*
>
> *Love always.*
>
> *Your son,*
>
> *Bo*

Holding Bo's face, my hands spasm, his words pulling at my heartstrings.

"Beautiful, Bo. Thank you. I will cherish this forever. You're a good boy. Remember that. I love you so much." We kiss. I press his letter to my heart.

Casey walks into the family room with a bagel in his hand.

"What are you two doing?"

"Mom's reading my card."

"Wow. No excuses this year, Bo? You actually came through? How long has it been? Let me answer that. Forever."

Bo stands, ignores Casey's comment, and goes to his room.

"You okay, Mom?"

"I'm good. Really good. But you know what I would really like?"

"What?"

"For you to be a little nicer."

"Oh, Mom, that's how Bo and I talk to each other."

Casey offers me his hand.

I place my palm in his and look up.

"Your hat?"

"What about it?"

"It's almost on straight."

I can't believe I didn't notice it before now. Is the walk-in preparing for his exit?

"I always wear it like this, Mom."

He pats the top of his cap and walks back into the kitchen.

Oh, no you don't.

The next morning, I walk into the family room. The kids are clustered around the coffee table, whispering. Bo speaks.

"Mom, let's go into New York City. I've already called the hotel. They're holding a room for us."

"I don't know, Bo. I've never driven into the city. You know how nervous I get when I don't know where I'm going."

Whenever I got lost driving the kids to their tournaments—basketball, soccer, or baseball—on the other side of town in Charlotte, I would turn the volume down on the radio, knuckle the steering wheel, and listen to my heartbeat throb in my ears. Now he wants me to drive into the city, filled with taxicabs that weave in and out of lanes and honk incessantly.

"How about taking the train?"

"Nope. Mom, you can do this. You drive. I'll navigate."

Four hours later, after getting lost once, we pull up to the hotel. Bo goes to the counter and gets the key to our room. We drop off our bags. Take the elevator down to the lobby. Step outside and hail a taxi.

"Twin Towers, please."

The kids stand in front of the wired fence where one of our nation's most horrific events took place. Annie shouts.

"Mom, take our picture."

"Got it. Where to next?"

"I really want to see the tribute to John Lennon—Strawberry Fields Forever in Central Park," Bo says.

"I want to go shopping," say Annie and Casey simultaneously.

We dicker over the options and finally agree. A taxi pulls up.

"Central Park, please."

As we walk toward our destination, enjoying the sunshine and abnormally high temperatures, we watch people riding their bikes and rollerblading. We stop in front of John Lennon's site. The kids lean on the fence, and I take several pictures. Bo's wearing his new toboggan. Annie has her T-shirt tucked under her jacket. Casey sports his new cargo pants.

We spend the rest of the day shopping. Later we grab a bite to eat then retire for the evening.

The day after we return to Albany from the city, I drive the kids back to the airport. At the curb, we hug and say our goodbyes. I wave and shout "I love you" until they disappear into the post-Christmas crowds.

While driving home, my throat tightens as I relive the last few days: sitting on the step with Bo, reading his card; seeing Casey's hat creep back in place; and listening to Annie's sweet voice as she gushes with gratitude for the tiniest thing. I can still hear the robust laughter and the constant chatter, feel the sweetness of every kiss, the tenderness of each hug, and those moments when our hearts beat as one—silently and deeply with love.

CHAPTER THIRTY-THREE

January 16, 2004 and . . .

Since I arrived in Albany, my weekday schedule has remained the same: wake up, meditate, go to work, put in a ten-hour day, come home, eat, call the kids, meditate, go to bed—until today.

Restless, I wake up at five o'clock. I make a pot of coffee, pour myself a cup, and sit down. No matter how hard I try to shake my dream—blink my eyes, read yesterday's newspaper, review my upcoming meeting with the volunteers—my nightmare persists. I settle back in my chair and allow it to play.

I park my car in front of Bobby's condo and rush to the door. It's wide open.

I clear my throat.

"Hello. Anyone home?"

No one answers. I step inside.

Lined against the dining room wall are Bobby's four sisters, dressed in black. They nod as our eyes connect, as though they've been waiting for me. I stop in front of each of them and put my hands on their cheeks. Not a word is spoken.

The scene shifts.

Outside, I'm sitting on the concrete step with Bobby. Tears flood his face. I stroke his knee, and he looks down.

"Everything is going to be okay," I say, choking on my words.

The scene ends.

Now, as when I woke from my dream, my body quakes.

The clock on the wall reads five fifty five. With no time to meditate, I shower, get dressed, and go to work.

My day is consumed with meetings, phone calls, and signing letters thanking the volunteers who adopted a child or family in our care for Christmas. Around five, my phone rings. It's one of my colleagues.

"Hey, Pattie. We're still on for tonight, right? I'll pick you up at seven thirty. The girls are so excited to meet you. Would you mind bringing an appetizer? I know this is short notice but—"

"It's fine. I'll stop at the store on my way home."

A couple hours later, I'm standing in the kitchen wrapping foil around the hot crab dip when the doorbell rings.

I answer. Judy steps in wearing a black tweed coat that touches the ankles of her black leather boots, with a multicolored scarf around her neck.

"Wow. You look great."

"Thanks. Hey, what's wrong? Your eyes are puffy."

"Nothing. Just give me a second to grab my purse and appetizer."

Judy stops me. "You want to tell me what's going on?"

"Just feeling off. Had this dream last night, and just can't shake it."

"You'll feel better once we get to the party."

After driving through the snowplowed backstreets of Albany, we finally pull into the driveway.

The ladies and I fill our plates with a variety of appetizers—Swedish meatballs, artichoke and spinach dip, fresh fruit and cheese—and settle in the living room. While we're talking about the most recent books we've read on spirituality, the hostess turns and looks at me. "Any good reads you want to recommend?"

"Sylvia Brown's most recent book. She talks about us having five different exit points during our life." When the last word rolls off my tongue, I feel someone punch me in the back. My torso arcs forward. Slowly, I turn my head and look behind. No one's there. I scan the room— all ladies accounted for. The sickening feeling that's been gnawing at me all day returns. I lean toward Judy.

"I need to go home. NOW."

Once inside the door at home, I hear the answering machine beeping. I press the button.

"This is your cousin Jim." He pauses then clears his throat. "Cathy and I are out of town, and she just called home to get our messages. There was one from Bobby, and it was quite garbled. I think something is wrong."

My heart quickens. I can feel my blood pressure rising. The second message plays.

"Mom, this is Annie. Where are you? You need to call me right away." She weeps through her words.

I can hardly catch my breath. I pick up the receiver and dial Bobby. He answers on the second ring.

"Jim said you—"

"He's d—" His whimpers chop his words.

"I can't hear you. What did you say?" My heart races. My palms sweat.

What tumbles out choppily are the words, "He's dead."

Bobby's moans come across the wires. My legs weaken. I grab hold of the counter. I want to scream that Casey can't be dead. He beat the odds. Instead, I ask the question I don't want to hear the answer to.

"Who's dead?"

"Bo's dead."

"Can't be. I just talked to him a few nights ago. He wanted to know how to cook lobster tails."

"He died at five o'clock this morning."

The exact moment I woke up from my dream.

Bobby continues, but I barely hear a word he says. "No need to fly in tonight. Nothing can be done at this hour. Catch a flight out in the morning. Annie can pick you up at the airport."

Shrouded in darkness, my spirit plummets into the abyss. I can't hear myself breathe. I can't feel my heart beating. I can't feel. Period. I want to ask what happened. All that comes out is "What . . . " But Bobby understands.

"He went out with three other guys. They got a hotel room. Guess they thought that was better than getting a DUI. Sounds like there was some heavy drinking and drugs involved. At five in the morning, Bo's friend Ryan tried to wake him up, but he didn't move. So . . . uh . . ."

He didn't move. My boy took his last breath, and I wasn't there. No. This can't be. This isn't the way it's supposed to happen. I want to ask, where is he now? Where's my boy? I need to be with him. I need to hold him. Rock him in my arms. I need to tell him over and over again, I love you. I feel sick. I want to hang up, but Bobby keeps talking.

"So, Ryan called his mom. She told him to call 911."

I want to say "stop." I can't bear to hear another word.

My eyes land on a picture of Annie, Bo, and Casey taken at Ground Zero. They're smiling. My emotions get lodged in my throat. I try to swallow, but my saliva backwashes over my tongue. I want to be with my kids. Hold them. Take away their pain. Tell them everything is going to be okay. But I would only be lying.

"Annie and Casey? Where are they?"

"Here."

"How are they . . ."

"A mess."

Somehow, I make it through the rest of the worst phone call of my life. I tell Bobby I'll book a flight to arrive in Charlotte in the morning and will call Annie with the details.

I hang up the phone and begin calling family. But I don't know who I talk to or what I say. It doesn't matter. None of it matters.

I walk toward my bedroom, knowing I have to pack. After I toss a few items in my bag, the room spins, and I fall on the bed. My body convulses. I pound my fist into the mattress.

"Bo. Honey, can you hear me? You can't be gone. I won't allow it. Please tell me this is all a bad dream."

I bury my face in my hands, press my fingers to my mouth, trying to silence the animal sounds within. My tears gush like water blasting from a fire hydrant. No matter how hard I try, I can't stop the agonizing cries. There is no way to stop the gut-wrenching pain. I yell into the darkness,

"God, I can't do this anymore. I feel like someone just plucked my heart from my chest, stomped on it, and it splattered into a thousand pieces."

With no life left in me, I succumb to the black of night, the rage in my heart, and the darkness of my soul.

Bo appears to me in my dreams, his eyes staring into mine. It's as if he's come to help me deal with my pain. I reach out, touch his face, and feel the warmth of his skin on my hands. "Bo, sweetie, is this really you?" I garble through my tears. "Oh, honey, I miss you so much. Come back. Please."

Bo smiles tenderly, his face illuminated against the backdrop of smoky clouds. For moments on end, moments beyond space and time, I get lost in his ocean-blue eyes, as if his spirit is drawing me deeper into his. He whispers, "Mom, I love you. I will always love you, and I'll always be with you. But listen to me. You and Dad need to find peace with one another. If you don't, you'll become prisoners of the past. You'll never be free." His face vanishes into the darkness, yet his voice trails. "It's all about love, Mom."

I open my eyes and sob through my words.

"Oh, Bo. I want you to know how much I love you. I'm not sure why God took you so soon. Maybe your work was over, and it was time for you to move on. God, I wish it didn't have to be this way. I wish I could turn the clock back and start all over. But dammit, I can't. There's so much I wanted to say to you, but I never had the chance. Listen to your mama. Okay? I want you to take all of this into your heart and hold it there.

"Thank you for being my teacher. Every part of your life was a reflection of what I needed to learn. When you came into my room with my purse strung over your shoulder and said, 'Bye. Bye. Fun,' you made me giggle and smile. When you went into treatment, I shuddered with fear as I let the blood-sucking skeletons out of the closet. When I showed up at Nar-Anon and finally heard the definition of insanity, I fell to my knees and wept, knowing what I had to do. When I took my power back, I felt my heart shatter each time I practiced tough love, no longer willing to cushion your blows. Sweetie, it's as if each time you stepped backward, I stepped forward, until eventually, I learned to love myself again.

"If it wasn't for you, Bo, I never would have learned these life lessons. Was that the pact you made before you journeyed to earth, to help your mama evolve? If so, it was such a selfless act of pure love, honey. I just wish I was aware that that was your purpose. I would have been a better student. I would have learned faster and then you wouldn't have had to endure so much pain.

"And now, even after you've gone, you are still teaching me. Teaching me that forgiveness, making amends with the past, is the next step I need to take on my journey. Without it, I will never be able to completely and wholly love, for it will be the looming dark cloud that smothers my heart.

"God, how I'm going to miss your presence! No more hugs. No more heart-to-heart conversations about your premonitions, your thoughts on spirituality, or just your everyday life. I feel like someone just yanked my heart out, honey, and left me here to die. I know that I'm supposed to trust, but damn, Bo, it's *so* hard. Hard!"

Feeling like every muscle, every bone in my body has been bruised and beaten, and still unable to sleep, I keep talking to my boy, not wanting to let go.

"Thank you, sweetie, for choosing me to be your mama, allowing me to share in your laughter and tears, and experience life through your eyes, your heart. You gave and you gave, and all you ever wanted in return was love. God, how I hope I loved you more than enough, Bo."

My body rocks. The pillow catches my tears, each filled with a mother's love, a love that never ends.

When Annie picks me up at the airport, her eyes are red and swollen. I take her in my arms. Neither of us says a word. We can't. The pain is too deep.

Annie's not one who's willing to express her feelings. I believe she stuffs them deep inside, pretending they don't exist. Or maybe she just keeps them at bay until she's willing to let them unfold. Either way, I worry about her. But I realize this is her journey, and I honor that. She knows if she needs to talk, I'm here for her, always and forever.

As Annie's driving to Bobby's condo, she inserts a CD and turns up the volume.

"Listen to this song, Mom. Bo made me this CD."

I try listening to the words, but I can't. My eyes are on Annie. Tiny droplets glide down her cheeks. I rub her knee. We ride in silence, each of us trying to deal with our grief in our own way. The car stops. We walk toward the front door—the door left wide open in my dream. I stop. Turn. Wrap my arms around my girl and hold her like I've never held her before.

As we step inside, Casey is coming up the stairs. His head is lowered. He stops at the landing. I wrap my arms around him.

"You okay, Case?"

"Not fair, Mom."

"I know, honey." I want to say more, but the walls inside me are caving in.

He breaks free from my hold, walks into the family room, and sits next to Bobby on the couch. His ball cap is front and center.

Bobby looks up, nods, and goes back to writing Bo's obituary.

I make my way down the stairs and stand in Bo's doorway. As I look out the sliding glass door, I see two barstools butted up to a table. My eyes glass over. It's as if I can see Bo there, shooting the breeze with his friends. *God, I miss you.* I glance to the right and see his red Fender guitar leaning against the armoire. Bo loved his guitar. Music was the beat to his soul.

Feeling faint, I lie down on his bed. I press Bo's pillow into my gut as if the soft down is my boy inside my womb. *Why, God, why? He was only twenty-two years old. He still had his whole life ahead of him.* I lift the pillow to my face and wipe away the liquid pain. I inhale, wanting to smell the scent of my boy. But the sheets have been changed. His smell is gone.

I crawl out of Bo's bed and make my way to his closet. Bunched on the shelf is a white fleece. I bury my face in it, draw Bo's cologne into my lungs and hold it until I can't hold it a second longer. Then I tuck it under my arm, knowing this is the only tangible thing I have left of him, a smell that will weaken with time. A stenographer's notebook sits on another shelf. I open it and see the words "I'm Moving On . . ." penned by Bo in red ink. I slam it closed and slide it under my arm with Bo's fleece. *I can't read this. Not now.* I saunter over to the door and place my hand on the doorframe. My shoulders curl forward, relinquishing to the weight of my sorrow. Slowly, I lift my head and turn. For the very last time, I inhale the final remnants of the life my boy left behind.

Later I meet Pop and Ginny at the hotel where they've graciously made arrangements for the family to stay. Over the course of the next few hours, family members and close friends arrive.

Mary and Kevin are first on the scene. Mary walks up to me. We sink into that place we love and hold on.

"We're so sorry." She loosens her grip. "You talked to Mom, right? So you know why she couldn't make the trip. With her failing heart, she thought seeing Bo would—"

"I understand. The last thing I want is Mom back in the hospital."

Next to arrive are Geri, number five in the family, and my baby sister, Margie. They're followed by my brothers, Charlie and John. Drace and Maggie trail behind.

I've always loved and appreciated my family and friends, but *never* as much as in this moment.

At five o'clock the next day, we caravan to the private family wake. Quickly the room fills with out-of-town family members from both sides.

Bobby mingles with his brother, sisters, and nieces; his eyes are swollen. Casey sits on a chair, conversing with my brothers, camouflaging his pain through his laughter. Annie is next to me, whimpering.

I put my arm around Annie's shoulder, and we walk into the viewing room. We kneel before Bo's casket. Like magnets, our bodies fuse, and I can't tell where Annie's body stops and mine starts. Our tears become our endless prayers. I stand and wrap my arms around my boy, dressed in a navy suit, white shirt, and pink tie; his body is cold as ice. I don't care. I cup his face and kiss his lips for the last time.

"You look so handsome, Bo," I whisper "I love you so much. My heart will never beat the same without you. You will always be my boy, now and forever." Broken and numb, I kneel back down.

Annie cries softly.

Even though I'm struggling to find my way through the maze, I know I have to be strong for my girl. I grab her hand.

"You know, Annie, Bo would be really upset if he saw the way they did his hair."

We chuckle softly. I know my son would want us this way, not crying.

Annie stands. Licks her fingers. Spikes Bo's hair. And smiles through her tears.

"There, Bo. Now you're looking good."

Loud commotion erupts in the other room. Annie and I rush in.

"What's going on?" I ask, my voice filled with panic.

"I don't know. Casey was talking about Bo. Then he stood up. Ran out of the room. Ran out of the main door." Charlie shouts.

The funeral home is on a busy street, and I'm afraid Casey will get hit by a car. I turn to Pop.

"Dad, you need to go get him. Please," I say, as waves of terror roll through my body.

My eighty-year-old father springs from his chair. Throws open the doors. Bolts down the street after Casey. My brother Johnny watches through the glass panes and updates us on the news.

"They're okay. Dad caught up with him. He has him in a football headlock. Looks like they're talking now. Dad just handed Casey something. They're heading back this way."

Casey goes to the men's room. Dad walks in, moving his head side to side while blowing gulps of air through his puffed cheeks.

"What happened?" I ask.

"He's okay now. He's just having a tough time. He said to me, 'Grandpa, this is all so surreal. I can't believe my brother is dead.' Then he asked me, 'Why, Grandpa?' I didn't know what to say or what to do, so I gave him my favorite lighter and told him to keep it."

I wrap my arms around Pop, my hug oozing with love and gratitude.

Another sleepless night! I rise, shower, and get dressed—white shirt, black jacket, ankle-length black skirt, and heels—and join the family in the main lobby.

By ten o'clock, we're back at the funeral home for the public viewing, followed by a spiritual service. I see familiar faces. I hear condolences exchanged. But nothing . . . *nothing* registers.

The funeral director approaches.

"It's time for the service to begin."

Robby, Bo's best friend, walks up to me.

"I can't do it. I can't be a pallbearer. You have to get someone else." I clench his hand.

"Yes, you can. And you will. You have to do this for Bo. He loved you so much. He'd be crushed if you weren't there by his side."

Robby walks back and forth then takes his place across from Casey. The pallbearers grab the handles and march forward.

Feeling like a robot, I take my place in the procession, directly behind the casket. With Annie by my side, I turn, looking for Bobby. He lags behind. It breaks me into two. I reach out and grab his hand.

"We brought this boy into the world together. We'll be together as he goes out."

We take our place, a couple rows behind Bo's casket. I'm sandwiched between Annie and Bobby. Annie rests her head on my shoulder. Bobby's head hangs low. Gently, I place my hand on his knee. Inside of me, all the past heartache between Bobby and me begins to dissolve.

The minister approaches the pulpit. His voice drifts into the background as I stare at Bo's casket, two feet in front of me.

Twenty-two years of Bo's life race through my mind. I see myself holding my baby in my arms for the first time. I hear his first words "da-da," "ma-ma", and "I love you." His laughter rings in my ears. I feel his arms around me, those little arms that grew into bigger arms, that lifted me off the ground. I see him playing sports—basketball, football, lacrosse, baseball, tennis—graduating from school, getting his first car, going to prom dressed in a tux with the limo waiting in the driveway, celebrating birthdays and holidays, leaving for college, and going into treatment: Yes, the good times and the tough times. Then Christmas 2003 flashes across the screen, and I see myself taking the last pictures I will ever take of my kids together. My heart slows as if it's losing its desire to ever beat again. My mind goes blank.

The sound of people whimpering and blowing their noses brings me back to the present.

I turn my head and scan the room. Every pew is filled with the people who mattered to Bo, from teachers, principals, friends—grade school through college—to family. My lips quiver with gratitude.

Lisa, Bobby's niece and Bo's cousin, stands next to the organ. She clears her throat. With great composure, she sings through her pain— her voice like an angel—to her cousin.

The minister speaks.

"And now I'd like to invite anyone who would like to say a few words to rise and step forward."

Casey, dressed in a navy suit, white shirt, tie, and polished shoes, strolls up to the podium. The baseball stitching, a reminder of his injury, is now camouflaged by his short, thick hair.

I can hardly catch my breath. My brain-injured child is going to speak? He's going to give his brother's eulogy?

Just over a year ago, I almost lost him. Yet today he stands before a room filled with Bo's friends and loved ones to honor his brother. My tongue catches a rolling tear.

I stare at the altar. Blink. Then blink again. Above and behind Casey is a white silhouette. It looks like Bo. He's here! And he's dressed like an angel.

Casey pulls a tattered piece of paper from his suit pocket.

"*I stand in front of you today to honor and express to you how much Bo, Robert Burns Hall, Jr., meant to a lot of people, especially my family. Bo is going to be missed by all of us.*

"*It hit me all at once—how I'm never going to get to be around you and laugh with you ever again. I won't grow old with you and share the experience of having kids and them having an awesome uncle.*"

Casey pauses. Collects himself. Then he proceeds to articulate his heartfelt emotions with great composure, tenderness, and love.

"They say you're in a better place now, and I sure hope so, Bo.

"You were one of the most generous people in the world. You weren't having fun unless your friends were, too. From the extravagant limos, to the New York City trip, you always wanted to make sure everyone was having fun, no matter what the cost.

"It seems so surreal that you are not going to be here anymore. Before, you were only a phone call away. Now all I have to do is talk to you, and you'll hear me. But what sucks is—I can't hear you."

Casey swipes the corner of his eye.

"This really made me realize how serious death really is, and what I want to accomplish before I die. . . . I know some day we will meet again. By then, we will have so much to talk about. I can't believe it's over—the 'Bo and Casey Show' has ended."

Sobs turn into laughter. Casey looks up from his notes and stares into the crowd, as if his mind is replaying movie clips of moments left behind, and joins in. As he lowers his eyes, his smile dwindles, as if it belongs to another time and place.

"I guess it has to come to an end one day for all of us. That's what God has planned for each of us. I just want you to know that I will never forget you. You'll be with me every day. I love you."

My hearts flutters. I think about the cards, for birthday and holidays, that I received in the mail from Casey after his accident. Each envelope was addressed to "Mom," as if that was my first and last name. His personalized notes were nothing but run-on sentences filled with misspelled words, all lingering symptoms of his traumatic brain injury. And yet today . . .

I hear applause. I turn. Some people are wiping their eyes. Others are smiling gently. But the majority claps. Are they applauding because Casey's speech was so heartfelt? Because they are proud of how far he's come? Or in celebration of Bo's life and the impact he made? Entrenched in this bittersweet moment, I join in.

As the noise dies down, Pop walks up to the podium. He pauses to look around the room, making eye contact with each person in the chapel. Then he speaks. "Hi. I'm Grandpa. And I'm an alcoholic." I cup my mouth and choke back the tears. For the next five minutes, Pop talks about the devastating effects of the disease. He pauses again. "I see a lot of young people in the crowd Bo's age. If any of you are struggling with an addiction, catch up with me after the service. I'd love to talk to you." Pop returns to his seat.

The congregation stands. One by one, the pews empty.

I walk up to the casket and drape my arms around it. Gently and tenderly, I kiss the cold metal, hoping my boy can feel my love penetrate the unwanted space that now separates us. Then in a voice so low that only Bo and I can hear, I talk to my son.

"I love you so, so much. Life will never be the same without you. I will never be the same without you. You hear me? Never. Please, Bo, remember your mama as I remember you. Okay, sweetie?" My body shudders. I kiss the casket as if I'm kissing my Bo for the *very* last time.

Even though I'm in the pit and not sure how I'm going to crawl out, I need to find my kids and make sure they're okay. I step into the sunlight, and the first sound I hear is a chorus of voices repeating, "Hi, Grandpa." Soon Pop is surrounded.

He starts, "The first thing you need to do is get to a meeting and find a sponsor. You need to get help before it's too late."

My chin quavers as his voice wanes.

I spot Annie and Casey mingling with their friends. Annie turns as if she heard my footsteps. I wrap my arms around my girl. We rock. I wipe away her stray tears.

"It's going to be okay, honey. It may take years, but it is going to be okay. I know your brother will never leave you. He loved you dearly, Annie. He had your back when he was alive, and he'll have your back until the end. This I know in my soul." I give my girl another squeeze. "I love you, sweetie. You're my girl. My brave girl."

"Mom," I hear over my shoulder.

I turn and see Casey. I brush my hand across his face.

"I've never been so proud, sweetie. You've come so far." My hands tremble as I feel the heaviness of my heart, which has endured its fair share of trials. "Casey, please know that your brother will always be with you. He'll guide you, cheer for you, and he might even smack you in the head when you get out of line. Just hold him here, sweetie." My hand taps his chest. We cry. We hug. We hold on.

Feeling like I'm on autopilot, I make my way through the crowds and find a quiet spot on the side of the funeral home. I drop inside and feel a hurricane brewing, ripping my life asunder. I want to cry for all my yesterdays. I want to cry for all my tomorrows. I want to cry until there are no more tears left to cry. I could scream until my throat grows raw. Pound my fists against the tree trunks until blood oozes. I feel like running away to hide, but I can't. Not today. I need to be here for Annie and Casey. I need to be strong.

Just then, a gentle wind blows. Even though Mom isn't physically here, I can feel her. I can hear her. She whispers her words of wisdom, words I've heard over the years.

"No one leaves this world without their share of trials and tribulations. At some point—young, middle-aged, or old—a situation will present itself, sometimes foreseeable, sometimes not, that will stop a person dead in their tracks and change life forever—physically, emotionally, spiritually, or sometimes, all three."

The wind sweeps down, catches her spirit, and takes it away.

But what Mom neglected to tell me was how to cope with those inconceivable, heart-wrenching changes. How do I breathe life back into my wings after they've been clipped and I've forgotten how to fly?

Annie honks the car horn and waves.

Casey shouts from the passenger seat.

"Mom, c'mon!"

And in that moment, I know the answer.

WITH LOVE.

THE NEXT DANCE

CHAPTER THIRTY-FOUR

*The journey between what you once were
and who you are now becoming
is where the dance of life
really takes place.*

~Barbara De Angelis

January 2004 - September 2011

Two days later, I return to New York, to my job. I'm here, but I'm not here. Minutes turn into hours. Hours into days. Days into weeks. I feel like an android: no heart, no soul, just a box filled with faulty wires.

But when I'm alone, I drop inside and let the monster free. The shrieks, moans, and cries that emerge from me are sounds I never imagined a human could make. Then, without any warning, the noises stop. Drained, I close my eyes and drop into silence.

Bo must be watching, because he flies into my third eye. I don't blink, afraid he will disappear. "Hi, Mom. Love you so much."

I gasp. Then a wave of sadness washes over me as Bo's image gets sucked into a black hole.

Twelve hours later, Bo's vision still ripe in my mind's eye, I pick up the phone and call Susan, a medium referred to me by my Healing Touch instructor. We book a session for the following day.

Her message leaves me speechless.

"Bo's here. He's wearing a red baseball cap. Says he's really sorry.

When he realized he crossed over, he was scared because he thought he was going to get in trouble. He wants you to know that your maternal grandmother is watching over him." Susan laughs. "Your grandmother said she wanted to 'box him in the ears' when he flew into your third eye."

So, I wasn't hallucinating. It was real.

"Bo says he's going to send you signs to let you know he's okay. 'Be on the lookout, Mom,' Bo says, giggling."

After I hang up the phone with Susan, I call Mom and share our conversation. When I get to 'box him in the ears,' Mom chuckles.

"What, Mom?"

"Oh, when we got in trouble as kids, one of Mom's favorite expressions was 'box him in the ears.' Hmm . . . her confirmation just might make me a believer. So you feel better, sweetie?"

"I do, Mom. I know Bo arrived safely home. Even though I miss him more than life itself, I know he's okay, and he's in the light with your mom, Jesus, the angels, and his guides."

"Sounds like he still has his sense of humor, too."

"It does, doesn't it, Mom? Can't wait to find the signs he's going to send my way."

Weeks go by, and nothing comes. I keep asking. Finally, signs appear.

On my walks, I find white feathers that I didn't notice before. Now they are everywhere. Taking them as a symbol that Bo's with me, I gather them and put them in a vase.

While driving the car, I call out to him. "Please, Son. Let me know you are near." A car pulls out in front of me. The license plate reads, "R B Hall."

I climb into bed and smack into a block of energy. I know it's Bo. I can feel his tenderness. He holds and comforts me.

I sit in a parking lot. The scent of his cologne fills the car. I breathe in the air, remembering . . . remembering.

I'm stuck in traffic, and a white feather falls from above, skimming my windshield. I nod a silent thank you through my tears.

On my birthday, the fifth of the month, I find five pennies by my car door. I smile, knowing Bo's celebrating his mama from afar.

The more signs I get, the more I want to know about energy, the afterlife, and connecting with my son on a spiritual level. This desire propels me in a new direction. I take classes at the Holistic Studies Institute and earn certification as a Reiki Master and Therapeutic Touch Practitioner. I travel to Sedona, where I take a week-long workshop on spirituality and climb to the top of St. Michael Mountain. Although I fall into a cactus bush while raising my hands in gratitude, I also get to sleep under the stars in a teepee. I journey with a spiritual group to Medjugorje and watch the sun spin in the sky on Easter morning. After I come home, I take classes in Crystal Resonance Therapy and shamanism. I am still searching.

Even though my healing is slow, and I wonder at times if I will ever be the same, the search goes on. Signs continue to come in unexpected ways. But the one that takes my breath away happens at work.

As the director of volunteers at Northeast Parent & Child Society, I have the great honor of working side by side with the volunteers and the children in our care. It is there that I step into my next phase of healing.

One day I am working in the basement of our Shelter Home along with some of our General Electric volunteers and a group of older teenage kids in our care. While I'm stacking food and supplies on the shelves, a young lad—around Bo's age and new to our program—joins me.

"Bet you're wondering where all this came from." I point to the hundreds of boxes stacked on the floor.

Without making eye contact, he nods.

"For years now, Price Chopper Supermarkets has included Northeast Parent & Child Society in their annual food show in Connecticut. Because of their generosity, we are able to create Thanksgiving and Christmas baskets for the families and children we serve, like you."

His lanky frame bows. He digs in the box and hands me several packets of toothpaste.

"For free? Why?"

"Michael, there are kind people on earth with huge hearts. They understand that life has been good to them. But they also know at any minute, the tables can turn. So, in essence, I guess you could say that they believe 'what goes around comes around.'"

His eyebrows become seamless. His already distant eyes become more withdrawn. Is he thinking about the many nights and days he struggled to have his basic needs met?

He clears his throat.

"Would it be okay if I took a tube of toothpaste and a toothbrush? I haven't brushed my teeth in three weeks."

I give him four of each. He puts three back on the shelf.

Humbled by his actions, I will the dam ready to break behind my eyes to hold.

During our brief encounter, I realize that the kids in our care—battered, abused, and broken—carry pain in their hearts, just as I do. But each time I engage in conversation with a young lad and he relays his struggles of leaving his past behind to create a new life, as unfamiliar as his experience may be, I'm inspired.

Over the next five years, I draw my strength from the kids. They become my heroes. My teachers. I know if these children can triumph through adversity then so can I.

In the spring of 2009, having learned the lessons I needed to learn, I pack my bags, leave New York, and move to Charleston to be close to my daughter. Excited to share my skills and compassion with a new nonprofit agency, I send out my resume—only to hit one brick wall after another.

I'm a big believer in the domino theory. When you're in alignment with the universe, you hit one domino and the rest follow. Because that process isn't happening, I tune in to my gut feelings. What I discover is that I can't move forward until I can find closure with the past, with Bo. I'm guided to pen a children's book, a tribute to my son.

I sit down at my computer and write a simple story about the loss of a child, a heart's healing journey, and the bond of a mother's love.

Satisfied with the words, I pull out my paints and draw simple watercolor illustrations.

During my lifetime, I've taken only one art class, which was in watercolor. Midstream, Casey had his accident and I never completed the course.

Frustrated, I call Drace.

"Drace. I can't do this. I need to hire an illustrator."

"You can do it. Keep trying. This is your story. No one will be able to capture your heart and the emotions you feel."

Drace has always been my cheerleader. When I'm blind and can't see, she points out my strengths and cheers me on.

Still not trusting my abilities, I call in my creative spirit guides. I call in Bo.

Page after page, I drop a blot of ink and watch it morph into the image I have in my mind. When I'm satisfied with my creation, I sit back and high-five my spirit guides and high-five Bo. And for the first time since his death, I feel lighthearted, a feeling I wasn't sure I would ever experience again. I keep drawing, and I make good progress until I get to page twenty.

I read what the grandchild says to his grandmother.

"Did you cry, Oma?"

"Yes . . . yes, I did. Some days I still cry. It's hard to lose the ones we love."

The image that comes to me is a heart. I drop a blot of pink paint on the paper. What stares back at me is worse than a toddler's drawing. I toss it in the garbage and try again. After my third attempt, I hear myself talk out loud.

"I need a little help here."

Someone or something pushes my chair. I believe it's Bo. I have felt him around me. Then I hear: "Use the thick brush."

I want to say, "I have never used that brush. How do you expect me to draw a heart with that?" But I do what I'm told, trusting.

Again, I drop a blot of pink paint, and in one brushstroke an image is created, an image that leaves me gasping for air. On the right side is the face of a child. On the left side is a blank heart, scattered with holes. Yet . . . they are one. It's as if Bo's saying that nothing can ever separate the love between a mother and her child. Like Oma, I cry.

Finally, on January 15, 2010, the day before Bo's birthday in heaven, I receive the book *Believe* in the mail. Flipping through the pages, I'm reminded that the sadness never completely goes away, and there will always be a hole in my heart. Even though the scars remind me of where I've been, these marks don't have to predict where I'm going. Honoring my son's journey and celebrating the gifts he left behind, I hold our creation to the heavens and give wings to Bo's spirit. It's a bittersweet moment, but I realize it's time for him and for me to *move on*. After all, Bo's spirit will always live on in his mama's heart.

On September 3, 2011, the family gathers once again—this time to celebrate the good times.

The DJ taps the microphone, silencing the room.

"Ladies and gentlemen, I'd like to present Mr. and Mrs. Casey Hall."

I'm front and center, sandwiched between my sisters, Mary and Geri. I'm wearing a cobalt-blue, one-shoulder silk-linen dress and silver pumps. Not wanting to miss one expression, one word, or one sound, I turn the movie camera on and wait in anticipation. The side door swings open and in floats my boy and Lyly, his bride. Their fingers are interlocked. They're in a world of their own . . . a world where fairy tales *do* come true.

Filled with emotion, I try steadying the camera as I witness an event I never dreamed I'd see. Mary nudges me, and I watch as our chins move in perfect harmony. No words are spoken, but I know in my heart our thoughts are in sync.

Almost nine years ago, the Irish twins stood at Casey's bedside. We prayed and cleared his energy fields of stagnant debris. We spritzed him with Lourdes holy water and called on Mother Mary and asked for a miracle. I grab Mary's hand and give it a tight squeeze, saying a silent "thank you" for being there for me. She smiles. She understands.

My eyes scan the room filled with family and friends. Some are crying happy tears. Others have their hands fisted upward. Hoots, hollers, and shrill whistles vibrate off the wall of windows overlooking the lush gardens near my son's new home in Texas. Again, I'm reminded that Casey never walked alone.

Lyly wears a white satin gown. From her bustline to her hips, the satin folds and tightens around her petite frame then loosely drapes down and skims the terra cotta tile. Casey's decked out in the new stylish trend for grooms. He sports a khaki suit, matching vest, white shirt, and beige tie.

My heart swells as I watch my son and my new daughter dance to their wedding song, "Looking for Paradise," by Alicia Keys. Casey spins Lyly, and her dress balloons. Lyly taps her chest as Casey points his finger toward his bride, and together they sing the verses. The camera wobbles in my hand. My joyful tears, waiting in a queue for years, spill down my face.

The DJ blows into the microphone, silencing the crowd.

"Now for the mother-and-son dance."

I hand Annie the movie camera. "Can you—"

"Love to. Just go," she grins through her own tears, waving me onto the dance floor.

With twinkling eyes and a glowing smile, Casey stretches out his hand to take mine and draws me close. I wrap my arms around my boy's broad shoulders. As we dance on a dime, I place my hands on his cheeks and stare into his sparkling hazel eyes. Trying to express the emotions bubbling from my heart, my tongue grows thick. "My Wish for You," by Rascal Flatts, plays in the background. At first our steps are slow, our moves tender. The beat quickens, and Casey spins and twirls his mama. I swing out too far, throw my hands up in the air and then move back into my son's arms. Behind me, I can hear Annie laughing and cheering. We continue our fancy footwork.

I'm caught up in the miracle of the dance of my lifetime, this dance with my precious son. He's not only walking and talking, he's also dancing—*we're dancing*. To some people, this dance may seem to be such a little thing. But for us and everyone in the room who knows, it's a miracle from heaven!

My son retrieves his bride. I leave the dance floor, my insides nearly bursting, and I catch a glimpse of Bo in my mind's eye. I wish he were here with us, reveling in his brother's miracle. But then again . . . I believe he is! Bo never missed a party, especially a family gathering.

The music gets louder. The dance floor fills. Shoes click against the tile. A circle forms around the dancers, and the guests bellow out every word to the song, lifting the vibration higher.

I step back and get caught in the whirlwind of my thoughts.

Twenty-nine years ago, Casey struggled to come into this world. Nineteen years later, he danced between life and death again. Both times, he beat the odds. Miraculous? I believe so. Even Dr. Bailey admitted he still has the bottle of Lourdes holy water I gave him. It's sitting on his desk. I smile. The family has endured their share of heartaches and has shed their own personal river of tears, but today we are celebrating life. I'm celebrating so much more . . . what was . . . what is . . . and what is yet to come.

My own personal journey through tragedy—almost losing one son, then losing another, disconnecting and reconnecting again—has taught me that nothing lasts forever and that what was once broken can become whole again: somehow, someday, somewhere. I now embrace each sunrise, each sunset, and everything in between, grateful for the sweet miracles of life.

Casey and Lyly glide by me. I'm brought back to the moment.

I bow and silently thank the heavens for a mother's dance—one step back, two steps forward, full circle.

Epilogue

*Every experience, no matter how bad it seems,
holds within it a blessing of some kind.
The goal is to find it.*

~ Buddha

Casey, my middle child, my miracle boy, finally did earn his associate degree in liberal arts. It took some years, taking a class at a time, just as the doctor predicted. To this day, Casey is still beating the odds. The doctor claimed that most brain injury victims reach their full recovery in two years. But Casey is still improving, surprising the best of them; and for the most part, the old Casey has returned. He has grown into a fine young man, and now lives and works full-time in Houston. Casey shares his life with his loving wife, Lyly, and the new loves of their lives, the twins: Camila and Liam.

Even though the "Bo and Casey Show" came to an abrupt ending in the winter of 2004, the memories of a love once shared still lingers.

We buried Bo on January 20, 2004. His death tore away a huge piece of each of us who loved him. There still isn't a day that goes by or a family celebration that occurs that he isn't missed. Even though I can't physically glance into his dazzling ocean-blue eyes, see his smile, hear his laughter, or feel his arms wrapped around me, his sweet and loving spirit still echoes in my heart. I find great comfort knowing he's smiling down on Annie, Casey, his dad, and me, and all the people he loved.

My youngest, Annie, is still as sweet today as she's always been, maybe sweeter. She graduated from the College of Charleston in 2007 with a degree in communications. Annie went on to earn a veterinarian technician degree. She's followed her heart, her passion for caring for animals and rescuing them. In April 2013, she married the love of her life and best friend, Carey. Attached to her wedding bouquet was a miniature silver frame with Bo's picture.

Bobby, my ex and the father of our three beautiful children, lives in Houston with his wife, Lisa. We are still working on forgiveness, chiseling away the final fragments of past hurts and pain, knowing we both did the best we could with the tools we had. But I believe in my heart of hearts that we are on the mend. Sometimes we just have to give time, time to work.

There isn't a day that goes by that I don't long for one more yesterday. But by the grace of God, I've been able to move forward, growing stronger each day. After finding closure with Bo, I felt a deep desire to fill my emptiness and step back into my joy. In the spring of 2011, I created an Internet radio talk show, *Joy Radio: People Inspiring People.*

The truth is, I'm not sure where I'm going, That's still being defined and written. But I do know that being a mother has been my greatest blessing, my greatest journey, *my greatest dance.*

ACKNOWLEDGMENTS

For me, writing a book was a bit like having a baby. After the seed was planted, I spent the next nine months eating healthy foods, refreshing my spirit with moments of silent reflection, and pushing my mind by writing, all the time believing the faster I penned my words, the sooner I would be able to give birth to my baby. But I was wrong. Totally wrong!

My literary pregnancy surpassed the longest woman's pregnancy in history (375 days) under the guidance of my first editor, Mary B. Johnston, who inspired me to keep writing. It then moved past an elephant's gestation period (twenty-three months) under the direction of my second editor, Shari Stauch, who challenged me to dig deeper into the pain and heartache by saying two simple words —"Splain Lucy!"— chapter after chapter. It tumbled into the hands of my third editor, Pat Gallant, whose watchful eyes pointed out a myriad of grammatical errors, which threw me into Braxton Hicks. I arrived at the maternity ward and was welcomed into the arms of my fourth editor and aunt, Mary Welek Atwell, author of *Wretched Sisters, Evolving Standards of Decency, Equal Protection of the Law?* She masterfully and with a playful sense of humor coached me through my contractions, as she pointed out areas that needed to be clarified, suggested cutting or adding text, and encouraged more character development to enrich the story. Later, I was ushered into the delivery room, where I caught a glimpse of the sign above the door—WriteLife Publishing, an imprint of Boutique of Quality Books Publishing Company—under the direction of Terri Leidich, president and publisher, a gifted and heartfelt entrepreneur. With no time to spare, Terri introduced me to her team of experts—Ellis Dixon, project manager, and Paige Duke, editor—who skillfully walked me through the process.

After five months of heavy breathing (editing), exhaustion set in, but I was determined to give birth to my four-year-old fetus, soon to turn five (yikes!). Seven months later, *A Mother's Dance* was birthed.

Finding the perfect editor and publisher is one part of the process, but without colorful characters, and the passionate and loving people behind the scenes, there really isn't a story at all.

Throughout Casey's spell in the hospital (when my journey into the unknown, the unbearable, and the unforeseeable began), God's angels and Earth angels became my beacons of light. The Earth-bound angels included Dr. Byron Bailey; the staff of doctors and nurses who administered the highest quality of care at the Medical University of South Carolina; Vanessa in the ICU Waiting Room at MUSC; and Marriott prayer angels in aprons.

During the various stages of development, it was my readers—Bonnie Compton, April Eberhardt, Anne Drace Hess, Catherine Underhill Fitzpatrick, Jim Johans, Deb Mangolt, Kathleen Martin, Mary Welek McBride, Bren McClain, Lori Nelson Spielman, Patrick Sullivan, and Annie Hall Vincent—and their constant echo, "Don't give up," that encouraged me to keep breathing and writing. Thank you!

Without the support, love, and understanding from my family and dear friends during those trying times—Robert B. Hall, Jr., Annie Hall Vincent, Charles and Ginny Welek, Rita and Bud Barry, Charlie and Diane Welek, Mary and Kevin McBride, Rita Kloster, Geri and Jeb Schary, John and Fran Welek, Margie Fagan, Anne Drace Hess, Maggie Hess Kennedy, James and Cathy Johans, Dr. Timothy Johans, Lili Corbus, Wendy Magee-Hagen, Marie Magee, Barbara Jo Halton-Bailey, Danny, my boss at Barnes & Noble in Huntersville, and my Arboretum colleagues, and *so* many more . . . you know who you are—I could still be wondering if I had the strength to carry on. Instead, I was able to mend my brokenness and restore the magical and miraculous to my life. Again, thank you!

To the brave and courageous brain injury and PTSD survivors who have endured the unimaginable; to the parents who have experienced the worst nightmare of their lives—losing a child; and to the family and friends who have supported you along the way, I wrap you in my arms with love.

Even though writing the book was a long and sometimes painful labor, it was in so many ways a labor of love. My prayer is by setting *A Mother's Dance* free, her wings will find her way into your hearts, inspire you, and bring you hope, *always hope*.

I am forever grateful to each and every one of you, and for your unfailing belief in me and this work.

BOOKS THAT HELPED ME ON
MY JOURNEY

1. Al-Anon Family Group Inc. *One Day at a Time*. Virginia Beach: Al Anon Family Group Headquarters, 1987

2. Beattie, Melody. *Codependent No More: How to Stop Controlling Others and Start Caring for Yourself*. Center City: Hazelden, 1986

3. Beattie, Melody. *The Language of Letting Go*. Center City: Hazelden, 1990

4. Brennan, Barbara. *Hands of Light: A Guide to Healing Through the Human Energy Field*. New York: Bantam New Age Books, 1988

5. Chopra, Deepak. *The Seven Spiritual Laws of Success: A Practical Guide to the Fulfillment of Your Dreams*. San Rafael: New World Library/Amber-Allen Publishing, 1994

6. Chopra, Deepak. *How to Know God: The Soul's Journey into the Mystery of Mysteries*. New York: Harmony Books, 2000

7. Chopra, Deepak. *The Path of Love: Spiritual Strategies for Healing*. New York: Harmony Books, 1997

8. Choquette, Sonia. *Your Heart's Desire: Instructions for Creating the Life You Really Want*. New York: Three Rivers Press, 1997

9. Cloud, Henry and Townsend, John. *Boundaries: When to Say Yes, How to Say No to Take Control of Your Life*. Grand Rapids: Zondervan, 2002

10. Das, Ram. *Awakening the Buddha Within: Tibetan Wisdom for the Western World*. New York: Broadway Books, 1997

11. Gawain, Shakti. *Creative Visualization: Use the Power of Your Imagination to Create What You Want in Your Life*. Novato: Nataraj Publishing, 1978

12. Hanh, Thich Naht. *The Heart of the Buddha's Teachings: Transforming Suffering into Peace, Joy, and Liberation*. New York: Harmony, 1998

13. Hay, Louise. *You Can Heal Your Life*. Carlsbad: Hay House, 1984

14. Hay, Louise. *Gratitude: A Way of Life*. Carlsbad: Hay House, 1996

15. Mata, Sri Daya. *Only Love: Living the Spiritual Life in a Changing World*. Los Angeles: Self Realization Fellowship, 1976

16. Mata, Sri Daya. *Finding the JOY Within You: Personal Counsel for God-Centered Living*. Los Angeles: Self Realization Fellowship, 1990

17. Millman, Dan. *The Laws of Spirit: A Tale of Transformation*. Novato: H J Kramer and New World Library, 1995

18. Moody, Raymond. *Life After Life: The Investigation of a Phenomenon—Survival of Bodily Death*. New York: Bantam Books, 1976

19. Myss, Caroline. *Sacred Contracts: Awakening Your Divine Potential.* New York: Three Rivers Press, 2003

20. Newton, Michael. *Journey of Souls: Case Studies of Life Between Lives.* St. Paul: Llewellyn Publications, 1994

21. Newton, Michael. *Destiny of Souls: New Case Studies of Life Between Lives.* St. Paul: Llewellyn Publications, 2001

22. Peck, M. Scott. *The Road Less Traveled: A New Psychology of Love, Traditional Values and Spiritual Growth.* New York: Touchstone, 1978

23. Prophet, Elizabeth Clare. *The Lost Years of Jesus: Documentary Evidence of Jesus' 17-Year Journey to the East.* Gardiner: Summit University Press, 1984

24. Ramacharaka, Yogi. *The Bhagavad Gita.* Chicago: The Yogi Publication Society, 1930

25. Redfield, James. *The Celestine Prophecy: An Adventure.* New York: Grand Central Publishing, 1997

26. Ruiz, Dan Miguel. *The Four Agreements: A Practical Guide to Personal Freedom (A Toltec Wisdom Book).* San Rafael: Amber-Allen Publishing, Inc., 1997

27. Tolle, Eckhart. *The Power of Now: A Guide to Spiritual Enlightenment.* Novato: New World Library, 1999

28. Vanzant, Iyanla. *In the Meantime: Finding Yourself and the Love You Want.* New York: Simon & Schuster, 1998

29. Vanzant, Iyanla. *One Day My Soul Just Opened Up: 40 Days and 40 Nights Toward Spiritual Strength and Personal Growth.* New York: Fireside, 1998

30. Virtue, Doreen. *Healing with the Angels: How the Angels Can Help You in Every Area of Your Life.* Carlsbad: Hay House, 1999

31. Virtue, Doreen. *Messages from Your Angels.* Carlsbad: Hay House, 2002

32. Virtue, Doreen. *Archangels and Ascended Masters: A Guide to Working and Healing with Divinities and Deities.* Carlsbad: Hay house, 2003

33. Walsh, Neale Donald. *Conversations with God: An Uncommon Dialogue, Book 1.* New York: G. P. Putman's Sons, 1996

34. Weiss, Brian L. *Many Lives, Many Masters: The True Story of a Prominent Psychiatrist, His Young Patient, and the Past-Life Therapy.* New York: Fireside, 1988

35. Williamson, Marianne. *A Return to Love: Reflections on the Principles of "A Course in Miracles."* New York: Harper Collins, 1992

36. Wing, R.L. *The I Ching Workbook.* New York: Broadway Books, 1979

37. Yogananda, Paramahansa. *Autobiography of a Yogi.* New York: The Philosophical Library, 1946

38. Zukav, Gary. *The Seat of the Soul.* New York: Fireside, 1989

39. *Law of Life, Book One and Two.* St. Petersburg: A. D. K. Luk Publications, 1960